The Guide to the
BEST EUROPEAN
BUSINESS SCHOOLS

The Guide to the
BEST EUROPEAN
BUSINESS SCHOOLS

William H. Cox

McGraw-Hill
New York   San Francisco   Washington, D.C.   Auckland   Bogotá
Caracas   Lisbon   London   Madrid   Mexico City   Milan
Montreal   New Delhi   San Juan   Singapore
Sydney   Tokyo   Toronto

Library of Congress Cataloging-in Publication Data

Cox, William H.
    The guide to the best European business schools / William H. Cox.
       p. cm.
    Includes index.
    ISBN 0-07-135720-3 (Paperback)
    1. Business education—Europe. I. Title.

  HF1140.C69 2000
  650'.071'14—dc21

                                 00-028282

McGraw-Hill

*A Division of The **McGraw·Hill** Companies*

1 2 3 4 5 6 7 8 9 0   AGM/AGM   0 9 8 7 6 5 4 3 2 1 0

ISBN 0-07-135720-3

This book was set in Minion by North Market Street Graphics.

Printed and bound by Quebecor World/Martinsburg.

McGraw-Hill books are available at special quantity discounts to use as
premiums and sales promotions, or for use in corporate training programs. For
more information, please write to the Director of Special Sales, Professional
Publishing, McGraw-Hill, Two Penn Plaza, New York, NY 10121-2298. Or
contact your local bookstore.

This book is printed on recycled, acid-free paper containing
a minimum of 50% recycled, de-inked fiber.

To my parents, wife Rozangela, and son Lee

CONTENTS

PREFACE

This is probably the first book published in the United States focusing on the ranking of the best European master of business administration (MBA) programs. Twenty leading programs are ranked based on surveys of potential applicants and recruiters (consultancies). This book should help you recognize the top schools and determine what to consider in selecting a school. You will also learn what it is like to study for an MBA in Europe.

Why study for an MBA in Europe when the 600 U.S. business schools are probably the most recognized in the world, with a history dating back to 1900? Europe has just 150 business schools and the oldest was established in 1956. The United States has both the largest alumni network and the largest number of graduates (75,000 annually compared to 30,000 in Europe). U.S. companies accept the MBA as a legitimate degree and know which schools are among the best. Established rankings and fierce competition among schools ensure the continued improvement of quality and standards. Starting and ending salaries for MBAs in the United States are the highest in the world. And, all MBA programs in the United States are in English.

However, there is another side to the story. This is the era of globalization. Most of the Fortune 500 companies have operations in Europe. As the DaimlerChrysler and Deutsche Bank/Bankers Trust mergers indicate, European firms can buy into American firms, just as Americans buy into European companies. As such, management is becoming a discipline requiring an understanding of how other nations conduct business. Managers who have this knowledge are bound to be more successful and to make more money than their counterparts who do not have such knowledge—not to mention the endless frequent flyer miles they will collect.

European MBA programs are thoroughly international. More than 10 of the leading European schools have a student body that is more than 90 percent foreign, and most have more than 50 percent foreign students. The student population at most top schools represents 25 or more nationalities, with a strong representation from Asia. On the other hand, some of the most international U.S. MBA programs, including Harvard's, have as little as 30 percent foreign students. And, the majority of these students are likely to come from neighboring countries, such as Canada and Mexico.

Most classes at European business schools are no larger than 30 to 40 students, which makes the learning experience more personalized. Many of the schools belong to ancient universities and do a commendable job of integrating the old with the new. At Cambridge University, for example, students live in a medieval college yet use the latest equipment when networking with the corporate world in seminars and meetings.

European business schools offer more innovative and modern approaches to learning management. INSEAD in France was among the schools which pioneered the conflict-learning approach of putting people with radically different backgrounds together in small groups and forcing them to reconcile differences in developing strategic solutions to business problems. At the Instituto de Empresa, Madrid, and at Cambridge all students are required to develop their own entrepreneurial plans. In Madrid, about 10 percent of the students actually become entrepreneurs. Because European MBA students are older than most U.S. students, the programs are postgraduate level and shorter. INSEAD in France, IMD in Switzerland, and Cambridge in England offer programs lasting less than a year that claim to cover what U.S. programs do in two years.

Case studies, the business school's main teaching method of looking at how a corporation developed and which challenges it confronted, are newer at European schools. GSBA Zurich, for example, uses mainly live cases. The case studies focus on companies in different countries and handle a large variety of legal and structural problems. As a student you might work on a case with a small group of four or five people, all from different countries with varying professional and educational backgrounds. If that does not teach you conflict management in a global world, no school experience will.

The European business school experience often includes projects that take students away from their home institutions. They learn other languages and establish a network of contacts that spans the globe. Finally, because European universities produce fewer faculty qualified in interactive teaching, its B-schools recruit faculty worldwide.

Despite all the pluses, the European B-school scene is still underdeveloped in its organizational structures. It lacks an established accreditation scheme and association such as the American Assembly of Collegiate Schools of Business (AACSB) in St. Louis, which is now called the International Association for Management Education. This deficiency is so evident that the German Ministry of Education recognizes AACSB-accredited MBA programs almost automatically.

While in the United States everything from cities to consumer goods are regularly and professionally ranked and open competition prevails, most European schools do not want to subject themselves to open examination and competition. The media are beginning to make inroads to break up this protectionism. The British newspaper *Financial Times* and the German magazine *Der Spiegel* are examples of publications which now regularly rank schools, much to the satisfaction of readers.

When *Business Week* began ranking U.S. MBA programs many years ago, American schools were not pleased either. Through the years, however, they have learned the value of the rankings, which point out their strengths as well as their weaknesses. Instead of putting their heads in the sand like some of their European counterparts, U.S. schools use the rankings to improve.

Rankings in this book are not perfect and only a beginning. Our philosophy is that because the quality of an MBA program most affects potential students and recruiters, they should be the ones to judge the programs.

Therefore, our ranking is based on two surveys: a survey of German university students and a survey of the largest consulting firms in Europe, which are major recruiters of MBAs in Europe. We compared what they wanted in an MBA program with what the programs actually offered, and then compiled the resulting ranking.

William H. Cox
Idar-Oberstein, Germany

ACKNOWLEDGMENTS

Books are never the work exclusively of the authors listed on their title pages. Normally, the authors' families, friends, professors, colleagues, and professional associates have at some point in the authors' lives helped in some way. They provided authors with funds, emotional support, and the many ideas which flow into their books. In my case, these people are too numerous to mention, although I do thank my parents for all their support, especially for supporting my education.

There is the more immediate support of the actual book: the researching, writing, commenting, and criticizing. Many ideas took shape only as the book was being written. In this connection I thank my colleagues, in particular Birgit Arens and Marita Klöckner-Kramer for their practical research work, and for keeping the daily business under control while this book was being written. My wife gave me the necessary motivation to deal with the task. The final text is the work of Leah Larkin, who had to work under pressure to complete the book on time. My colleagues had to shorten most descriptions with the reader in mind—a difficult conceptual task.

Finally, I thank the participants in our surveys who filled out questionnaires and quickly returned them. I also thank the business schools which have gone through substantial pains to answer all our questions quickly and accurately.

THE MBA IN EUROPE

THE EUROPEAN EXPERIENCE

THE LANGUAGE FACTOR

"It is wrong to see studying in Europe as all the same, just in a different language," wrote an MBA graduate from a top European business school recently. Actually, it is not even in a different language. Most European MBA programs are in English, or they are bilingual—English and another language. While the language requirements depend on the philosophy of the school, even bilingual programs are slowly switching to English only. Oddly, the London Business School requires that students demonstrate proficiency in a second language in addition to English. The MBA program at INSEAD in France, which has increasingly positioned itself as a global center of learning, has moved away from being bilingual French/English. IMD in Switzerland, with no more than two people from a single nation in its MBA program, has only been in English.

English has asserted itself as the world business language. At any major European airport you can overhear business people, whose native languages are not English, communicating with different accents in English. Learning a different language is not what a foreign MBA program in Europe is about, although it can be useful. Learning another language can be a part of a successful career strategy in a particular area of the world in which English is not widely spoken, such as Latin America. For a career in Latin America, it makes sense to do an MBA at a top Spanish school such as the Instituto de Empresa (IE) in Madrid or IESE in Barcelona, where parts of the MBA are taught in Spanish. Not everyone of importance in Latin America speaks and writes English, so knowing Spanish would be essential to success in this large market consisting of numerous countries.

A GLOBAL EMPHASIS

Do MBA students studying in London really get to know the British way of doing business, or do those studying in Paris get to understand the French way? Not really. Take an extreme example such as INSEAD, located roughly 40 miles outside of Paris. Its program lasts 10 months; it is intensive and offers virtually no free time. Students are either in class, working in small groups, or studying at home. Their faculty, who teach in English, are from the United States, Asia, Germany, the UK, and France. Normally, each student in a working group is from a different country. To intensify the experience of diversity and constructive tension in the group, the students selected for the group are also from different academic backgrounds. For example, a philosophy graduate from Oxford, an engineering graduate from Bangalore, an economics graduate from New York, and a medical doctor from Adelaide may be in such a group. They might be working on a case involving marketing chicken feed in northern China. The course could be taught by a professor from Japan. What does this teach about the French mentality or way of doing business?

While this example is hypothetical, it is not exaggerated. The more international the school, the less students are going to learn about the local or national culture, unless they take a specific course on that country's culture. With 70 to 95 percent of the students at many top European schools foreign, that is, not from the country in which the school is located, they will learn most about doing business in a global world rather than a specific region of this world. They will also learn how to reconcile different mentalities in meetings and working groups in the interest of a constructive business solution, and they will feel comfortable in *any* international setting rather than in one or two particular foreign settings.

In addition, most schools with open (as opposed to corporate) MBA programs, teach something about all aspects of management, be it strategy, marketing, human resources, or managing information systems. With this aspect plus the global dimension of their studies, students become true generalists and global managers, able to switch locations, disciplines, departments, and continents easily. Global business is what they learn at a top European business school.

NATIONAL AND BINATIONAL BUSINESS SCHOOLS

At schools addressing more limited markets and with fewer nationalities represented in their student bodies and faculty, the experience can be less global and more national or binational. An example of such a program is the GSBA Zurich, with a German, Swiss, and American faculty and with students mainly from Germany and Switzerland. Case studies represent mainly these regions. WHU Koblenz in Germany is similar. Many of the British B-schools, SDA Bocconi in Italy, and the Spanish schools fit this mold. Programs of most schools outside of the United Kingdom are likely to be at least partially bilingual, and students are likely to discuss issues closer to home. If a student wants a geographically and culturally more defined MBA experience, he or she would select this type of program.

However, even these schools are globalizing by setting up exchange programs with joint degrees that bring in students and faculty from more countries. This development forces the school to find a common language, namely English. Case studies and teaching approaches flow into a program that is more like a global melting pot.

German B-schools, which are just now being set up in the wake of a new liberalized law, are largely national. Their faculty, students, cases, and approaches are primarily German. In Spain, whose gross domestic product (GDP) growth is among the highest within the European Union, demand for MBAs has been so strong that schools have not needed to be global. The two or three top schools are the exceptions.

Other schools, such as EAP with centers in Paris, Berlin, Oxford, and Madrid, believe that an international education consists of the sum of national ones. Students can study in several of the EAP centers, receiving a single degree at the end. They must be fluent in every language of each location, where they meet students mainly from that country.

A COMPARISON OF U.S. AND EUROPEAN MBAS

In this book we compare U.S. and European MBAs simply because most students considering a European MBA will consider studying in the United States as well and vice versa. The *similarities* between the European and U.S. MBA programs are general and superficial. In both programs:

- A master of business administration degree is awarded.
- Admission requires the Graduate Management Admissions Test (GMAT), Test of English as a Foreign Language (TOEFL), and an undergraduate degree.
- The school's reputation is linked to its tough admissions policy and the success of its alumni.
- The basic areas of business administration covered in the curricula, such as strategy, human resources, and marketing, are the same.
- The MBA is a practical, career-oriented degree.
- The MBA is a popular degree and develops skills such as quick analysis and synthesis, presentation abilities, ability to work in teams.
- Learning is under pressure and students' performance is closely monitored and evaluated.

- Business schools foster close relations with the business world.
- English is the main language of instruction.

The *differences* between the U.S. and European MBA programs outweigh the similarities. The European programs have:

Differences
outweigh
the similarities.

- A more international student body and faculty
- Greater global reach of programs and more international exchange and cooperation partners
- Many shorter programs (1–1.5 years)
- Longer work experience requirements
- Older students
- Greater diversity and originality of teaching and learning methods
- Interdisciplinary courses
- A greater multitude of MBA types (one-year, two-year, executive, distance learning, etc.)
- Less established accreditation and certification system
- Overall, much less corporate acceptance of the MBA in hiring, promoting, remunerating, and donating funds
- Not even half as many students as in the United States
- Smaller numbers of students, facilities, faculty, and endowments, generally
- Newer facilities than U.S. schools
- Business schools that, with the exception of the United Kingdom and recently Germany, are not part of large universities

Are U.S. schools becoming more European or is the development the other way around? Generally, European schools can afford to be more dynamic because they are less developed. No historically rooted and accepted accreditation norm exists among them as it does in the United States. Europe is multicultural because it includes a large number of nations bordering each other within a small area. Moreover, European nations have been export-oriented because their domestic markets, such as those of Germany, are too small in relation to their industrial production. Thus, their perspective, and therefore that of their business schools, is more global than the United States. Finally, European economies and companies have a lot of catching up to do in relation to their American counterparts. The banking business, for example, must undergo major long-term reform, reducing the number and bureaucracy of the banks. Other industries must similarly consolidate to remain internationally competitive. Labor costs must come way down in countries such as Germany and France. Germany's inefficient and economically strangulating government structures must adapt to the realities of a business-driven world. And in all this, European business schools have a chance to play an active role in supplying qualified leaders.

On the other hand, the dynamism of European business schools may encourage U.S. schools to develop shorter programs, more innovative teaching methods, and a greater degree of internationalism in their programs.

FULL-TIME PROGRAMS: ONE-YEAR AND ONE-YEAR PLUS MBAs

Programs lasting about one year are the trend in most of Europe. One reason is that European MBA candidates are older (mainly between 28 and 35) than their American counterparts, and they are too rooted in their professional careers to give them up for a full two years.

Another reason is that the MBA is seen as a postgraduate or even postexperience degree for well-educated and professionally experienced people. Entering students are expected to know the basics of business and not to need to cover this in a full first year or the better part of the first year. Instead, core sections cover a wider range of more advanced courses. At Cambridge's business school, Judge Institute, some of the core courses are interdisciplinary and not considered basic. For example, the course Organizations, Behavior and the Management of People covers "an understanding of individual behavior, the working of organizations and the relationship between the two which is fundamental to management success."

Some of the most highly regarded international European programs, such as those of INSEAD and IMD, are even less than one year. Cambridge started off in the early 1990s with a much longer program and then introduced a one-year program, which also incorporates several projects and contact with the corporate world. However, one-year programs are not likely to offer students the opportunity of exchanging with other schools for a term or semester because the total time of study is too short.

A compromise between one-year and two-year programs is the one-year-plus program (of 14 months or so) that is offered by the Instituto de Empresa in Madrid. The final months are dedicated to working on the student's own entrepreneurial business plan and project.

FULL-TIME PROGRAMS: TWO-YEAR MBAS

The two-year programs were the first European MBAs, the oldest being that of IESE in Barcelona. They were modeled on their American counterparts with the first year being for core courses, the summer break for internships or other working experience, and the second year for exchange programs with other schools, electives, and interviewing with prospective employers. In addition to IESE in Barcelona, the London and Manchester Business Schools have largely maintained this variant. Their philosophy is that it takes two years to cover and digest this much material. However, the two-year programs are more expensive than shorter ones, both in tuition and living expenses. Typically, only very well known schools can offer these programs to students convinced that they need two years.

PART-TIME PROGRAMS: EVENING, WEEKEND, AND EXECUTIVE MBAS

There are several types of part-time programs. First, there are programs, which cover practically the same material as the full-time programs, but do so on weekends and evenings. They typically take a year longer to complete. London Business School offers a part-time variant to its full-time MBA. The only major difference, besides the length and structure, is that the students are often somewhat older.

The fact that a program is part-time does not make it an executive masters in business administration (EMBA). An EMBA caters to the needs, interests, and experience level of executives with a number of years of real managerial experience. The EMBAs at Koblenz and Zurich are typical examples. The structure is often modular, each module consisting of one or two or more week's full-time study at the school. Students prepare for their modules at home; mainly senior faculty teach the courses or modules; and the material presupposes knowledge of business administration. Some EMBA applicants to Zurich's GSBA program with a master's degree or even a doctorate and five or more years management experience are required to take an intensive executive bachelor of business administration (BBA) program if their knowledge of business administration is insufficient. EMBAs only make sense for those who live and work within reasonable transportation distance of the school and are fully employed. The breaks between modules can be several months. EMBAs are costly and often culminate in some thesis work relevant to students' work. Normally they allow students opportunities to relay what they have learned to their careers in a more direct manner than other MBAs.

DISTANCE-LEARNING MBAs

Thanks to astounding technological developments, distance learning has shaken its shoddy image and come to the forefront as one of the most innovative approaches to business training. Estimates are that two schools in Britain, Henley Management College and Open University Business School, together, may have nearly 10,000 students enrolled in their distance-learning programs and studying in various locations all over the world. The two schools are the world leaders in this type of MBA.

The main attraction of distance learning is that distance is no problem—a major advantage in globalization and a mobile world. Thus, IBM has strongly backed Open University's program, enrolling executives from various European offices in the program and sending them to the main campus for regular seminars, which constitute the "residency" elements of the program. Distance learning also allows those in emerging markets to more easily earn an MBA. The Association of MBAs (AMBA) in London has accredited several distance-learning programs against criteria designed specifically for such programs.

On the other hand, critics are loud and strong in asserting that distance MBAs lack some of the key components of MBAs, that is, the learning advantage of working with excellent faculty and students from all over the world in classrooms. Distance students who work alone are bound to learn fewer skills than on-site students who have the opportunity to work together with others. Even so, the distance-learning schools are countering by offering virtual classrooms with online video conferencing, chat rooms for group discussions among students, and remote tutoring—all technological tactics designed to at least partially offset the lack of personal contact. In any case, distance learning is the fastest growing form of MBA and is here to stay.

CORPORATE AND CONSORTIUM MBAs

A corporate MBA is tailor-made for the personnel of a particular company. One or more business schools put together a curriculum for one or more companies, concentrating on courses that suit the needs of the companies. Critics claim that these programs are too narrow and the MBA earned may not be very marketable outside of the sponsoring company(s).

BENEFITS OF THE EUROPEAN MBA

If you study with people from all over the world, you'll have access to an international alumni network. This is a career advantage for graduates of schools that have organized active alumni networks around the world. Perhaps the best global alumni network among the European schools is that of INSEAD. While the Harvard alumni network, with its Harvard Clubs, is bigger, older, and more established than INSEAD, most top U.S. schools are weak seconds and thirds after Harvard. So, the global second place probably goes to INSEAD.

Schools are realizing that strong international alumni organizations are valuable both as selling points to attract applicants and in expanding their influence in different regions of the world. For example, an alumnus in Kuala Lumpur, Sao Paulo, or Capetown may have access to influential people and institutions in these places and could persuade these people to join the advisory board of the school. Or, the alumnus could help set up ties with another business school in a foreign country.

Instead of having one advisory board of prominent business people and personalities, INSEAD has set up an advisory board for each country in which it has a strong presence. There are advisory boards in Germany, the United Kingdom, and the United States. The advisory boards of schools such as IESE in Barcelona, Instituto de Empresa in Madrid, London Business School, and many of the other high-profile schools, give the schools global prestige and influence. Board members bring ideas from the top levels of global business and politics into the schools' management. European schools can boast the most international advisory boards and committees.

While fund-raising at European schools and universities is much less developed than in the United States, Europeans are catching up. Alumni are giving more to their alma maters, and advisory boards are helping to drum up funds for new projects, such as the new Institute for Entrepreneurship at the Instituto de Empresa Madrid.

BACKGROUND OF THE EUROPEAN MBA

European business schools developed parallel in different countries, such as the United Kingdom, France, Spain, the Benelux, and

Switzerland. INSEAD and IESE were set up in the 1950s; London and Manchester, in the mid 1960s; and many of today's stars "grew up" in the 1970s and even 1980s.

An important impetus for the European business school came from two American reports released in 1959 by the Ford Foundation and Carnegie Corporation sharply criticizing the academic rigor, quality, and overall relevance of the American business schools. American schools responded quickly, and Europeans became interested in the idea of management education. In the United Kingdom Lord Franks released a study on the issue in 1963. In response to these studies, business schools were created in the two largest British business centers, London and Manchester, not in the more traditional learning centers of Oxford and Cambridge. This underscored that management training was to be close to the business world. Indeed, it wasn't until the early 1990s that Cambridge introduced its MBA, and Oxford did the same just a few years ago. In France the Chambers of Commerce in large cities such as Paris and Lyon created a network of *Grandes Écoles* (great schools), which offered business education along the lines of MBA studies. Later many of these programs were called MBA programs.

In Europe a dichotomy appeared between more academic, research-oriented schools and teaching-oriented, practical schools. The debate continues to this day between the two philosophies. Schools such as the London Business School and IESE in Spain belong to the former grouping, Henley in the United Kingdom and GSBA Zurich to the latter, although all possess elements of both categories.

In addition to schools established and sanctioned by governments, there are many schools, such as INSEAD, IMD, Ashridge, and Instituto de Empresa that were created by companies or groups of investors and entrepreneurs. These independent schools were always managed more like companies, while those connected with universities are run like traditional academic institutions.

QUALITY AND ACCREDITATION

While it did not take long for Americans to set up an accreditation organization for MBA programs (the first U.S. MBA program was established around 1900 and the AACSB accreditation association in 1917), Europeans have been slow to follow suit. Only in the United Kingdom has the AMBA (Association of MBAs) established a track record in accreditation. In Brussels, the European Foundation of Management Development (EFMD), an organization with European scope, resisted developing an accreditation system, claiming its quality auditing system was sufficient. It recently established the European Quality Improvement System (EQUIS) as the first real European accreditation institution.

Specialists from European business schools who put together EQUIS made the criteria tough and detailed, covering every aspect of a business school. EQUIS examines 10 categories of a business school, such as its curriculum, quality improvement mechanisms, external relations, faculty hiring and upgrading practices, and practically every aspect of its self-management. While the AMBA accredits MBA programs (in the same manner as the AACSB), EQUIS accredits the entire school. Schools submit detailed self-assessment reports of several hundred pages. Later a team of examiners from other schools spends several days verifying and debating the applicant's accreditation worthiness. The school may have a new MBA program, like Koblenz in Germany, but still receive EQUIS accreditation on the basis of its undergraduate degree program(s). Schools active within the "right" EFMD circles probably run only minimal risks of failing to get EQUIS accreditation. Given that EQUIS has no legal value, it will probably be up to the schools to market EQUIS accreditation by promoting the fact that they have earned it. Roughly 20 schools to date have been accredited by EQUIS, including INSEAD, IMD, London Business School, Instituto de Empresa, WHU Koblenz, and IESE. Unlike the AACSB, which itself secured acceptance by the U.S. Department of Education, no government authority controls or directly sanctions EQUIS. No industrial association controls it or publicizes its contents to its members. While AACSB accreditation in the United States, or AMBA accreditation in the UK, has significant merit, to date EQUIS accreditation has little practical significance for students or employers.

There are several other national accreditation or quality certification organizations including:

- *France:* Chapitre des Écoles de Management (Chapitre)
- *Italy:* Associazione per la Formazione alla Direzione Aziendale (ASFOR)
- *Spain:* Asociación Española de Representantes Escuelas de Dirección (AEDE)

Recent efforts toward a European accreditation system.

COSTS

The costs of European MBA programs range from zero to $25,000 annually for tuition alone. Living expenses can be very high in London, Paris, Madrid, or other large cities. The bargains in tuition are the very new German schools, many of which are state-funded and do not charge tuition. London Business School costs 25,000 Pounds Sterling ($42,000); IMD costs 38,000 Swiss Francs ($25,000) and INSEAD charges 151,000 French Francs ($28,000) for tuition alone.

As in the United States, scholarships are rare because most schools assume MBA students should be able to secure the funds if they wish to do an MBA. Loan schemes are numerous, particularly in the United Kingdom, but rare in Germany. Normally schools will recommend banks that will grant loans mainly on the basis of the students' admissions letters. Finally, given the more advanced age of most applicants, it is assumed that they should have sufficient reserves to fund most of the MBA themselves. These students will not be earning anything—or very little—for the duration of any full-time program. Executive MBA or distance-learning candidates can handle the financial burdens more easily because they need not give up their income during the MBA.

ADMISSIONS

Admission procedures at most European MBA programs are not unlike applying to American B-schools, requiring high GMAT scores, TOEFL scores if your native language is not English, an undergraduate degree, five or more years work experience, references, and interviews. The requirements differ from one another with respect to the (1) amount and level of work experience, (2) foreign language requirement, (3) application deadlines, and (4) emphasis placed on grades earned in the undergraduate degree.

Unlike U.S. schools, which require that applications be submitted by spring of the year you want to begin or earlier, even top schools in Europe (e.g., Cambridge) may have rolling admissions. Early application improves your chances at rolling admissions. Applications for distance-learning programs can be made at any time during the year. Most programs begin in September or October, but some start a second class in January. In each case, admissions deadlines might vary.

The most competitive schools, accepting the fewest candidates or only the most qualified, include INSEAD, IMD, London Business School, IESE, Rotterdam School of Management, Cambridge (Judge), Oxford (Said), Cranfield, Ashridge, and a handful of others.

Their average GMAT and TOEFL acceptance scores are above 600 points. Applicants have high grade point averages from their under-graduate degrees, have worked with international companies, and have excellent references from employers and professors. They also demonstrate high motivation and clarity about their career goals during admission interviews. The largest group of applicants has a degree in engineering or some other science, followed by law and the social sciences. Many employers consider the combination of a scientific background and an MBA ideal.

Many schools with large alumni organizations can arrange an interview off campus near you. However brochures, Web sites, books, and articles cannot replace a visit to the campus. The "feel" of the school and conversations with students will give applicants more security than rankings or other remote materials.

An increasing number of B-schools are moving away from requiring that students take the GMAT. For a time, even Harvard Business School did not require the test. The feeling is that its use of multiple-choice questions is an American approach that is not a way of thinking imbued in Europeans. The GMAT also empha-sizes nuances in the English language that Europeans cannot be privy to. Many German schools thus do not require the GMAT. Some schools, such as the Instituto de Empresa Madrid, adminis-ter their own test or accept the GMAT, giving students their choice.

CAREER OUTLOOK FOR MBAs IN EUROPE

European consultancies, auditing firms, and financial service institutions have been the primary recruiters of European MBAs. These firms offer the most jobs, do the most active recruiting and pay MBA graduates what they expect. On the other side, MBA graduates offer these firms exactly what they want: strategic think-ing, the ability to work long work hours, and practice in solving case studies, which are similar to consulting projects and work in high finance.

However, with well over 40,000 MBA graduates working in the United Kingdom alone, MBAs are increasingly entering other industries, particularly in the United Kingdom. Furthermore, the variety of MBA forms, especially part-time and distance-learning MBAs, has made the MBA available to wider categories of man-agers. Someone in public service might go for a part-time MBA as would someone in a machine tools firm. Even in Germany, where there has been resistance to the MBA outside of consultancies and financial services, MBAs are finding appropriate jobs in practically all industries. There the main factor is not the large pool of MBA graduates employed, but German companies' need to finally modernize and rationalize. MBAs are useful both for the tough process of modernization and for managing modernized companies and divisions in a competitive global world.

European career perspectives for MBAs are probably best in the United Kingdom, followed by the Benelux, France, Spain, Switzerland, and Germany. Starting salaries for graduates of top European programs are between 10 percent and 20 percent lower than for graduates of the top American schools, such as Harvard, Wharton, and Kellogg, who earn about $100,000. European schools whose graduates earn the highest starting salaries are INSEAD and ISA HEC in France, IMD in Switzerland, and London and Warwick in the UK. The dollar equivalent of these starting salaries in local currencies may be less than the dollar salary of graduates of U.S. schools, but the salary must be related to its buying power in the country where it is earned. For example, while starting salaries of the leading Spanish schools may be lower, they are high in relation to their buying power in Spain. In general, the more international the school, the higher the average starting salary of its graduates, because graduates will be distributed over a greater variety of jobs and salary levels in different countries and industries.

However, in Europe starting salaries may not be the most appropriate yardstick by which to measure the career success of European MBA graduates. In Germany, for example, starting salaries for MBAs may be only marginally higher than those of less qualified employees in the same jobs. Yet MBAs tend to advance more quickly on their own merits and are allowed—if not expected—to advance more quickly in the hierarchies. Human resource managers at Dresdner Bank and Deutsche Bank in Frankfurt confirmed that this was the case in their firms. MBAs work longer hours, give better presentations, suggest more intelligent strategies, work more effectively in groups, and handle international tasks more easily than those without the MBA.

The broader presence of MBAs in all industries is demonstrated by the growing number of companies recruiting at the top schools: 350 at Madrid's Instituto de Empresa, 190 at IESE in Barcelona, 150 at Manchester Business School, 128 at London Business School, 110 at SDA Bocconi in Milan, and 102 at INSEAD (Source: *Which MBA?* Addison-Wesley, London, 1996). The fact

> Career perspectives are best in the UK.

that some of the more international schools have fewer companies recruiting does not mean that they are less popular in the corporate world. It may mean that some larger companies recruit at these schools centrally for all or sections of Europe. By contrast, leading schools with a more national slant are likely to attract national and international companies of all sizes. However, the school should have a "critical mass" of companies recruiting, to reflect the breadth of image in the market.

THE MBA IN THE UNITED KINGDOM: EUROPE'S LARGEST MBA MARKET

The United Kingdom is Europe's largest MBA market, with more than 10,000 students enrolled in roughly 110 MBA programs. Some 8000 students graduate with MBAs there each year. Americans are among the largest foreign groups studying for MBAs and a host of other degrees in the United Kingdom. Language is no problem. The UK educational system enjoys a strong reputation in the United States, yet it is located in Europe and offers the European flair Americans normally look for when studying abroad. The substantially older and professionally more experienced students in British programs promise foreigners a richer learning experience and insight into the management cultures of many countries.

POPULARITY AND VARIETY OF MBAs

The number of MBA programs has grown dramatically, with demand so high that most major universities and some independent institutions now offer one or more MBA programs. Estimates are that between 40,000 and 50,000 MBA graduates are employed in the United Kingdom in many successful positions. This mass of managers is one factor helping the infiltration and acceptance of the MBA in corporate United Kingdom. Many of those seeking to hire people with MBAs hold MBAs themselves. The generation holding negative opinions of MBAs, thinking that they are arrogant, too consultant-like and expensive, is slowly changing its views or retiring. More and more ads for management positions include the MBA as a desired qualification. More UK employers than ever before support their employees in earning an MBA, and MBA programs are adapting their curricula to what the corporate world wants and expects.

One advantage of doing an MBA in the United Kingdom is the large variety of MBA program types available. There are one- and two-year, full-time programs, executive MBAs in different forms, modular programs, consortium MBAs, corporate MBAs and distance-learning programs. Estimates are that over half of the MBA students are enrolled in the increasingly part-time and distance-learning variants. MBA students in the United Kingdom are older than their counterparts in the United States—the feeling is that the degree should be earned once you have substantial experience in the business world. As such, the flexibility of part-time or distance learning fits with the profiles of the students.

ONE-YEAR, FULL-TIME MBAS

Among the full-time programs, the trend is toward shorter, one-year programs. With the exception of London Business School and a few others, full-time programs are tending toward the one-year variant. On the European continent, some of the best-known schools such as INSEAD and IMD, offer MBA programs lasting only 10 months. While shorter programs might save time and initially seem like a good idea, proponents of longer, or at least somewhat longer programs, maintain that it is hard to digest so much new material and so many new lessons in such a short period of time. In addition, these compact programs hardly allow students to integrate the new knowledge into their business lives.

Shiela Cameron writes in *The MBA Handbook* (Cameron, Shiela, *The MBA Handbook,* 3rd ed., Pitman Publishing 1991, 1997), "If the more difficult techniques are not practiced while 'fresh,' there will be insufficient impetus ever to make the effort of applying them. By the end of a year's full-time study a student's head may feel completely stuffed with all that has been covered."

TWO-YEAR, FULL-TIME MBAS

The older programs, such as those of London Business School, Manchester Business School, and Birmingham still follow the two-year American model. Like the American programs, the first year is dedicated to a core curriculum; the summer break is the time for a management internship; and the second year is for specializations, projects, and meeting with recruiters. This variant requires a nearly complete career break because employers are hardly going to hold a job open for two years. For foreigners studying in the United Kingdom, the long two-year program gives them a chance to get to know the UK business culture and perhaps those of other countries as well. Most longer programs, like those at London and Manchester Business Schools, offer a worldwide network of schools for student exchange. Participating in this kind of an exchange program for one semester (one or two terms) will definitely make the longer period of study appear more worthwhile.

PART-TIME AND DISTANCE-LEARNING OPTIONS

For those living and working near a business school in the United Kingdom, a weekend or evening MBA may be the right way to go. These programs, such as those at London, Manchester, or Cambridge, generally last a year longer, but cover the same material as their full-time counterparts and are somewhat more expensive in tuition fees. Even so, they are generally more demanding than distance-learning programs, which can be spread out to last as long as seven years. Holding down a high-pressure job and attending a three-year part-time MBA at London Business School will probably require active employer support. Inevitably, the MBA studies will cut into your available time at work.

Generally, the popularity of executive, distance-learning and other part-time MBAs has to do with the positioning of the MBA in the United Kingdom as a postgraduate and indeed postexperience education. The typical age for doing an MBA in the United Kingdom is between 28 and 35, and most students will have well over five years professional and management experience, plus a bachelor's degree from an accredited university or college. A survey by the British business school association AMBA in 1995 showed that the 36 to 40 age group accounted for over 30 percent of all MBA students, as compared with only 20 percent in 1992.

Eighty percent of the students enrolled in MBA programs in the United Kingdom are in part-time or distance-learning programs. The world market leader in distance-learning programs is Henley College, an independent business school conferring a Brunel University MBA. Thousands of its students study online or use other forms of communication worldwide. Distance learning is normally for mobile and fully employed executives. Wherever they are, they can continue to work on their MBA. A tutor can be reached around the clock to help with course materials. Materials are complete; there's no searching for books, cases, or numbers. Most programs require that students spend a certain number of residency hours on campus or in classroom seminars. This is to ensure that the mutual learning experience is not completely lost. These programs involve the latest information technology. Problems arise if communications standards in the student's country do not match those required by the program. However, there is no comparison here with full-time or other part-time programs that involve constant classroom presence. The distance-learning seminars are spread out over a long period of time, and the entire learning experience can be quite watered down if the student's workload does not allow working on the MBA more intensely. Its utility for foreigners wanting a United Kingdom or European learning experience is at best marginal.

CONSORTIUM OR CORPORATE MBAS

Corporate sponsors support roughly 80 percent of the distance-learning students, and there are other forms of direct corporate involvement in the MBA. If you work for a UK corporation, even in a foreign subsidiary or division, it might be that they offer a corporate MBA, a consortium MBA with several business schools, or sponsor students at one or more particular schools. Several B-schools have created specialized MBA programs catering to their sponsor industries. Examples include the MBA in financial studies at the University of Nottingham Business School, the public sector MBAs at Aston, Henley, Birmingham, Nottingham, and Exeter, the MBA in legal practice at Nottingham University Law School and the MBA in healthcare and housing management at Glasgow Business School. Although this sector has not grown like the distance-learning MBA, it has become an accepted part of the MBA scene in the United Kingdom.

Corporate or "single-company MBAs" have not taken hold as was anticipated. Even so, there are plenty of prominent examples: British Airways and Lancaster Management School, Standard Chartered Bank and Henley, and the BBC and Bradford Business School. Standard Chartered's commitment to the program is so great that they will fly in participants from as far away as Australia to participate in the seminars. Critics assert that these MBAs are too narrow and address only the interests of the associated company or companies. This is perhaps one reason why many top B-schools have shied away from offering corporate MBAs. Other drawbacks of corporate MBAs are that they take longer to complete than other MBAs and offer fewer electives; that is, they are more specialized, tailored to the culture of only one institution, and thus might limit later employability with other companies.

QUALITY AND ACCREDITATION

Aside from a small number of schools such as London Business School, Manchester, Cranfield, Warwick, Ashridge, or Imperial, most of the UK business schools are not that well-known outside of the United Kingdom. Nevertheless, this says little about their actual quality. Between 30 and 40 are accredited by the AMBA. The AMBA accreditation is not as tough or encompassing as that carried out by the AACSB in the United States, but it does contain a self-assessment study and evaluation committee visit. It can be considered as one of many criteria to consider when selecting a business school. Yet many of those not accredited are associated with reputable universities. The lack of accreditation of an MBA program might indicate that the program is too new.

Being associated with a large public university in the United Kingdom means access to faculty, library, living, and research resources. The British universities compete for public funding, must demonstrate their research abilities, and are regularly rated by the newspaper *The Times.* It is thus important not only to look at what the business school offers but also to consider the reputation of the university it is a part of. If the B-school belongs to a large university, it may have access to top faculty and resources from other departments.

THE STUDENT BODY

Much of the United Kingdom's internationalism derives from the Commonwealth era when it encompassed countries as diverse as Canada, India, and Malaysia. Accordingly, the world has studied in the United Kingdom, and its MBA programs continue the tradition. Students from 20 to 30 different countries attend many of the programs. Birmingham claims to have 94 percent foreign students; Glasgow, 90 percent; and London, 78 percent. To avoid programs with too many foreign students from one country or region of the world, consider how many nationalities are actually represented in the percentage of foreign students.

According to AMBA (in their study *MBAs: Salaries and Careers, 1995*), students at UK universities took their first (bachelor's) degrees in the following areas:

- Engineering (32 percent)
- Other sciences (24 percent)
- Social science/law (13 percent)
- Humanities (12 percent)
- Business (8 percent)
- Computer science (3 percent)
- Other (9 percent)

The science bias reveals that a great number of MBA students are doing their MBA to escape being trapped in a specialized technical job. The AMBA survey also found that 88 percent of the MBAs polled cited "improving job opportunities" as the reason for pursuing the degree. Most planned to stay with their existing employers with hopes of achieving more responsibility and perhaps even a better position.

COSTS

At first glance, British programs may seem like a bargain compared to their American counterparts. Annual fees are around 10,000 Pounds Sterling (approximately $17,000) for European Union residents with non-EU students paying 10 to 20 percent more. Obviously living expenses will vary depending on whether you study in London or in less expensive cities such as Nottingham. Estimates are that in any case a one-year program might cost a total 20,000 Pounds Sterling (approximately $34,000).

Most financial aid schemes in the United Kingdom are for UK students. Fulbright scholarships are granted for several schools, and the big consulting firms award a limited number of grants on the basis of merit for studying at particular schools, such as McKinsey at Cambridge's Judge Institute of Management Studies.

ADMISSIONS

As in the United States and almost everywhere, the GMAT is required by most programs and considered a good yardstick for the quality of a student. The top UK schools have average GMAT scores about or in excess of 600 points, which puts them on par with the best American schools. Examples of schools with the highest average GMAT scores include:

London Business School: 625
Cambridge (Judge): 620
Cranfield: 620
Oxford: 620
Aston: 610
Dublin (Trinity): 610
Warwick: 610
Manchester: 593

The grade point average from the undergraduate degree and the reputation of the university where these were earned are also important. Work experience is crucial. The trend is to require upwards of five years of professional experience, preferably with increasing management experience. If students meet these requirements, the interview is given critical importance. Of those invited to interviews, probably more than half are offered places at top schools.

Starting dates for most UK full-time and regular MBA programs are in September and October. A few, such as Ashridge and Bristol, start in January as well. Distance-learning programs can be started practically anytime.

USEFUL INFORMATION SOURCES

ASSOCIATIONS

Association of MBAs
15 Duncan Terrace
London N1 8BZ
Tel: (44) 171 837 3375
Web site: http://www.amba.org.uk

AMBA accredits UK and Continental European MBA programs, gives information, and awards loans.

Association of Business Schools ABS
London WC 1X 8BP
Tel: (44) 171 837 1899
Fax: (44) 171 837 8189
E-mail: abs@mailbox.ulcc.ac.uk

Most UK B-schools are members; gives information and puts out a guide of schools.

SCHOLARSHIPS AND LOANS

Association of Commonwealth Universities
John Foster House
36 Gordon Square
London WC1H 0PF
Tel: (44) 171 387 8572
E-mail: awards@acu.ac.uk

Grants scholarships for study within the Commonwealth and gives information on universities within the Commonwealth.

The Grants Register
Globe Book Services Ltd.
Macmillan Publishers Ltd.
Brunel Road
Basingstoke, Hants RG21 2XS
Tel: (44) 1256 817245

Provides a comprehensive listing of awards and scholarships.

BOOKS AND NEWSPAPERS

The Association of MBAs Guide to Business Schools 1997/98, Pitman
Publishing, London, 1997. Contains an extensive list of UK
schools plus helpful background information.
Business School Directory 1999–2000, Postgraduate and postexperience courses, Jonathan Slack, 1999. Lists and partially evaluates practically all UK business schools.
The Financial Times. Every Thursday this daily paper publishes a
weekly page on career and business schools by Della Brad-
shaw. In addition, the paper has begun to conduct surveys
yielding rankings of European and American full-time MBAs
and executive education programs.
The Guardian. It contains regular educational sections, which
often cover UK or other business schools and MBA programs.
The Times. On Saturdays the paper publishes a special education
section. Sometimes this section is dedicated largely to MBAs.

THE MBA IN GERMANY: STILL AN EMERGING MBA MARKET

Germany is economically the largest nation within the European
Union. Its GDP alone comprises about one-third of the GDP of
the European Union. Its blue-chip corporations have enjoyed a
global presence since the 1950s. Since Germany has virtually no
natural resources, it has essentially been a producing and export-
ing country. Over half of its industrial production is exported,
which means that its management culture is externally oriented.

This outward bias, however, has translated neither into modern
management techniques nor into a large market for business
schools. Most of the DAX 30 (stock index of German blue chips),
such as Allianz, Bayer, Deutsche Bank, and Siemens, are only now
doing what U.S. corporations did in the 1980s—restructuring for
efficiency. Mergers and acquisitions within Germany are just getting

under way, although DaimlerChrysler and Deutsche Bank/Bankers Trust are cases of major takeovers by German blue chips. It is interesting to note that these deals were engineered by American investment firms and businessmen with non-German MBAs.

The number of Germans pursuing MBAs has doubled over the past few years to just over 2000 per year, but this is still very few for a population of over 80 million. There are only two German business schools comparable to schools in the United Kingdom, France, or Spain—WHU Koblenz and European Business School, both within an hour's drive of Frankfurt.

OLD LAWS AND OUTDATED MENTALITY BLOCK MBA DEVELOPMENT

As an MBA market, Germany has been inhibited by several factors. One is the government. Germany is among the most overly bureaucratized nations in the world. Combined with the Germans' basic trust in government as a source of legitimacy, this is a major hindrance to modernization. And, due to laws that date back to Hitler and forbade the awarding of foreign degrees, German schools were not even permitted to officially award the MBA degree with the sanction of the Ministry of Education until 1999. The only way around this had been to award foreign—mainly American—degrees by holding some courses in Germany and some at the foreign campus.

To make matters worse, Germans who applied to foreign MBA programs were overly concerned that the degree be recognized by the German government. Dr. Albert Stähli, dean of the GSBA Zurich, Switzerland, a school with roughly 50 percent German students in its Executive MBA program, said, "I have highly qualified managers applying for admission and being very concerned about what the German government will think about their MBA degree." The Ministry of Education only accepted MBA programs with American AACSB accreditation or British programs, and these only within limits. World-renowned MBAs such as those of INSEAD in France or IMD were not formally recognized. Yet no inclusion or exclusion criteria for accreditation were released by the Ministry of Education. The impression was that the Ministry knew little, if anything, about MBAs. Formally printing the title "MBA" from a nonrecognized school could be punished by law in Germany and result in a hefty fine.

This attitude is changing. A study by Cox Communications and the German magazine *Audimax* (used in the ranking of this book) shows that potential applicants believe that de facto recognition of the MBA by the business world is much more important than recognition by the government. Yet even in Germany things are changing. The government now permits German state colleges and universities to offer MBAs themselves.

Even so, for years German corporations resisted actively recruiting MBAs because they thought that they might be too expensive and pushy—not easily integrating into the rigid German corporate structures. This too is changing, albeit slowly. Outside of consultancies and major foreign companies like Johnson & Johnson, MBAs still have a hard time at German firms. They are not given substantially higher starting salaries or responsibilities as they normally are in the United States or even in the United Kingdom.

FLEDGLING MBA MARKET

Germany lacks even a single long established MBA program. Most programs are just starting out or are only a few years old. The schools lack alumni, proven faculty, advanced teaching methods, specialized facilities—practically everything their foreign counterparts have offered for years.

There are two first-degree (undergraduate) business schools with national and international standing. Koblenz and European Business School (EBS) have been offering undergraduate three-year business programs with a partial MBA flavor for years. Students go to these schools almost directly from German *Gymnasium* (high school) and receive a *Diplom-Kaufmann* (business diploma) at the end. Within the context of these studies, Koblenz has set up a worldwide network of exchange programs with reputed MBA b-schools. Koblenz students are encouraged to take a semester abroad during the final part of their studies toward the *Diplom-Kaufmann*.

Koblenz recently began offering an executive MBA program together with the Kellogg School of Northwestern University. Actually, the degree awarded is a Kellogg degree and Kellogg faculty teach most of the modules. As one Koblenz spokesman said, "There are too few faculty qualified in teaching interactive and strategic MBA classes in Germany. We wanted to go together with an international partner."

Under its new dean, Jacob de Smit, formerly MBA program director at the renowned Rotterdam School of Management, EBS is expected to soon offer its own MBA. Thanks to de Smit's leadership, EBS is beginning to overtake its archrival Koblenz in rankings by major German magazines as Germany's best place to study for a first business degree.

DIFFERENT MBA TYPES

While the MBA in Germany is still in a start-up phase, a number of types of the MBA degree are being offered by German or foreign schools on German soil:

- MBAs offered by German state universities and colleges
- MBAs of foreign schools offered in conjunction with German state universities and colleges
- MBAs of foreign schools in conjunction with private German schools
- MBAs of international business schools with branches in Germany
- Corporate or consortium MBAs

MBAS AT GERMAN STATE UNIVERSITIES AND COLLEGES

With the liberalization of the *Hochschulrahmengesetz* (German law on college and university education) allowing German state colleges and universities to offer foreign bachelor's and master's degrees, there has been a rapid influx of new MBA programs offered directly by these institutions. Practically overnight this has grown to become the largest category of MBAs in Germany, with between 20 and 30 MBA programs available at the time this book was written. This figure could well double or triple by 2001 or shortly thereafter. As pointed out, these programs appear to be MBAs in name only. They have not yet proved their quality; most have not even graduated a single class. Their faculty members are often already teaching in the university within the conventional first-degree programs and are not uniquely qualified to teach at business schools. One observer said after negotiating with a German university, "They (the German universities) seem to be only concerned with buildings and classrooms, facilities, not teaching quality or the methodology of their program."

Many of the *Fachhochschulen,* or FHs, state colleges awarding mainly first degrees, have gotten into the business of offering MBAs. They are more practical and vocationally oriented, preparing students more directly for a specialized profession such as engineering, finance, or business. Their studies are shorter than those of comparable universities and their diplomas are marked "FH." While many in Germany consider a university education more prestigious than that of an FH, the low quality of education offered by overfilled German universities and the high unemployment of their ill-prepared graduates enhance the merits of the FH.

These programs normally last between 14 and 18 months. Many hardly require professional experience, such as the FH Kiel or Saarland. In many cases, the proportion of international students is only 10 percent, if even that. Even so, most programs are both in English and German, some are even exclusively in English and involve foreign faculty or part-time faculty who are mainly business people. Further examples of these programs include:

- FH für Wirtschaft Berlin: First semester in Berlin, second in London, later studies partially in China. The school specializes in China, offering a "China MBA."
- FH Pforzheim: Exchange programs with universities and B-schools in Europe, the United States, and Asia. Class size is 18.
- Universität des Saarlandes: Has offered an MBA for several years; 60 percent of the students are foreign.

GERMAN SCHOOLS OFFERING FOREIGN MBAS

This category is substantially smaller than that above. Koblenz, in cooperation with Kellogg, is by all standards more established and less experimental than the FHs or state universities. While the Koblenz MBA is small (class size: 60 students or less), the school has substantial experience from its pre-MBA days in dealing with foreign business schools. Kellogg is among the world's best business schools with an excellent faculty. However, the Koblenz program is part-time and modular, and thus it is only practical for those actually living and working in Germany or at least nearby. The numerous modules would make flying in from a distant country to attend impractical. Furthermore, Koblenz, which is highly regarded in the German corporate world, prefers that students in the executive MBA program be sponsored by their employers, normally major blue-chip firms or consultancies. This limits the attractiveness of the school's program both nationally and internationally. It also means that the classroom is not likely to be a melting pot of cultures. The program remains a German and American exchange experience. Part of the program is conducted at Northwestern.

The Henley Management College of England has a German division offering distance learning from the United Kingdom. To offer the degree in Germany, Henley set up a separate *eingetragener Verein* (a sort of registered "club," such as those for hiking, auto, or other uses in Germany), giving it the name *Gesellschaft zur Förderung der Weiterbildung an der Universität der Bundeswehr München e.V.,* in short gfw. The gfw uses the classrooms of the military university in Munich. Some 90 percent of the faculty are part-time, and students only come to the school for occasional seminars (residency periods). Henley evaluates the faculty annually. Graduates receive a Brunel University degree.

OTHER GERMAN MBAS

Schiller International University in Heidelberg is an example of an American private university offering U.S. degrees in Germany. Schiller is not a "U.S. military school" as many have thought, but an independent institution. Interestingly, Schiller has always been tolerated by the German authorities as an exception to the national educational law. The school has offered U.S. programs and conferred degrees for decades without difficulties. The programs are full-time and part-time. The learning environment is American and German.

A small number of private German business schools, which have offered only first degrees, mainly in business (roughly equivalent to a bachelor of business administration), cooperate with big foreign schools and offer their degrees (MBAs) as a continuation of their studies. An example is the Akademie für Internationales Management (AIM) in Mannheim and Stuttgart, which cooperates with DePaul University in Chicago and the University of Newcastle in the United Kingdom.

QUALITY AND ACCREDITATION

Only Koblenz's MBA enjoys true international accreditation. Through Kellogg, the Executive MBA is governed by American standards, and the school recently achieved EQUIS accreditation. At this early developmental stage, the MBAs offered by German state schools guarantee little quality assurance. Faculty, curriculum, facilities, alumni, and virtually every aspect of MBA education remain to be proved.

Although the German government now permits the awarding of MBAs and recognizes the degree, this has no bearing on quality assurance of the programs. The government has no experience in assessing MBA programs and has not examined the programs, as has been done by the AACSB in the United States since 1917 and by the AMBA in the United Kingdom.

A more reliable source of program accreditation might be the Foundation for International Business Administration Accreditation (FIBAA), a program-accreditation body sponsored by the large and powerful industrial associations in Germany, Switzerland, and Austria. In the years of its existence, FIBAA has not accredited more than a handful of schools throughout Europe, but MBA assessment by employers is bound to become more prevalent.

THE STUDENT BODY

Due to the underdeveloped and muddled MBA situation in Germany, many—if not most—MBA candidates have enrolled in U.S. programs or programs in bordering countries such as Switzerland or the Benelux. Schools in the UK, France, and Spain are also gaining popularity.

There really is no "typical" student in a German business school. Programs are small and different. Students, ages 27 to 39, have varying degrees of professional experience. A German in his or her late 20s is not likely to have any serious job experience because earning the first degree may take more than five years. German universities often lack research materials and the student/faculty ratio is so poor that professors cannot test candidates for graduation. The study pace is slow, and there is very little competitive pressure. The government pays most fees and expenses. Thus, "real" MBA students are likely to be in their mid or late 30s. If they are fully employed, it is difficult to enroll in a full-time program. Thus, the bulk of the motivated managers in Germany either attend executive development courses paid for by their employers or executive MBA programs. German companies are said to spend billions of dollars each year on executive education and development.

Of the younger MBA students with little or no job experience, most have studied business or economics or engineering. An engineering degree followed by an MBA is considered a valuable combination in Germany.

THE RECRUITER VIEWPOINT

Only major consulting firms, such as Boston Consulting, Booz Allen, Roland Berger, McKinsey, or auditing/consulting firms, such as Andersen or KPMG, consistently recruit a significant number of MBAs in Germany.

Deutsche Bank, for example, hires more MBAs at their London or New York branches than at their large headquarters in

Frankfurt, where they recruit only 100 to 150 MBAs. The same is true for the other big banks, such as Dresdner Bank and Commerzbank, both in Frankfurt. And, these MBAs are mainly hired for investment banking, mergers and acquisitions, and perhaps capital markets positions. However, with major restructuring and modernizing of German banks, more MBAs are likely to find opportunities in the German financial sector. New services and more efficient operations will require new talents.

The attitude in other industries is even less enthusiastic. Exceptions are foreign firms with divisions in Germany, such as Johnson & Johnson, or German firms recruiting for foreign operations or strategic tasks, such as Bertelsmann, Quelle, or Volkswagen. Elke Strathman, head of human resources for Johnson & Johnson in Germany, said the firm tends to pay higher salaries for MBAs than for those without MBAs. However, most German firms start MBAs off at regular salary levels, but move them up the ladder quickly, depending on their performance.

THE ATTRACTION OF GERMANY FOR AMERICANS

The main reason to earn an MBA in Germany is to facilitate getting a job in Germany or with a German firm outside of Germany. The business school situation in Germany is too underdeveloped to be attractive. Germany, as Europe's largest economy currently in the midst of modernization, could be a good place to advance one's career, particularly in the service or financial sectors. The best strategy is to earn an MBA outside of Germany, which is partially in German and involves Germans, rather than to invest time and money in the untested German B-school market.

COSTS

Costs for MBA programs are among the lowest worldwide. State university education is free, so currently the only cost is living expenses, similar to those throughout Europe. However, even the State MBA programs are beginning to charge for their programs. The Universität des Saarlandes charges DM 6000 (about $3350) tuition for the total year and a half program. The FH Pforzheim is free. However, the foreign exchange partners charge tuition of between $5000 and $15,000 annually. Henley's GFW program costs roughly $16,000 and Koblenz charges about $12,500 per year. In *Das MBA Studium* (Staufenbiel, Cologne 1998), a guide on national and international MBA programs, the MBA program of the Universitaet Augsburg, which will start in late 1999, will cost over $20,000 for tuition, a high price in Germany. Financial aid for foreigners is highly limited for MBA programs in Germany.

ADMISSIONS

Some schools require some evidence of proficiency in English or a TOEFL test score of 550 or higher. The GMAT rarely appears as an admissions requirement. Also required is a primary degree such as the German *Diplom,* a master's, or bachelor's degree. The University des Saarlandes claims to accept only 30 out of 150 applicants. However, it could be that most of these 150 persons were in no way qualified. Saarland, for example, requires GMAT, TOEFL, references, and a personal interview. Some programs begin in October, some in January. Some may only begin when they receive sufficient applications.

USEFUL INFORMATION SOURCES

ASSOCIATIONS

FIBAA Foundation for International Business Administration
    Accreditation
Adenauerallee 8a
D-53113 Bonn
Tel: (49) 228 104490
Fax: (49) 228 104493
Web site: www.ihk.de
E-mail: kran@wb.diht.ihk.de

Accreditation organization of the German, Swiss, and Austrian industrial and employers associations

Sekretariat der Ständige Konferenz der Kultusminister der Länder
    in der Bundesrepublik Deutschland
Lennestr. 6
D-53113 Bonn
Tel: (49) 228 5010
Fax: (49) 228 501777
Web site: www.kmk.org
E-mail: presse@kmk.org

German Ministry of Education

FINANCIAL AID

Carl Duisberg Gesellschaft e. V
Weyerstr. 79-83
D-50676 Cologne
Tel: (49) 221 20980
Fax: (49) 221 2098111

Philanthropic organization for students at all levels

Haniel Stiftung
Franz Haniel Platz 1
D-47119 Duisburg-Ruhrort
Tel: (49) 203 806463
Fax: (49) 203 806720
E-mail: cornelia_gielter.fhac@haniel.de

Philanthropic organization

International Student Exchange Program (ISEP)
Georgetown University
1242 35th St. NW
Washington, DC 20057
Tel: (202) 667 8027
Fax: (202) 667 7801

PUBLICATIONS

Das MBA Studium, Giesen, B., Staufenbiel, Cologne, 1998.

The Saturday editions of large German daily papers such as the *Frankfurter Allgemeine Zeitung* and *Die Welt* regularly carry articles on business schools and the MBA.

THE MBA IN FRANCE: HOME OF THE GRANDES ÉCOLES

With its central location and extensive network of modern communications, France is a vital hub in Europe. As one of the founders of the European Union and a member of the Group of Seven (G-7), France plays a leading role in the international, political, and economic arena. The "glorious years" of its national economy, however, ended more than two decades ago when its annual growth rate slowed down—currently around 2.3 percent—and companies had to face increasing international competition and the need to improve productivity. Unemployment soared. Most analysts believe that France needs to modernize its welfare state, public service, labor market, and even its business sector. Indeed, it is already doing so, but in ways that the French often find uncomfortable. "The role of the State," explains Jean Luc Lagardère, head of the Lagardère defense group, "has been fundamental since the 17th century" and continues to be so. Faith in a dirigiste model remains a source of pride, not of resentment, among many French. It is worth noting that the French state spends 54 percent of the country's GDP and employs one in four workers.

However, a new wave of liberalization has swept through many industries in recent years, and French business schools may be partly responsible for the changes. Markets in electricity, telecommunications, and gas have been opened to competition and some of the companies previously owned by the state, such as Air France, Aerospatiale, and France Télécom, have been partially privatized. A further example of these changes occurred last year when Banque Nationale de Paris launched a hostile bid to take over two other French banks, Société Générale and Paribas, which themselves had just decided to merge. This episode attracted enormous attention from the general public and the media, not only because it would potentially result in the world's largest bank, but also because it revealed a more Americanized way of dealing with competitors. Indeed, the French are caught between their urge to resist "American hegemony" and the reality that they should adapt to many of the American ways of doing business.

THE TRADITION OF THE GRANDES ÉCOLES DE COMMERCE

Business education in France is mainly the domain of the *Grandes Écoles de Commerce* (GEC)—literally "Great Schools of Commerce"—with very few exceptions. The primary exception is INSEAD in Fontainebleau near Paris, which is the top European school according to this book's ranking. Most of the members of the "executive caste" have been educated at the highly regarded

GEC or at INSEAD. This includes the top managers at the French blue chips: L'Oréal, the world's largest cosmetics group; Danone, the world's largest dairy-products firm; Vivendi, the world's largest water supply company; AXA, Europe's largest insurer; and LVMH, one of the more successful luxury-goods groups worldwide.

Most of the GEC were founded by the local chambers of commerce to satisfy the educational needs of their business communities, and they still depend financially on them to a large extent. This may mean that the more powerful a chamber of commerce is, the more influential the school might be, as are the cases of ISA HEC, ESSEC and ESCP; all three are attached to the Paris Chamber of Commerce. Another example is E. M. Lyon, founded by the Lyon Chamber of Commerce. Indeed, chambers of commerce play an important influential role in the business community, and they act as a network both in their own cities and at a national level.

The most prestigious GEC belong to *Chapitre des Grandes Écoles,* which currently comprises 28 members. More information on its members and programs can be found at www.cge.asso.fr. Many GEC offer master's degree programs, but for most the core is undergraduate. After large corporations and applicants with international aspirations began asking for the MBA, the MBA became popular and the GEC began to offer it. Prior to that French companies recruited students with undergraduate degrees from prestigious GEC for their executive positions.

VARIETY OF MASTER'S DEGREE PROGRAMS IN MANAGEMENT

French schools currently offer an amazing variety of specialized master's degrees in management. You can choose from a master's specialized in luxury-brands management, such as the one offered by ESSEC in Paris (www.essec.fr), to a master's in management of sport companies, such as that run by ESCNA, the business school of Nantes (www.escna.fr). Undoubtedly, if you are thinking about working in a luxury-goods company it makes sense to study in France, the undisputed center of the world in this field. Apart from the number of specialized master's degrees, however, the program that is becoming increasingly popular is the general MBA, preferably in its one-year version. INSEAD, ISA HEC, and E. M. Lyon are examples of schools offering this type of MBA.

French schools are also offering more part-time MBA programs and a variety of executive courses. Since the GEC are attached to chambers of commerce, and consequently have close links to companies, they are active providers of executive education programs. Schools such as ISA HEC, E. M. Lyon, and ESSEC offer part-time MBA programs, and they also run executive centers that provide open and tailored programs for companies. The younger Theseus Institute, based in the Sophia Antipolis technology park in southern France (www.theseus.fr), is becoming increasingly active in offering consortium programs for its corporate clients. The most visible school in this segment, however, is INSEAD, which probably leads the European league in this field, even though it does not offer a part-time MBA.

THE FRENCH LIFESTYLE

The French share an *art de vivre*—art of living—that is special to a country with a highly developed culture considered by many as Europe's quintessence. If you can live in France as the French do, you will have the opportunity to experience an interesting and sophisticated way of life. Food is paramount—not to mention wine—and the cultural life is as rich as the cuisine. Although Paris is the center and the country's *pièce de résistance,* the entire country is a delight—with beautiful countryside and interesting cities to explore. Thanks to the TGV, the world's fastest train, it is easy to get from one part of France to another.

ADMISSIONS AND COST OF LIVING

French schools that offer MBAs require the GMAT or the TAGE-MAGE (French test of managerial aptitude) for entry. In addition, they require an undergraduate degree and, in many cases, previous professional experience—more than two years. Proficiency in French is not required at the beginning of the program by those schools that offer English or have bilingual programs, such as the schools covered in this book. However, it is advisable to arrive with at least a basic knowledge of French, as the French are very proud of their language. Living expenses in Paris are comparable to those of London or New York. If you intend to apply for a scholarship, it is best to contact the schools for information.

THE STUDENT BODY

With the exception of INSEAD, which has one of the more multicultural student bodies worldwide, GEC that offer international MBA programs usually have a large proportion of French students—often over 50 percent—but with an increasing number of foreign students. Applicants from Asia and Africa are on the rise due to France's historical presence in these continents.

French applicants to MBA programs should have completed their secondary education degree. Many French students who pursue an MBA have earned the *diplome supérieure* degree at a GEC. If the GEC offers an MBA, they may continue for another year to earn that degree. Foreign students who pursue an MBA at a GEC often mix with French students who are concluding their university studies, as well as those in the MBA program. French students who do an MBA as an extension of their degree program often have professional experience acquired through company internships during their studies.

USEFUL INFORMATION SOURCES

ASSOCIATIONS

Chapitre des Écoles de Management
60 Boulevard Saint Michel
75272 Paris Cedex 06, France
Tel.: 33-1-432 62 557
Web site: www.cge.asso.fr

This is the Association of GEC (Grandes Écoles de Commerce—the French equivalent of business schools).

FNEGE—Fondation Nationale pour L'Enseignement de la Gestion des Entreprises. This is a foundation jointly created by the French government and companies. It provides services and information for people interested in management education in France. For more information you can visit www.fnege.fr.

NEWSPAPERS AND MAGAZINES

The most popular daily newspapers in France are *Le Monde* (www.lemonde.fr), *Le Figaro* (www.lefigaro.fr) and *Liberation* (www.liberation.fr). They are good showcases of social, economic and business life in France. The economic newspaper *Les Echos* is the one mostly read by business people (www.lesechos.fr). The weekly magazine *L'Express* (www.lexpress.fr) has more extensive information on French business life and publishes surveys on management education from time to time.

THE MBA IN SPAIN: EUROPE'S MOST DYNAMIC ECONOMY

Since the mid-1980s Spain has experienced an unprecedented boom. Impressive social, economic, and political changes of the past three decades have come to fruition under a stable democracy. The country is an active member of the European Union. Indeed, Spain led the European Union in rapid growth in 1986, and still maintains one of the highest growth rates among Western European countries at 3.5 percent. Rising domestic demand has been accompanied by real increases in incomes, greater employment—although the unemployment rate is still at about 15 percent—and growth in company investment, industrial production, and corporate profits. Despite the need for further structural changes to liberalize its economy, Spain has undergone profound changes in recent years, including the privatization of many companies previously owned by the state.

What strikes the foreign observer above all, however, is the genuine enthusiasm and outward-looking philosophy of Spanish business people and their companies. The incorporation within the European Union was viewed by most Spaniards as a real opportunity to join the world's leading economies and to parade their country's virtues to the outside world. The year 1992 brought a splendid opportunity to showcase a new image of Spain to the rest of the world with the celebration of the 500th anniversary of the discovery of America, the Olympic Games in Barcelona, Expo '92 in Seville, and the choice of Madrid as the cultural capital of Europe.

THE ADVANTAGE OF STUDYING FOR AN MBA IN SPAIN

Spain's historical links and current commercial exchange with Latin America, as well as friendly relations with the Arab world, are important factors that give Spain a distinct advantage over other European countries in terms of study. This is acknowledged not only by many of the students who study there but also by some foreign companies, which invest in Spain precisely to gain a foothold in markets that are difficult to penetrate.

In addition, studying in Spain brings the opportunity of learning a language that is increasingly used in business. The three Spanish business schools covered in this book—Instituto de Empresa, IESE, and ESADE—offer bilingual MBA programs (English/Spanish), providing a soft landing in a different culture for those prospective applicants who are not proficient in Spanish. These schools report that their graduates are perfectly suited to work in Spanish-speaking environments, which brings the choice of working in one of the fastest-growing regions of the world. Undoubtedly, Latin America will continue to be one of the most attractive regions for companies and investors, since there is still much room for growth and most of its countries are becoming socially and politically stable. Evidence of this is the huge investment of a significant number of Spanish companies in Latin America in recent years. The Spanish have become one of the main groups of investors in the region. Companies such as Telefonica, Repsol, Endesa, BBV, or BSCH currently are leading players in many Latin American countries and are among the largest European blue-chip companies (for more information about the largest Spanish corporations and economic indicators, see http://www.recoletos.es/economica).

THE INCREASING POPULARITY OF MBAS IN SPAIN

A new breed of entrepreneurs is emerging in Spain, as a business career becomes fashionable for many university graduates. Not surprisingly, recent statistics reveal that 12 percent of university graduates in Spain show interest in enrolling in MBA programs, although the number of master's degrees in management produced by Spanish business schools and its public university network is estimated at about 11,000. This impression is reinforced by the common archetype of the new Spanish business executive, who has an MBA from a U.S. university or from one of the top Spanish business schools. In fact, the leading Spanish B-schools have barely been able to cope with the avalanche of prospective students, and management training is expanding at a phenomenal rate. The aim is to turn out "Euromanagers" able to operate with equal facility in a variety of business environments.

It is difficult to assess the exact number of institutions and educational centers operating in the Spanish market, since information regarding postgraduate management education in Spain is fragmentary. A recent report accounts for more than 200 different Spanish business schools and similar institutions, offering a variety of programs. The top Spanish business schools, Instituto de Empresa, IESE and ESADE, which are ranked in this book, have been accredited by EQUIS and by AMBA. Another reliable source to assess the quality of management education in Spain is AEEDE, the Spanish Association of Business Schools, a private organization that runs its own accreditation system. This association includes the three above-mentioned schools, along with other well-reputed institutions such as ICADE in Madrid (http://www.upco.es), EADA in Barcelona (http://www.eada.es), and the University of Deusto in Bilbao (http://www.deusto.es).

The well-established and cheap Spanish university network—with more than 39 public and private universities—is probably the reason for the scarce presence of foreign universities there. An exception is the University of Chicago, which offers an executive MBA from its branch in Barcelona. This program lasts 18 months and is scheduled in a modular fashion, since its participants continue working during the program. For more information about this program, contact barcelona.inquiries@gsb.uchicago.edu.

The increase in enrollments shows that part-time master's degree programs in management have become very popular in recent years, since they allow participants to take courses without leaving their jobs. The three schools covered in this book offer such programs, called executive MBAs at both Instituto de Empresa and IESE. Companies finance a high proportion of the participants in these programs.

WHERE IN SPAIN

Writers on Spain have often claimed that a more accurate name of the country would be "the Spains," since within its frontiers the differences of landscape, climate, peoples, languages, and cultures are probably greater than in any other country in Europe. The two major Spanish cities are its capital, Madrid, where Instituto de Empresa is located, and Barcelona, home of IESE and ESADE.

Madrid is the hub of the country's financial network and major Spanish corporations. Located in the geographical center of Spain, its congested airport channels many European travelers to Latin America. The city has rich cultural offerings, as well as an extremely lively social scene. Spanish traditions and the new business spirit come together in this city where most of the worldwide consulting and auditing companies, who actively recruit at Spanish B-schools, have branches.

Barcelona is the capital of Catalonia, one of the largest and most industrially developed regions in Spain. The cornerstone of the Catalan economy is a well-developed industrial network, with an impressive number of family-owned businesses. Catalonia accounts for almost a quarter of Spanish exports. It is closely linked to the rest of Europe culturally, psychologically, and economically, evidenced by the fact that the European Union accounts for 60 percent of its foreign trade. Barcelona enjoys a privileged location on the Mediterranean coast, and it is increasingly becoming a fashionable and cosmopolitan city for many foreigners. Although the main language in this region is Catalan, a dialect that belongs to the Romance family of languages, most Catalans also speak Spanish.

LIVING IN SPAIN

Spaniards indeed "work hard and play hard." After a lengthier daily working schedule than their European counterparts, they socialize until the early hours of the morning quite regularly, often in the company of family or friends. Spain has the third longest working day in the world (behind Japan and the United States). Though comparisons are difficult, they probably sleep less than most of their European neighbors, and, apart from holiday periods, the siesta is no longer observed. Above all, Spaniards are friendly and generous hosts, both with their time and their pockets.

Understanding how Spanish people conduct business and their business relations may be as important as good communicative skills in the foreign language. Generally considered open minded, Spaniards are on the whole as much concerned about maintaining their own distinctive traditions as they are in modernizing their country. The Spanish habit of spending time with people, for evening drinks and meals or tapas, is of crucial importance in developing business relationships. Like Latin Americans, business people in Spain do not appreciate the formal, desk-bound approach to discussion and decision making which is characteristic of the Anglo-Saxon executive. Spaniards believe that a good business relationship is very much tied up with the development of a good personal relationship, and social situations facilitate this. Of course, this is just a generalization, and the multicultural composition of the student body at schools such as Instituto de Empresa or IESE may create different circumstances.

The costs of living in Madrid or Barcelona are comparable to those of other major European cities. An increasing number of foreigners settle in Spain because the quality of life is good, people are open and friendly, the weather is more bearable than in northern Europe, the gastronomy is excellent and varied, and the rates of security are higher than in other western countries.

As to financing the MBA program, the three business schools surveyed in this book offer scholarships and loan schemes. If interested, it is best contact the schools.

THE STUDENT BODY

The top Spanish business schools—Instituto de Empresa, IESE, and ESADE—attract a high percentage of students from Europe, the United States, and especially from Latin America, in addition to their domestic student body. At Instituto de Empresa and IESE, the proportion of foreign participants in some programs is above 50 percent, which means that their environments are more multicultural.

Since university degree studies in Spain take an average of five years, longer than in most other European countries, Spanish students who attend full-time programs there tend to have less professional experience than their foreign counterparts. For example, at Instituto de Empresa and IESE, the average previous professional experience of the students is about three years, slightly below the five to eight years average at INSEAD or London Business School. On the other hand, the academic backgrounds of Spanish applicants are varied, although the highest single group is represented by those with degrees in economics or business.

USEFUL INFORMATION SOURCES

ORGANIZATIONS

Circulo de Progreso. A publishing company with its own directory of postgraduate programs in Spain and an extensive database available through the Internet (http://www.dices.com).

AECI (Agencia Espanyola de Cooperacion Internacional). The Spanish Office for International Cooperation offers diverse scholarship schemes for foreign students, mainly to those coming from Latin American countries. (Telephone: + 34 91 583 81 00)

NEWSPAPERS AND MAGAZINES

El Pais. The Spanish newspaper with the largest daily circulation, it also publishes an international edition that is distributed overseas. Its weekend edition contains a special survey on business that includes a section on management education. It is also available through the Internet (http://www.elpais.es).

ABC. A very influential newspaper in Spain, its Sunday edition is the weekend's most-read newspaper and includes information on business education. It is also available through the Internet (http://www.abc.es).

Expansión. The economic newspaper owned by the Pearson Group, which publishes the *Financial Times.* It is the newspaper most read by business people and publishes diverse surveys on management education during the year. It is available through the Internet (http://www.recoletos.es/expansion).

Actualidad Económica. A weekly business magazine with the largest circulation in the country. It provides a very good opportunity to get more familiar with Spanish corporations. It publishes a survey on Spanish business schools every year (http://www.recoletos.es/economica).

THE MBA IN SWITZERLAND: SMALL AND HIGH QUALITY

THE SWISS CONTEXT

Switzerland, a small mountainous country in the middle of Europe, is an important international center with one million of its six million residents carrying foreign passports. Many large multinationals have located their European headquarters within the alpine country, no doubt because Switzerland levies lower taxes on corporate profits than most other European countries. Dow Chemical Europe and General Motors Europe, for example, are both in Zurich, the country's economic powerhouse where most major business decisions are made. The Zurich stock exchange is one of the large European courses, following London and Frankfurt. Although Switzerland's failure to join the European Union has meant that it operates on the sidelines of European economic and business developments, the Swiss have maintained their discretion in banking. Money from around the world still pours into this safe haven. And, doing business surrounded by magnificent mountain scenery is a major attraction.

BUSINESS SCHOOLS IN SWITZERLAND

In the context of internationalism and business, the country appears ideal for business schools. On a per capita basis Switzerland has one of the largest number of MBA applicants of any European country (1000 annually). Swiss corporations, like companies in many European countries, are modernizing, which increases the demand for business education.

Harvard Business School once tried to set up an executive training center on picturesque Lake Geneva, but the venture failed. Others were more successful. Europe's oldest business school, the International Management Institute (IMI), was established in Geneva by the Canadian aluminum corporation Alcan back in 1946 to train its executives. Later IMI opened its doors to managers and students from all over the world. Similarly, in 1957 Nestlé set up IMEDE (full name) in Lausanne with the help of Harvard. Both institutions merged in 1989 to establish the Institute for Management Development (IMD) located at the former IMEDE campus in Lausanne.

Another private initiative, which grew to become one of central Europe's largest executive-level business schools, is the Graduate School of Business Administration (GSBA Zurich). It was established in 1985 as the first major initiative in Switzerland's economic capital. Swiss state universities and colleges, like their German counterparts, have not made a significant contribution to the European MBA scene. Even so, unlike the German schools, Swiss state schools such as the Hochschule St. Gallen (HSG) and, to a much lesser degree, the University of Zurich have offered a variety of modernized management programs that contain "MBA-like" elements. Although HSG seems to derive up to one-third of its revenues from private sources, a number of hindrances have impeded it and other Swiss State schools from offering the MBA proper, including laws against offering foreign degrees and the lack of MBA-qualified faculty and financial resources.

On the other hand—and unlike Germany—the Swiss never forbade private institutions from setting up shop and offering a wide variety of national and international degrees. This liberalism has fostered the establishment of world-renowned private high schools and hotel schools. It has also led to the establishment of business schools of all sizes and quality.

THE "FIRST LEAGUE" OF SWISS MBA PROGRAMS

IMD is undoubtedly one of Europe's most prestigious business schools and also enjoys considerable national prestige. With about 80 students, it is among Europe's smaller MBA institutions. However, its main business is educating managers in highly profitable executive development courses, which are attended by an estimated 3500 business people annually. While research was once the main emphasis of IMI, one of its predecessors, IMD Director Peter Lorange, emphasizes that offering teaching excellence to managers from all over the world is the school's main goal.

HEC Lausanne, not to be confused with ISA-HEC in France, is younger and not well known. The school is part of the University of Lausanne, which was founded in 1890 but dates back to 1537. It is recognized by the French Conférence des Grandes Écoles (leading schools association), an indication of western Switzerland's cultural and economic ties to France. HEC Lausanne's MBA program is among the shortest in Europe, lasting only nine months. Besides the full-time program, the school offers a two-year, part-time variant.

Newer and tailored to the German-speaking market is GSBA Zurich, located on a new campus on Lake Zurich and in downtown Zurich. Among its programs are the Executive MBA (250 students), Executive BBA (700 students), Master of Science, and Swiss programs such as the *Betriebsökonom* (a pre bachelor professional business degree). The programs attract students mainly from Switzerland, Germany, and Austria. The master's and bachelor's programs are in German and English.

OTHER SCHOOLS

Switzerland's other schools and programs can be listed under three categories: (1) business programs by state institutions, (2) small but solid private initiatives with quality programs, and (3) various foreign initiatives.

The main player among the state programs is HSG in St. Gallen near the German border. The school is 100 years old with 4000 students studying economics and business-related courses. A joint finance master of science was developed with New York University, but neither school attracted significant numbers of students or other revenues. More successful, but not an MBA by a multitude of criteria, is a two-year, part-time course culminating in an "NDU" diploma (*Nachdiplomstudium in Unternehmensführung*—an executive development diploma). The limited appeal of HSG is due to its location more than 100 kilometers from Zurich—too far for busy managers to travel to get a postgraduate degree.

Business School Lausanne (BSL) is an example of a small but solid school offering full-time bachelor's and MBA programs, plus evening and weekend MBA degrees. Unlike many other schools in Switzerland, BSL has maintained a low profile, relying on word-of-mouth propaganda to promote its programs. BSL has attracted top German students from prominent families, and its graduates secure top jobs and pursue highly successful careers. BSL enjoys American ACBSP (Association of Collegiate Business Schools and Programs) program accreditation.

A small program with poor value for the money is the University of Rochester (Simon School) MBA program in the provincial town of Thun near Bern, the capital of Switzerland. Its countryside location is poor. The school is expensive (68,000 Swiss Francs or $46,000) and poorly marketed. While Simon is top-rated in the

United States, and graduates from the "Bern program" receive the Simon MBA, the Swiss program is just a few years old and—like that of the University of Chicago program in Barcelona—cannot be considered a major player in European markets. Bern is a small market and too far from Zurich to attract the clientele the school seeks. Furthermore, programs like those of Rochester in Bern and Chicago in Barcelona rely mainly on the home institutions' images but have not equipped themselves with corporate connections and effective strategic plans in Europe. They remain sideliners at best. Lacking are reports about their financial success, indicating they may be unprofitable and ultimately doomed. A more successful approach to transatlantic cooperation is that of GSBA Zurich, which carries out its executive MBA program with the State University of New York at Albany and awards both institutions' degrees.

The third category consists of foreign schools of varying quality, such as European University near Lausanne, Webster University in Geneva, and City University in Zurich. Of these, European University (EU) has been making the most "waves," expanding into eight European countries with 13 campuses. Originally EU was set up in Antwerp, Belgium, but the school's head of international operations separated from the original school and pushed ahead with innovative programs and international cooperation, such as with the University of Dallas. New innovative programs attempt to combine management with hospitality and tourism, public relations, telecommunications, healthcare, human resources and multimedia. In addition to Dallas, EU cooperates with the U.S. Sports Academy in Mobile, the London College of Printing, and Saratov State Technological University, an engineering school in Russia.

INFORMATION SOURCES

Unlike in other countries such as the United Kingdom or even Germany, there are few consistent and recommendable sources of information on the Swiss business school scene. Information on IMD can be obtained in international catalogs and guides. GSBA Zurich is listed in guides and rankings. Swiss sources are meager. Newspapers and magazines occasionally run articles on business schools. Only the magazine *Index,* published in Basel and aiming at graduates of business programs, carries lists of programs and covers the subject consistently and somewhat objectively.

RANKING THE MBA PROGRAMS

The list of the 20 "top" MBA programs in Europe is actually a list of 20 very good programs. It is not an exhaustive list, and another survey methodology would probably yield a slightly different list or at least a differing order of programs. Importantly, the list is of MBA programs, not entire schools.

The schools and programs will probably hardly differ from other rankings. However, this book gives descriptions of the programs, covering what makes each program and school special. It offers information about life on campus, teaching methods, faculty, financial aid, contact details, and more. Appendix B contains a detailed discussion of the methods used in the rankings.

Most readers of books on business schools and MBA programs are looking for help on deciding whether to go for an MBA and where to do so. Accordingly, most books offer some advice on how to judge and select the school and/or program you really want. No set of criteria can do more than help you make a decision. The most difficult part is actually making that decision.

There is a practical difference between *judging* schools and MBA programs and *selecting* them. Judgments involve theoretical criteria such as reputation, campus, and the feel of the school or program. Selecting the right program involves practical criteria such as return on investment and whether the particular program will help your career aims. In this section we suggest examples of both:

- Criteria for judging schools and programs
- Criteria for selecting the right school for you

The criteria are derived from years of speaking with thousands of applicants, MBA students, faculty, and recruiters in many countries. Some lean on other books that give advice on how to select a business school or MBA program. The criteria are not based on a formal survey.

Judging a business school is only partly the same as assessing an MBA program. A school consists of its reputation, facilities, other departments, various services (e.g., career services), and administration, to mention just some of the important elements. While the MBA program may be the most important part of the business school, it is a separate entity and judging it means applying additional criteria.

The difference between judging schools and programs is best understood by learning how accreditation systems work. There are both institutional and program accreditation systems. The most famous accreditation organization in business administration, the St. Louis-based International Association for Management Education (whose accreditation system is known by the initials of its previous name AACSB), accredits only MBA programs. So-called regional accreditation organizations in the United States, by contrast, only accredit the institutional aspects, that is, the school itself, its facilities, management, etc. The Association of MBAs (AMBA) in the United Kingdom accredits only specific MBA programs, while the European Quality Improvement System (EQUIS), the new European accreditation system, accredits all aspects of the schools—institutional and program. Thus, if a school claims that it is "accredited by AACSB," this is actually incorrect. Only its program or programs can be accredited by AACSB. If a school claims that its program is accredited by a regional association in the United States, this is also incorrect. Regional accreditation applies only to the school as a whole. The individual programs are not examined and accredited in the same way as they would be had a program accreditation organization looked at them.

CRITERIA FOR JUDGING A BUSINESS SCHOOL AS AN INSTITUTION

Criteria for judging a business school as an institution include the following:

REPUTATION OF THE SCHOOL AS A WHOLE

Is the school well-known and well-reputed as a university or college? Harvard is an example of a school whose institutional name is probably greater than that of any of its colleges. Yet its colleges and individual components are each highly regarded in their own rights and constantly support Harvard's overall name. Oxford and Cambridge are perhaps even better examples. The schools are the United Kingdom's best, famous throughout the world as centers of learning. Although Cambridge's MBA program is only 10 years old, its reputation exceeds that of many other, much older MBA programs. It attracts students with high GMATs and excellent backgrounds. Recruiters flock to the school and sponsor professorships, facilities, and scholarships. Oxford's MBA is even newer, yet one alumnus recently gave the school a gift of 20 million Pounds Sterling ($33 million). Its MBA program attracts applicants with high GMAT scores and the school already was awarded accreditation by EQUIS.

In Europe many schools are not parts of large universities and thus must build their reputations on their own, mostly through the excellence of their program(s). INSEAD in France, IMD in Switzerland, and Ashridge and Henley in the United Kingdom have built up reputations as independent institutions by relying primarily on their short executive programs. Executive programs are a good way for a school to build its reputation among businesses. If the programs are good, managers can be "sold" on the school in only a few days. The business people already have influence and thus the school does not have to wait many years for their alumni to achieve career maturity and indirectly promote their alma maters. IMD and INSEAD are again good examples. IMD is the result of a merger between IMI in Geneva and IMEDE in Lausanne. Both schools were strong in the area of executive education. IMD maintains formal relations with more than 100 global corporations. Its MBA program enrolls fewer than 100 students in total. Its executive training programs enroll several times as many. The situation at INSEAD is similar. However, INSEAD's MBA program was increased to 450 students a decade ago, so the MBA program now carries more weight in the school's overall reputation.

While there is a great deal of discussion on how good a school's reputation really is, many would probably agree that the reputation of a school could be based on the following:

- Treatment in the media
- Positions in rankings
- Number of blue-chip companies who recruit there
- Career successes of graduates
- Satisfaction of graduates
- Loyalty and dedication of alumni to the school
- Financial grants given to the school
- Scholarships for students
- Facilities and location

Many schools are not parts of universities.

- Research by faculty
- Uniformly high quality of graduates from all programs of the school (no "top" and "trash" programs)

CAMPUS AND FACILITIES

While a picturesque campus with well-kept lawns and impressive old or modern buildings may seem to have little to do with the quality of a school, many people feel comfortable and can learn well in this kind of atmosphere. However, an American style campus is rare among European business schools, which are often located in the middle of important business centers. INSEAD, ISA HEC outside of Paris, Ashridge, and a few others are examples of schools located in rural areas or smaller towns, offering the schools room for relatively large campuses. Others, such as Instituto de Empresa in Madrid, IESE in Barcelona, and London Business School, all located in large cities, are not all concrete thanks to small gardens around or behind their buildings. Yet others are totally urban, such as EAP Paris and Imperial in London. A well-kept campus can reflect healthy finances or at least a pronounced school culture.

ALUMNI NETWORK

There are smaller alumni associations in Europe.

Harvard Business School is old and has many alumni who benefit from the Harvard Clubs and Harvard alumni associations around the world. This means networking possibilities among people from diverse backgrounds and an extensive alumni network. Cambridge is another example. With only 40 MBA grads annually, the Judge Institute at Cambridge could hardly set up a very dense global alumni network, but Cambridge MBA graduates are automatically members of the Cambridge University alumni system.

CAREER SERVICES

Students at full-time programs normally are not employed and will need jobs when they graduate. Therefore, most schools offer career services that try to bring together MBA students with prospective employers. While these services are highly professional in the United States, European schools are in varying stages of developing their career services. These can range from the secretary of the school administration making individual appointments for students to meet with companies, to a placement office with permanent staff. These staff members organize company presentations at the school, arrange individual meetings, coordinate with the alumni organization, release books containing profiles of all upcoming MBA graduates, and counsel students. A good placement office can mean more and better job offers, higher starting salaries, and graduates getting the job they really wanted.

COOPERATION WITH OTHER DEPARTMENTS AND SCHOOLS

Being part of a larger university or college can have other advantages: namely, exchanging personnel or other resources with other schools or departments. One form of this phenomenon, which is most pronounced at U.S. universities, involves joint degree programs by different schools within the same university, such as a joint MBA/JD (doctor of jurisprudence) program. It normally entails that students can apply once to both programs and perhaps save a semester or year by better integrating both programs.

At European schools, the cooperation between schools and departments is more likely to involve the business school borrowing faculty from other schools or departments. In general, the newer a school or program is, the more likely it is to borrow faculty and facilities from others. The Judge Institute does this with Cambridge. Most of the German MBA programs do not have any permanent faculty of their own, but nonetheless can give a long list of faculty from the very beginning of the program. This is something to view with caution. Is the faculty experienced in the interactive and case study teaching mode expected of an MBA program? Have the faculty worked together regularly in the past? Are they accustomed to coordinating with one another?

FINANCIAL SUPPORT

Business schools should practice what they preach and demonstrate sound financial and business management. New programs subsidized by larger institutions are more likely to survive than those

> Some business schools borrow faculty from universities.

which must quickly turn over a profit. In many cases, support may even come from the government. Caution is advised in cases of too much government support, which can erode the performance ethics of an institution. Bad faculty are retained and supported, spending is inefficient, the business world and students become secondary, etc. Limited government support, however, is normally useful if a program is new, if it involves scholarships based on merit, and if the government is only one of many sources of income.

LINKS WITH BUSINESS

Normally the school itself will promote its involvement with the business world and then implement these connections to enhance its programs. The central idea of business schools' involvement with the business world is that management education is a practical undertaking and must be partially carried out with the business community and accepted by it. If a school does not have established relations with high levels of the business community, this could indicate:

> There is room for improvement in links with corporations.

- Poor relations with recruiters and thus fewer job opportunities for graduates
- A weak overall reputation
- Graduates who performed poorly in their jobs
- Weak school management, which could equally affect the school's overall standing and image

In most cases, good relations with the business community indicate:

- Advisory boards with leading business and other personalities
- Advisory boards which meet regularly and donate money
- Numerous high-level guest lecturers at the school and in all of the school's programs
- Numerous companies, 50 or more annually, recruiting on campus
- Sponsored professorships, "chairs" carrying the corporate name of the sponsor

- Scholarship programs by companies
- Awards by companies to outstanding students

CRITERIA FOR JUDGING AN MBA PROGRAM

FACULTY QUALITY

The quality of the faculty may be the single most important characteristic of both a school and an MBA program. If all else about a school and program are good, but the faculty is poor, your education will not be good.

The faculty directly affect the:

- Teaching and learning process
- Reputation of the program and the school
- Students' abilities and graduates' career successes
- Quality of research conducted and materials used in class
- Students' recommendations of the school/program; students' ratings of faculty quality
- Ranking of the school and program
- Future recruiting efforts by the school for faculty (good faculty will not be willing to join a program where the faculty has a poor reputation)

Good faculty are hard to come by. Moreover, some top faculty may be employed in the program on paper only. They may be away on lucrative consulting assignments or teaching at other schools and departments.

What constitutes a "good" faculty member? A good faculty member:

- Possesses a top academic education
- Has significant experience in consulting or practical business matters
- Can activate the class, motivate students to learn
- Knows the field inside and out
- Is reputed in the academic and perhaps even management communities
- Has published popular and academic texts
- Conducts research that can be used in class
- Has perhaps taught at other top schools

- Is consistently rated highly by students
- Is accessible to students for questions and meetings

ADMISSIONS, SELECTIVITY

European average GMAT scores are high.

Normally, the harder it is to get accepted in a program, the higher the number of applicants and the better the students are who want to get admitted to that program. This presupposes that there are other good reasons, such as top faculty, for wanting to gain admission. Admissions offices working for top programs take pains to put together a class of very particular people who will enhance one another in the course of the program. IMD in Switzerland normally ensures that there are no more than two people from one nationality in its 70-person MBA program. GSBA Zurich looks for people with the right amount of management experience who will be able to make a real contribution to its small classes of 25 persons and the working groups of 4 persons.

The general criteria which many, if not most, top schools in Europe (and the United States) adhere to include the following:

- GMAT score of between 550 and 600
- TOEFL score of over 600
- A first degree (bachelor's, master's, or equivalent) from a renowned college or university
- Two to five years of work experience
- Strong references from employers and former professors
- Clearly defined goals—applicants who have a career plan and focus
- A favorable personal interview with school officials or alumni

The GMAT is a tough hurdle. This aptitude test was recently revamped to include more essay parts after it had been criticized as being too quantitative. Most of the top schools in Europe still require a high GMAT score, although some schools, such as the Instituto de Empresa in Madrid, offer students the possibility of taking the Instituto's own test as a substitute. The GMAT remains the accepted yardstick for programs to judge whether an applicant is likely to make it in the MBA program or not. Accordingly, programs with high average GMAT scores (the average GMAT scores of the last entering class) reveal a reputation strong enough to attract and admit only those with high scores. However, given the strong American approach and emphasis on English language nuances in the GMAT, schools with a large proportion of national students are likely to have average GMAT scores that are 50 to 70 points lower than their international counterparts. Similarly, executive MBA programs normally have lower GMAT averages because older European students are not used to this kind of test and rarely score over 600. For these two types of programs, a GMAT score higher than 530 or 540 is good.

The following ratios may also reveal something of the competitiveness of the program and thus its quality:

- Number of applicants applied/number of applicants accepted
- Number of applicants accepted/number of applicants who finally enrolled

These ratios also have limits, though. A high rejection rate may also suggest that many applicants were of inferior quality and did not meet the minimum standards. Thus, even a high ratio may say little about the program's ability to attract highly qualified applicants. Similarly, if not all applicants accepted actually enrolled, this does not necessarily mean that they did not cherish the offer of acceptance into the program. It may mean that they were so good they had too many other equally enticing offers or that the program was too expensive or that they had sudden job commitments, which prevented them from attending the program.

CURRICULUM

European schools are more difficult to judge by their curricula than their American counterparts because of the larger variety of programs. Generally, MBA specialists will probably agree that a good MBA program should do *at least* the following:

European schools have highly diverse curricula.

- Cover the core subjects of business administration such as accounting, economics, finance, human resources, information systems, marketing, organizational behavior, quantitative analytic elements, and strategy
- Feature a minimum number of classroom ("contact") hours of 500 for an MBA, which even modular, part-time executive MBAs normally achieve
- Offer sufficient opportunity to specialize, either in the form of elective courses or thesis papers
- Include quality control of student work, such as grading on class participation, sufficient testing, evaluation of presentations or thesis papers
- Offer project work in which students apply what they have learned in the program, such as in a consulting project, entrepreneurship project, business plan, or thesis paper
- Include small groups or strategy groups of four to seven people in which students work on case studies or jointly work out and present strategic solutions
- Offer international case studies, not just national case studies
- Offer recent research or case studies, not just old material which may have too little relevance to today's management challenges
- Emphasize skills ("soft skills") such as team work, presentation abilities, negotiation, and reasoning in most courses
- Provide guest lecturers from the business world with discussion and Q&A sessions
- Offer cooperation, exchanges of students and/or faculty with other reputable schools/programs in other countries
- Require students to put in long hours (10–14 hours) in class and homework every day

The program should be neither too long, which would remove the pressure from learning, nor too short, which would prevent students from covering all subjects. Some claim that the INSEAD and IMD programs (10–11 months) are too short to cover all subjects adequately and for students to digest and implement what they have learned. London Business School, Manchester, and Rot-

> A good MBA program should include a lot of strategy work in small groups.

terdam, for example, take the view that an MBA requires nearly two years of intensive study.

Most school and accreditation officials as well as recruiters will agree that the soft skills are one of the principal benefits of a top MBA program. Learning facts and acquiring knowledge is not what makes an MBA different from other academic degrees. Learning how to perform and apply skills to a multitude of management situations using superior skills is what distinguishes a top program from a program that only looks good on paper.

For the book *Which MBA?* (George Bickerstaffe, Pearson Education Ltd., London) regular surveys are conducted of students' satisfaction with program content. While a good idea, the method does not consider the differences in student expectations. As such, a student group expecting a lot in terms of strong public relations, a superior school image, or the high level of professional experience may be more difficult to please than another group expecting less. The former would give higher marks; the latter, lower marks. Accordingly, the top European programs such as IMD, London, Rotterdam, and IESE scored lower than Harvard, Kellogg, and many other top U.S. programs.

Students learn from each other.

STUDENT BODY

Students learn as much from each other as from professors and materials. Top programs attract an excellent and diverse student body with at least the following traits:

- Varied backgrounds and first degrees from different fields
- Representative of 20 to 30 nationalities (at European programs)
- High proportion of international students (over 70 percent at European programs)
- Interesting and diverse professional backgrounds

One of the big attractions of European programs is the diversity and internationalism of their student bodies. This generates unconventional ideas in class and in the work groups. Students thus acquire a broader perspective and have to defend their own ideas against a wider variety of attitudes and views.

STARTING SALARIES OF GRADUATES

Like many of the above criteria, the actual starting salaries of MBA graduates of a particular program are hard to verify. Schools or the individuals could be exaggerating, and there is no way to tell. Average income per country may differ substantially. Starting salaries in Italy or Spain may be lower than in the United Kingdom, but in relative terms they could be the same or higher. Thus, the starting yearly salaries of MBA graduates of the top U.S. schools (over $100,000) may not be comparable with European counterparts. Furthermore, a particularly large proportion of U.S. MBA graduates may be employed in expensive cities like New York, Chicago, Boston, or Washington, DC. Their buying power may indeed even be lower. Thus, this data must be considered very carefully, if at all. Rankings of differently structured programs in various countries based largely or even solely on starting salaries can be dismissed a priori.

SUCCESSFUL ALUMNI

Like starting salaries, it is difficult to determine whether the program has in fact produced a significant proportion of successful alumni. Although U.S. schools cite the percentage of CEOs of Fortune 500 companies who graduated from their MBA programs, many or most students of European programs may work in consulting or not want to become CEOs of Fortune 500 firms. Furthermore, smaller programs have a slighter chance of getting large absolute numbers of graduates into CEO positions, and most European programs enroll under 100 students. Even so, an impressive list of successful alumni is a strong sign of a program's quality because it indicates that the program:

- May have taught them how to be successful
- Recruited the "right" students
- Has a strong reputation which might benefit later generations of graduates

A MODEL FOR SELECTING AN MBA PROGRAM AND A BUSINESS SCHOOL

As pointed out earlier, there is a difference between judging a school and determining whether you want to attend. The following selection considerations are in some way related to the points of judgment just outlined, but then are framed as questions to help you consider each criterion:

SELECTION CONSIDERATION 1: RETURN ON INVESTMENT IN YOUR MBA EDUCATION

- *Cost of program:* Can I afford it? Will I get what I want later in my career? How long will it take to pay off loans? What are the other costs such as dropping my job or sacrificing my family life?
- *Length of program:* Can I afford one or two years off the job? Can I pay for my expenses while studying (normal expenses plus school and possibly travel costs)? Would it be better for me to attend a part-time program? Modular, evening, or weekend? In another city? If so, how far away?
- *Starting salaries:* Is a higher salary what I am looking for? If so, will it really be higher in my case? Are the school's claims about salaries credible? Is the school recognized in the industry and area where I later want to work? Will my employer pay for a full-time or part-time program? Will he then pay me more? What are my long-term salary prospects?
- *Financial aid availability:* Are scholarships available? If not, what is the best way to finance the program? My savings, loans? Does the program allow me to earn some money while studying, such as in consulting or other projects integrated into the program? Will these projects possibly put me in touch with prospective employers?

SELECTION CONSIDERATION 2: INTERNATIONALISM

- *Curriculum:* Do courses take an international perspective? Are cases international? Are internationally oriented electives offered?
- *Student body:* Are students from numerous foreign countries? How high is the percentage of foreign students?
- *Percent of international job offers:* How many graduates receive international job offers? How many work in a country different from where they came from before enrolling in the program?
- *International partnerships:* How many schools in how many countries is the program associated with or have exchange programs with? What is the percentage of stu-

---

Many European programs are shorter and offer a quicker return on investment.

European schools mean variety of languages and international faculty.

dents actually taking part in these programs? Are the partner institutions in the countries that may later benefit my career? Are faculty also exchanged?

- *Language requirements:* Is the language requirement a hindrance or do I really want to learn another language? Is there an all-English program variant? How could a foreign language help my career? Do I have to learn the language before beginning the program? How much time, effort, and money will this take?

- *Faculty:* How international is the faculty, that is, what are their nationalities, where did they study, and where have they worked?

- *Foreign field projects:* Does the program offer or even require "field projects" in foreign countries? How much do they immerse me in those countries' business worlds? Are the projects taken seriously by the management of the companies involved? How much can I learn? Do they pay?

- *International companies recruiting on campus:* How many and which international or globally active companies regularly recruit on campus? And for which positions? Are the most jobs really international or national/local?

- *Program management processes:* Which processes exist in the program or school to further the program's internationalization?

SELECTION CONSIDERATION 3: SKILLS TAUGHT

- *Self-management skills:* Do courses help students develop the following: self-confidence, integrity, identification with employer, entrepreneurial abilities, skills to coordinate and organize projects, discipline to optimally use time?

- *Interpersonal skills:* Are the following promoted: people management, leadership values/abilities, influence and persuasion, team working, interpersonal communication, cross-cultural communication and work, flexibility, creativity, ethical awareness, ability to produce high-quality results under time pressure?

• *Intellectual skills:* Are the following promoted: analysis and synthesis, strategy, interdisciplinary thinking, conceptualization, knowledge of business administration fields?

• *Techniques:* Are the following promoted: knowledge of how to find information, decision making and problem solving, use of information technology?

SELECTION CONSIDERATION 4: OVERALL EXCELLENCE OF THE MBA PROGRAM AND BUSINESS SCHOOL

• *Accreditation:* Are the program and the school accredited? By which organization? Is the accreditation organization itself credible? Does it enjoy governmental recognition or strong de facto recognition in the business community? How long has the program or school been accredited?

• *Selectivity, admissions?* How selective is the program? What does it require for admission? What are the average GMAT, TOEFL, or other scores of incoming students? How many students are turned down? How much work experience is required? Is the admissions process purely quantitative or does it consider strengths and skills?

• *Initial career development:* How many job offers do graduates receive? From which kinds of companies? What are some typical starting salaries?

• *Reputation:* What do my friends and colleagues say about the school's and program's reputation? How positive is the coverage in the media? What do recruiters say? How well-founded is the reputation? How many alumni, in which positions, support this reputation? Are alumni criticisms, for example, in the media? Are these frequent? Do they criticize academic quality or just personalities in the school? How do supporters and critics arrive at their conclusions?

• *Potential:* Are the school and program in a growth market, i.e., attracting increasingly qualified students from growing markets? What does the school's management do to promote and build the school and program? What

Accreditation is less important in Europe than in the United States.

59

processes has the school put in place to ensure its dynamic development and competitiveness? How have student numbers, average GMAT scores, reputation, faculty numbers, revenues, starting salaries, number of job offers per graduate developed over the past years?

When and how should you apply these questions:

- In research using books, guides, and program brochures
- In conversations with recruiters, alumni, media, as well as with friends and colleagues
- In interviews with school officials

PROS AND CONS OF RANKINGS

RANKINGS AND THE APPLICANT

There are thousands of MBA programs worldwide and roughly one million students applying to these programs. How to decide which program is best for you? The information in this chapter is designed to help you in the process. Before you even attempt to seriously evaluate a manageable list of schools and programs, however, there is a need for *preselection*. Rankings can help with both preselection of schools and programs. There are numerous rankings available, which you can use to compile a short list of good programs and schools. Whether a school is number 1, number 5, or number 16 depends on the method used in ranking and will vary from ranking to ranking. These differences are of greater concern to the schools than to the applicant. All of the schools in a top 20, top 30, or top 50 are likely to be strong and worth considering. It is unlikely that you will make more money, enjoy more prestige, or be more successful if you earn an MBA from a school rated 3 rather than a school rated 10 in any specific ranking. However, there are real differences in career development and salary between MBAs graduating from the top schools and those graduating from "no-name" schools.

Applicants and readers like to see lists with winners and losers. Magazines such as *Forbes* and *Fortune* discovered this instrument for increasing readership decades ago. The *Business Week* issue with the ranking of the 25 best business schools in the United States is among its best-selling issues. Recently the German magazine *Der Spiegel* started regularly ranking German universities and colleges. The British *Financial Times* has started to rank MBA programs and executive programs at business schools worldwide. Competing, winning, and losing appear central to human nature and thus capture human interest. Most mature industries have accepted this. Many European business schools and their associations have not. As Jonathan Slack, chief executive of the Association of Business Schools in the United Kingdom, wrote in a letter to the British newspaper *The Guardian* (10 October 1998), "Pre-selection of schools or programs should be avoided on the grounds of in-built discrimination and subjectivity." The view is typical for European—and perhaps other—business school associations whose interests include equally promoting all their members.

Most opponents of rankings like to refer to the wide array of information sources on business schools and MBA programs available to applicants. Mike Jones, director general of the "other" business school association in the United Kingdom, AMBA (Association of MBAs), takes this view: "They [potential applicants] would be better advised to undertake thorough research on the many possibilities open to them at business school prior to making what may be the most important decision of their careers" (Letter to *The Guardian,* 10 November 1998). Jones fails to point out how this "thorough research" should proceed and which of the "many possibilities" should be included and which excluded from this research.

RANKINGS AND THE SCHOOLS

Most schools both love and hate rankings. They love them if they do well; hate them if they do poorly, or do not know how they will do.

When *Business Week* editor John Byrne started surveying recruiters and MBA graduates on the best U.S. business schools over a decade ago, the American schools were up in arms. Meanwhile they have matured, accepted the BW ranking as a reality, and tried to improve their programs to make them more beneficial to the user. The "users" are the students, whose careers and lives are affected by their MBAs, and employers, whose bottom lines may be greatly affected by good or bad managers with MBAs.

Many, if not most, European schools are way behind in this maturation process—a situation which makes selecting the right school more difficult.

VALID ARGUMENTS AGAINST RANKINGS

Every ranking methodology used to date, including the one in this book, has its weaknesses. These days applicants must not only confront the problem of preselecting and selecting schools and programs, but also judging between the "good" and "bad" rankings which are intended to make preselecting schools and programs easier.

In essence, there are three arguments against rankings, which readers and applicants might want to consider in judging rankings.

First, a ranking may consider only one or *too few dimensions* of a business school or program. Rankings of schools by starting salaries of their graduates, or the number of articles published by the faculty within a certain time, or whether the MBA has produced an adequate financial return on investment, should be discounted. Much more must be considered.

Second, some rankings *depend primarily on what the schools say about themselves.* Rankings in which schools or their associations can distort the results by giving information which no one can verify are merely public relations instruments.

Third, rankings based on a *small or too narrowly defined sample* must be put into perspective. Our ranking suffers from this weakness. Surveying German potential applicants and deriving a ranking of European MBA programs from this is fine, but only if the reader realizes that this is only the opinion of this target group. Thus, our profiles of the MBA programs are descriptive rather than evaluative.

POOR ARGUMENTS AGAINST RANKINGS

All methodologies, whether in the natural or social sciences, can be criticized. Some of these arguments may even be valid. However, the challenge lies in suggesting at least equally workable alternatives. Indeed, rankings are popular because they meet a need. Thus, the challenge lies in suggesting alternative methods for conducting a ranking, not citing endless reasons why it cannot or should not be done. Arguments not containing suggestions on how to conduct a better ranking are academic and of no use to applicants and of little merit to philosophers.

Such "critics" are often schools or school associations whose interests are obvious. Mike Jones of AMBA is a good example of a typical association representative holding this view. He writes, "The academic community is surprised that a broad newspaper . . . would wish to be a party to such a ranking." He points to the need to consider "vital characteristics" such as the schools' research basis, standing in the business community, alumni network, and salary and career prospects of graduate students. He fails to point out how these might be objectively judged. For example, how many points will a 10-page paper published in journal *A* get and how much a popular book published in Hong Kong by faculty members of a school? How many points is having Bill Gates on a school's advisory board worth? Or is a grant by the Ford Foundation worth more? Is an alumni association with 15,000 members better than one with 13,500 or 1000 members? How much is "better" and how can lines be drawn?

Secondly, some critics like to attack the ranking author instead of the ranking itself. Typically, authors are accused of being "biased." Normally, an argument such as this is an easy way out. The critics have not really taken the time or effort to analyze the ranking method itself. They simply do not like the idea of the ranking.

Beyond this, it might be worth considering what the critic's motives for criticizing the ranking are. Freelance journalists, in particular, could be influenced or "sponsored" by schools or associations. As Stuart Craiter and Des Dearlove point out in *Gravy Training: Inside the Shadowy World of Business Schools* (p. 167), "Deans have been known to call journalists to petition for more coverage. They have been known to turn nasty if they don't like the coverage they do get." Given that rankings "will have a significant impact on Business Schools' revenue generation (i.e., tuition fees from paying students)," as Mike Jones of AMBA admits, schools are willing to go to great ends to promote and safeguard their reputations. The problem is that readers and applicants cannot be expected to weed through the politics of public discussions on rankings.

Thirdly and amusingly, although schools and associations want to offer their programs in a free market, they do not always want this market to judge their products. Michael Pitfield, Director of Marketing at Henley Management College in the United Kingdom, clarifies in relation to a questionnaire sent to him that "Neither do we wish you to include reference to our programs as a result of your own compilation of material from existing published data." Pitfield, who is not an exception, apparently thinks that existing published data does not do justice to his program or school. More probably, he is concerned about not being able to control the outcome of a ranking involving his school. Yet the idea of "participating" or "not participating" in a ranking itself is amusing and contradictory. If schools had this choice, the ranking would by definition be school-controlled and thus possibly invalid.

Some schools seem to be afraid of facing the market.

EUROPE'S TOP 20 MBA PROGRAMS

This book seeks to strike a compromise between brevity and comprehensiveness. The alternative to a book with a ranking such as this is to study hundreds of similarly sounding brochures and Web sites of European schools. But this would not help to know which schools correspond to what applicants and recruiters actually want in a school.

The author visited many of the schools listed along with the researchers. The profiles are not all the same length because in some cases we felt that it would be unfair to the reader to exclude interesting information. In others it would have been pressing the reader's patience to draw out the profiles just to make them the same length as those of other schools. This does not mean that schools with longer profiles are "better" than those with shorter profiles.

INSEAD—EUROPEAN INSTITUTE OF BUSINESS ADMINISTRATION

MBA Information Office
Boulevard de Constance
F-77305 Fontainebleau Cedex, France
Web site: http://www.Insead.fr
E-mail: mbainfo@Insead.fr

**1.
INSEAD**

Program

Program ranked: MBA

Structure: 1 year full-time; 15 core subjects; 7 electives (minimum)

Size of class: 650 per year (two intakes)

Participants: More than 50 nationalities (56% western Europe, 5% central and eastern Europe, 16% North America, 13% Asia, 10% rest of the world), with average work experience of 4–5 years; aged over 28

Costs: Tuition fee: 25,500 Euros (approx. $26,700); estimated living expenses for a single person: 15,240 Euros (approx. $15,960)

Program director: Prof. H. Landis Gabel

Accreditation: AMBA (British), EQUIS (European)

Admissions

Admissions requirements: University degree; GMAT (average score 680); TOEFL (minimum 620); 2 references; work experience (average 4–5 years); fluency in English and understanding of French by the start of the program; third language to graduate

Applications deadline: April for the September program and August for the January program

Starting date: Two intakes per year: January and September

Application fee: French francs 700 (approx. $110)

Recruiting

Placement office: Database with job descriptions from recruiters, recruitment guide published for companies, organized recruitment logistics

Number of companies recruiting: 250+

Examples of recruiting: McKinsey, Boston Consulting Group, Bain, Booz Allen, L'Oréal

Contact:
Admissions Office
Phone:
(33) 1 60 72 4273
Fax:
(33) 1 60 74 5530

BRIEF DESCRIPTION OF THE SCHOOL

INSEAD is among the best-known European business schools and among its four oldest. Like a number of European schools, it was founded by businesspeople as an independent institution, not as part of a university. Accordingly, tough management in the areas of image development, alumni networking, fund-raising, and executive training have successfully advanced the school's name throughout Europe and, increasingly, outside of Europe.

Our survey of European consulting firms revealed a strong preference for recruiting INSEAD graduates. This could be partly due to the fact that the largest group of INSEAD graduates go into consulting (45 percent). Even so, graduates include the CEOs of L'Oréal, Cartier, the Economist Group (publishers), Ford France, and the leader of the British Conservative Party. INSEAD produces nearly 500 MBA graduates annually, and 5000 grads of the 29 executive development programs help to spread the INSEAD name. The school reportedly has over 19,000 alumni and 30 national alumni organizations. A recent fund-raising drive for FF 700 million (approximately $112 million) targets alumni and businesspeople with which the school cultivates close relations.

The fact that INSEAD makes the top spot in many rankings does not mean it is the best alternative for everyone. Surveys emphasizing different criteria, involving a slightly different sample group or response rate, could effect INSEAD's position.

The organizational structure at INSEAD is designed to uphold the quality of its wide-ranging activities as well as to cater to the every need of its impressive network of corporate clients. Two of its most visible units are the European Center for Continuing Education (CEDEP) and the Euro-Asia Center. The CEDEP runs diverse executive development programs, including the so-called consortium programs—courses tailored to meet the requirements of a group of selected companies in a sole program. Although this type of program is now a common feature of other business schools, INSEAD was one of the pioneers in the field. The programs are an example of its efforts to offer courses suiting the business community.

The Euro-Asia Center, which runs programs and conducts research on business issues in that region, is another one of the school's strengths. In fact, INSEAD's commitment to, and experience in, the Asia-Pacific region has led to one of the most important things that has happened at INSEAD in recent years: the opening of a new campus in Singapore—an expensive and potentially risky venture. This new campus first offered an MBA program in October 1999 and will presumably attract a significant number of students from the region in years to come. In accordance with its new credo "One school, two campuses," suggested by Dean Antonio Borges, INSEAD will try to maintain its culture and levels of excellence, while increasing its international presence in a business world heading irreversibly toward globalization. The school has even more ambitious plans for its future international expansion. The model they adhere to for their long-term strategy is that of a multinational consulting firm which has branches in different countries, yet still retains one culture and one standard across the board. "We would like to one day open a campus in South Africa, and another in Brazil. A long-term strategy for INSEAD would be to have one school but many campuses," explains Landis Gabel, Associate Dean of the MBA program.

An important element in INSEAD's success is combining extensive promotion with tough admissions procedures. INSEAD grads are therefore probably good because they were already good in the first place. The incoming class includes graduates from many of the most prestigious schools in the world. Roughly 50 nationalities are represented in an intake of over 600. INSEAD reports its average starting salary is over $80,000—certainly another motivation for good people to apply to INSEAD. The school attracts over 200 companies to recruit on campus each year and its executive development seminars have radically expanded the number of alumni leaving and later supporting the school. Thus, in terms of return on investment and the related quality of students, INSEAD is a "strong buy."

One of the school's major assets is its alumni. According to a recent survey, 20 years after graduation 36 percent of the school's MBA alumni attained positions of CEO or equivalent. International mobility and entrepreneurship also distinguish INSEAD graduates. Alumni spend from 30 to 65 percent of their careers abroad, and 20 years after graduating, 42 percent are running their own businesses.

The international dimension at the school is reflected in the composition of the student body, the composition of the faculty, and the content of its programs. According to Landis Gabel, Associate Dean of the MBA program, "The atmosphere is completely international. We have no conception of someone being foreign. This is because there is no dominant, single, most common nationality in our program." It is worth noting that one of the requirements for admission to the MBA program at INSEAD is the ability to speak at least two languages. The concept of global village is taken very seriously there. No nationality is allowed to exceed 15 percent, so the student body is pretty multicultural.

THE CAMPUS AND LIFE ON CAMPUS

The INSEAD campus is nestled in the forests of Fontainebleau, a small town steeped in history just 65 kilometers from Paris. The forest, formerly the hunting ground of French aristocracy, surrounds the buildings which are spread out over an acre of land. While the buildings may not be the most modern, pretty gardens and open spaces create a pleasant ambiance.

INSEAD classrooms are especially spacious, so spacious that in INSEAD-speak they are called "amphis" as they resemble small amphitheaters. The cafeteria, offering delicious French food, and the student lounge are the campus hub, located halfway between the classrooms and residence halls. This is where students socialize, mingle with professors and participants in other programs, or even listen to an impromptu performance by a fellow student on the grand piano as they keep an eye on stock and business channels.

Although the school has its own residence halls, most MBA students live off campus in Fontainebleau, a quiet town with an impressive royal palace. Fontainebleau offers little in the entertainment line, but Paris is just 45 minutes away. Fontainebleau does offer outstanding restaurants, including some that feature foreign cuisine.

The working language at the school is English, but a great deal of French is spoken, and you'll hear numerous other languages as you walk the corridors. The student's life revolves around the "amphis," the cafeteria, the library, and the study rooms reserved for teamwork. With the exception of a squash court, there are no sports facilities on campus. However, the surrounding forests are ideal for jogging, and there are sports centers nearby.

THE PROGRAM

The MBA at INSEAD is an 11-month, full-time program with two intakes: One begins in September and ends in early July; the other begins in January and ends in December, with a seven-week summer break. Students work together in an international atmosphere, being initially assigned to small study teams of six to seven members from different countries. The method of mixing students and backgrounds into small groups is a much-copied idea initially developed and practiced at INSEAD. It teaches students to maximize consensus despite a priori differences—an important asset of any business school education.

The program is divided into three main phases. Phase I of the program involves covering 10 basic courses in four months. These courses are similar to those taught at most other B-schools, and include people and organizations, prices and markets, and applied statistics.

Students are closely monitored and graded. Those failing to uphold adequate standards risk being dropped from the program. However, according to one alumnus, "If you manage to obtain good results in the first four months, you should not have any problem to graduate at the end of the year. You can even enjoy the last six months of the program."

Phase II goes a step further but consists only of core courses such as corporate strategy and economic analysis. The final phase is called "individual orientation" and is completely devoted to electives, which carry interesting titles such as business in China, starting and growing entrepreneurial enterprises, creating new products and services, and the ethical dilemma. Sadly, the extremely short program prohibits students from taking more than a very small selection from this list of 60 highly interesting courses.

FACULTY, TEACHING, AND LEARNING PROCESSES

INSEAD's 113 faculty members represent 24 different nationalities, reflecting the school's international orientation. Besides teaching, a typical faculty member does extensive consulting—certainly a factor in the school's overall orientation toward the consulting business. However, this entails high faculty salaries and potentially long periods away from the school and students in order to pursue consultancy projects.

INSEAD's pedagogical approach is pragmatic. The objective is to prepare students through the simulation of business reality. The MBA program is based on problem solving in small groups, active class participation, and

individual preparation and research. As mentioned, students work in small study teams during the first four months of the program.

An MBA school day includes two or three classroom sessions that may be lectures, case discussions, or computer simulations. Case studies may involve role playing, action learning, and simulations. Some courses include the presentation and defense of individual or group projects.

The school is a productive and successful factory of case studies which are related to highly diverse cultural environments. Students, for example, learn how to deal with the manufacturing problems of a Japanese company, how to implement the strategy of an eastern European retail distributor, how to face downsizing at a South African company.

PLACEMENT

The Career Management Service (CMS) is INSEAD's placement office. It conducts career counseling, seminars, and workshops and it maintains extensive company information. It also publishes a recruitment guide with the INSEAD students and organizes roughly 8000 interviews between students and potential employers. Each student receives an average of four job offers.

FINANCIAL AID

INSEAD offers a variety of scholarships based on merit. The scholarships vary by year and student category. In addition, many European banks recognize the value of an INSEAD MBA and readily grant loans.

2.
LONDON
BUSINESS
SCHOOL

LONDON BUSINESS SCHOOL

Sussex Place, Outer Circle
Regent's Park
UK-London NW1 4SA
Web site: http://www.lbs.ac.uk
E-mail: mba-info@lbs.ac.uk

Program

Program ranked: MBA
Structure: 21 months full-time; 13 core courses, 11 electives, internship
Size of class: Maximum 70 students
Participants: Average age 29; some 80% from overseas, representing approximately 45 nationalities, predominantly North American and Asian (22% and 25%, respectively); 25% female; average work experience of 6 years
Cost: Tuition fee: 31,500 Pounds Sterling (approx. $50,797); estimated living expenses for a single person (including 600 Pounds Sterling [approx. $968] per month for own room in modest shared accommodation): 29,000 Pounds Sterling (approx. $46,765)
Program director: Julia Tyler
Accreditation: AMBA (British), EQUIS (European)

Admissions

Admissions requirements: University degree (can be waived in exceptional cases of proven high potential); GMAT (typical score of native English speaker 680); TOEFL (minimum score of 600 for the paper exam or 250 for the computer exam); or IELTS if English is not the student's native language and, if it is, proven fluency in at least one other language; minimum 3 years relevant work experience
Applications deadline: First week of April
Starting date: September only
Application fee: 75 Pounds Sterling (approx. $120)

Recruiting

Placement office: Recruiter database, company presentations, distribution of résumés
Number of companies recruiting: 102
Examples of recruiting companies: McKinsey, Kellogg, Johnson & Johnson, Citibank

BRIEF DESCRIPTION OF THE SCHOOL

London Business School (LBS) is undoubtedly one of the best-known European business schools. It was created in the wake of the 1965

Contact:
Admissions Office
Phone:
(44) 171 262 5050
Fax:
(44) 171 724 7875

Franks report, which pointed out that Britain was lacking business schools and that it would be a good idea to set up at least two—one in London and another in Manchester. The school was duly set up in temporary premises close to Trafalgar Square before a permanent campus was created at its Regent's Park site in 1970.

Although LBS operates under the aegis of London University, it would appear that it runs under its own steam. The full-time MBA is the cornerstone of the school, which is committed to the American two-year (or 21-month to be more precise) MBA system. There is a 24-month part-time program in which the vast majority of its students are sponsored by companies. The Sloan Fellowship Master is a full-time program for candidates with a minimum of 10 years relevant experience; the vast majority are self-employed. The school also offers both a full-time and part-time MBA in finance as well as a highly respected Ph.D. program.

In addition to the core programs, the school offers a wide portfolio of shorter programs aimed at general management. The school is also starting to offer highly specialized sector or issue-based programs lasting between three and five days, and LBS has recently introduced what it calls "Master Classes," two-day programs designed to provide executives with a quick update on the latest findings in business research.

LBS has traditionally emphasized economics and finance, strategy and marketing, and operations management and organizational behavior. While these areas are still core, the school is also focusing on entrepreneurial skills. The school recently launched its own Foundation of Entrepreneurial Management to provide students and alumni with money to fund new business ideas. One recipient of these services is Mike Roberts, who looked to the school for help with his venture iglu.com, now the largest Web site for ski chalets in the world. LBS helped fund the project. Tony Wheeler of "Lonely Planet" fame and Sir John Jennings are other well-known LBS alumni who have set up their own businesses.

London Business School is one of the few consistently high-ranking European business schools located in the heart of a capital city, in this case one of the financial capitals of the world. With approximately 80 percent of its student body from overseas, international diversity is the order of the day at LBS. The impressive plethora of its electives, 75 in all, is proof that the school believes in allowing students to specialize. Candidates should be aware that, in keeping with its international identity, LBS is one of the few schools to insist on proof of a high level of competence in at least one language other than the student's mother tongue.

THE CAMPUS AND LIFE ON CAMPUS

For location and aesthetics, there can be no denying that LBS has it. The pristine elegance of its Nash building façade, built in the early 1820s, is guaranteed to impress. And, with Regent's Park as a backdrop, what more could the school's marketing department ask for? Anyone familiar with the magnificent parks of London need hardly be reminded of the pleasure of taking a stroll amid this particular park's lovingly cared for gardens or alongside its lake, an appropriate antidote to counteract the blood, sweat, and tears lost in the course of a typical day's work.

London is one of the world's most vibrant capital cities, a hub for the movers and shakers of the business world, culture vultures, and a wide range of society addicts. "If you're tired of London, you're tired of life" still holds true nearly a century after Dr. Johnson first said it.

At LBS, most of the master's program buildings are no architectural jewels, but they offer superlative computer facilities, ample amphitheater-style lecture theaters, and what is generally recognized as one of the best business school libraries in Europe. Networked syndicate rooms, numerous audiovisual teaching rooms, and reprographic services all serve to make the most of the learning experience. Leisure facilities include a fitness center complete with pool, a wine bar, restaurants, and a common room where students can meet and put the business world to rights.

The school has its own on-campus accommodations, but they are reserved for students who visit the school as part of an exchange program. Other students live off campus. Those lucky enough to have a limitless budget will be able to look for accommodation in the immediate vicinity of the school. As in most large cities, however, less salubrious neighborhoods permit students who have all but sold their soul to finance their master's the hope of finding accommodation of a more modest, student-like nature, reasonably near the campus.

THE PROGRAM

The school has adopted the classic American approach of a two-year master's. However, it points out that this does not mean it is simply a European style one-year master's spread out over a longer period. LBS believes a two-year program is the only way to study master's subjects with the amount of attention they deserve. The student can expect an intensive learning experience consisting of three main stages.

The first year is devoted to 13 typical core courses designed to equip the student with strong analytical skills, the ability to work both in a team and alone, experience in the use of new technology, and a solid understanding of international marketplaces and cross-cultural working practices.

On completion of the first year the student is catapulted into a three-month internship. Although the school will help in the search for host companies, the student is expected to play an important role in securing a place in a company. Salaries paid during these summer assignments average at 900 Pounds Sterling (approx. $1452) per week, and it is fairly typical for companies to

offer students the possibility of a permanent post when they have finished the program.

In the second year students undertake 11 electives from an extremely impressive list of 75 courses covering many areas. In keeping with the international character of the school, second-year students have the opportunity to participate in an exchange program and spend a term at one of LBS's 32 exchange school partners.

Language instruction is also available for those who still need to attain the minimum required capacity for communication in a second language before the end of the MBA program.

FACULTY, TEACHING, AND LEARNING PROCESSES

Although the case method forms part of the program, it is not considered the be-all and end-all. Students are, above all, encouraged to share their personal work experience and to learn from classmates. LBS relies on the high caliber of its students to make the program work. The wide variety of top-level professional and cultural backgrounds of participants gives the program—and students—a competitive edge by providing an exchange of information and viewpoints that is enriching from both a professional and personal perspective. It also means a productive environment for networking.

Group work plays a pivotal role in the learning process. Students are assigned to a group of six or eight people on arrival and work with them throughout the first year. Guest speakers and field visits also form an integral part of the learning process, and London is a rich source of both.

International best describes LBS faculty. According to the *Financial Times* LBS has the highest percentage of international faculty of the top 10 American and European business schools. Research is important at LBS. The school occupies third place for research in the world with nine separate research centers. One of its most noteworthy projects is that of the virtual laboratory which investigates commerce on the Internet.

LBS professors are actively encouraged to collaborate with the many companies who seek their help on consultancy projects. The school believes that this not only provides access to contemporary thinking and business realities, but also brings real-life business situations into the classroom. As Dr. Kent Grayson, assistant professor of marketing at LBS, said, "When course material and real-world practice collide in the classroom, it's pretty exciting, for both students and faculty."

PLACEMENT

The LBS Careers Management Center organizes workshops to help students focus on their next career move. The Center uses London GOLD, a database that provides employers with access to information via a telephone hot line and organizes presentations and career-related events such as networking dinners.

The school has created "The WorkPlace," a pioneering Web-based service where companies in search of senior managers and alumni on the lookout for career opportunities can find each other. All this is on both a national and world-wide level, in keeping with the international spirit of the program and school.

FINANCIAL AID

LBS states that 50 percent of each class typically receives permanent job offers after the summer, and that four years after graduation its graduates enjoy an average salary increase of 174 percent. However, graduates who do not attain this success could have a hard time paying back their investment. The summer assignment and consultancy project will help pay for a few odds and ends, but in view of the considerable outlay required, money from this source represents a small percentage of total costs.

About 90 percent of LBS's full-time MBA students are self-sponsored. The LBS application form provides information on loans that cover tuition and living costs including GMAC MBA loans, which are aimed primarily at citizens of the United States, and the AMBA loan scheme, run in conjunction with the Association of MBAs and UK banks. There is also information on scholarships available printed on an insert in the MBA prospectus. These scholarships are small, ranging from 1000 to 7500 Pounds Sterling (approx. $1612 to $12,095)—a mere drop in an ocean of expenses.

3.
IMD

IMD—International Institute for Management Development

MBA Information Office
Chemin de Bellerive 23, PO Box 915
CH-10001 Lausanne, Switzerland
Web site: http://www.imd.ch
E-mail: mbainfo@imd.ch

Program

Program ranked: MBA
Structure: 11 months, full-time; eight modules; 10 electives; international consulting projects and TIE (team initiated enterprise)
Size of class: 83 per year
Participants: 35 different nationalities represented (54% Europe, 11% North America, 9% South America, 6% Australia, 18% Asia, 2% other); average age, 31; average working experience, 7 years
Costs: Program fee: 41,000 Swiss Francs (approx. $26,775) for self-sponsored students; 61,000 Swiss Francs (approx. $39,840) for company-sponsored students; estimated living expenses for a single person, 30,000 Swiss Francs (approx. $19,600)
Program director: Prof. Dominique V. Turpin
Accreditation: AMBA (British), EQUIS (European)

Admissions

Admissions requirements: University degree; GMAT; 3 recommendation letters; work experience (minimum 3 years); fluency in English; ratio of applications to those admitted, 10:1
Applications deadline: 1 September
Starting date: January
Application fee: 250 Swiss Francs (approx. $164)

Recruiting

Placement office: Yes
Number of companies recruiting: 50+
Examples of recruiting companies: Nestlé, AT&T, American Express, J. P. Morgan, Ernst & Young, Andersen Consulting

Contact:
Admissions Office
Phone:
(41) 21 618 0111
Fax: (41) 21 618 0615

BRIEF DESCRIPTION OF THE SCHOOL

IMD was created in 1989, the product of the merger of two management education centers: IMI Geneva, founded by Alcan in 1946; and IMEDE Lausanne, founded by Nestlé in 1957. The school has earned still further the right to describe itself as "born of industry" by striving to maintain close links with more than 120 partner and business associate companies, which have a marked influence on the curricula of IMD's degree and nondegree courses.

Numerous executive development seminars make up the main core of IMD's activities, attended by some 2000 participants annually. It is these highly profitable programs, rather than the 80 to 90 students in the one-year full-time MBA program, that constitute the main source of revenue to finance the 45-strong full-time teaching faculty. Both faculty and student body are highly international in content, comprising 18 and 35 nationalities, respectively.

IMD has successfully promoted itself with a high-visibility study entitled the *World Competitiveness Yearbook,* which ranks 40 to 50 countries according to their "competitiveness." The results are a regular feature in the key media of all of the countries involved. This is just one example of IMD's extensive research activities, renowned for their practical approach to management.

DISTINGUISHING FEATURES

IMD fits in with the familiar pattern among top-ranking schools in that it is as international as any program can be, with regard to student body, faculty, and content. Multicultural is the norm here. One way in which IMD breaks the top-ranking-school mold, however, is its insistence on the fact that "small is beautiful." There are no plans for expanding its MBA program, although its other executive education programs allow the school to grow in other directions.

A student to faculty ratio of 3:1 makes for an intense learning environment, with plenty of personal attention and close working relationships between professors and students. Research projects conducted jointly by students and faculty are common. Note that this level of attention is not intended to help lame ducks keep up with the demanding program, but rather to push highfliers to greater heights.

Strong links between things academic and the business community are further fostered by the large number of executives from a wide range of business sectors who attend the school's executive development courses and with whom MBA participants will share the campus. The program content includes different hands-on projects developed in collaboration with client companies, and students are also drawn into the school's Learning Network activities organized on campus.

THE CAMPUS AND LIFE ON CAMPUS

IMD is situated in Lausanne (population 125,000), located on Lake Geneva, roughly 40 miles from Geneva itself, in the heart of the French-speaking part of Switzerland. Surrounded by the French and Swiss Alps, Lausanne is a truly beautiful city, with a privileged lakefront location that provides real picture-postcard scenery. As well as being the home of the International Olympic Committee (IOC), it is also a renowned center of learning, business, congresses, and medical care. Visitors can relax in its pleasant, traffic-free shopping streets and parks and enjoy a broad choice of entertainment ranging from museums, galleries, and theaters, to ballet, music, and nightlife. Living in Lausanne is one long cultural experience, during which things tend to happen in a somewhat traditional and orderly fashion and at a stately pace. The downside of this lovely city has to be the sky-high cost of everything from a Big Mac to an apartment, and the fact that beautiful fresh summers are inevitably followed by severe winters.

The IMD campus comprises six modern, functional buildings situated amid pine trees in a quiet area overlooking Lake Geneva. The main one, known as La Residence, houses the bulk of the administrative team, while the MBA is located at Bellerive 32. Each of the school's 20 MBA group study rooms are equipped with two personal computers networked to the IMD computer center, a laser printer, and direct telephone lines. On the catering side, the campus has a restaurant and café lounge/bar, and on the practical side, banking facilities. The limited number of MBA students results in a friendly and relaxed atmosphere on campus, where participants and faculty mingle informally on a first-name basis. From the moment participants set foot in the place, they find themselves immersed in an international environment and faced with a serious and intensive study program.

There is no on-campus accommodation available, so most MBA students rent apartments as near the campus as possible. The admissions office provides students with an updated listing of available apartments and assists them in finding suitable accommodation, but be prepared for those prices.

Fitness enthusiasts can ward off stress at the nearby University of Lausanne sports facilities, and there are swimming and tennis centers located minutes from the campus, plus a gym next door to the MBA building. IMD has created the MBA Partner Program for companions of MBA participants, to prevent their feeling out of things and to make them feel more like members of the IMD community, as well as to help participants get to know each other better.

THE PROGRAM

The MBA at IMD is an intensive full-time program lasting 11 months (January–December). The program is structured into eight modules covering the core management disciplines. Every module builds upon the skills acquired in the previous phases of the program, making the learning process a cumulative experience.

Initial modules equip participants with the necessary tools to understand how business functions operate and interface. They then move on to a broader analysis of the business environment, the impact of strategic decisions within a certain industry, and finally, the challenges of managing a company in a global environment.

Students are given the opportunity to gain in-depth experience in a chosen management field through the wide range of elective courses offered in the seventh module of the program. The final module, Leading Self, is a personal analysis of the participants' careers. Participants examine their past and future careers to set an agenda for self-development.

The MBA program at IMD includes two types of applied management projects that students develop during the second half of the year: the International Consulting Projects and the Team Initiated Enterprise (TIE) Projects. The International Consulting Projects enable participants to serve as consultants to the top management of client companies and advise them on critical management issues. TIE participants work in self-selected teams to create, define, and implement an enterprise that adds value to the larger community, and they must complete and submit a business plan for a new company.

FACULTY, TEACHING, AND LEARNING PROCESSES

The 45 IMD professors derive a great deal of their recognition from research sponsored by and conducted in collaboration with companies belonging to the school's Partner and Business Associate Network. In addition to this, approximately 20 percent of the school's budget is pumped into research and development. The teaching faculty contributes to the MBA program not only as professors and mediators of class discussions but also as supervisors of the International Consulting Project.

The learning processes are based on the development of cross-cultural and global skills. As in the case of most top-ranking schools, the fact that students work in multicultural teams is considered a core learning tool. A wealth of very different personal experiences are shared in teamwork, and classmates take on a teaching role every bit as important as that played by professors. The average student has seven years' work experience and some 85 percent of each cohort has lived or worked outside his or her home country, so everyone usually has something to say for themselves.

Like Ashridge, IMD is game for innovative approaches to teaching methods. One group of course participants, for example, on learning how to compare the management methods involved in bringing about a musical performance, found themselves with a chamber orchestra and jazz band ready to give them a practical illustration of the results of their efforts.

PLACEMENT

Participants in the MBA program reap the benefits of the school's strong links with the corporate world in the final stage of the program. More than 50 companies recruit on campus every year. About 95 percent of the participants receive an average of 2.5 job offers by the time they graduate. The average starting salary after graduation is $92,000, which constitutes an average increase of 75 percent over pre-MBA salaries, plus an average sign-on bonus of $21,000, making IMD graduates among the highest paid MBAs within the European business school scene.

While INSEAD and London Business School students, for example, have backgrounds in financial services or consulting, 65 percent of IMD students hail from the industrial sector. Curiously enough, a large percentage of IMD graduates return to industry, in stark contrast with their counterparts from other schools, who tend to gravitate toward the services sector.

FINANCIAL AID

Despite the fact that the program takes only one year, the MBA at IMD is still quite a costly option, as Switzerland is not exactly a cheap place to live by any standards. IMD offers several scholarships each year to MBA participants, and the school also helps accepted participants from developing countries through the IMD MBA Alumni Loan Fund, founded by the MBA class of 1989, which provides low-interest loans to cover part of the tuition fees.

4.
ROTTERDAM SCHOOL OF MANAGEMENT

Contact:
Admissions Office
Phone:
(31) 10 408 1927
(or 2042)
Fax: (31) 10 452 9509

ROTTERDAM SCHOOL OF MANAGEMENT

Erasmus Graduate School of Business
International MBA
Burgemeester Oudlaan 50
NL-3062 PA Rotterdam, Netherlands
Web site: www.rsm.eur.nl/rsm
E-mail: RSM@FAC.RSM.EUR.NL

Program

Program ranked: International MBA
Structure: 18 months full-time; 13 core courses, 10 elective courses, 2 minicourses, consulting project
Size of class: 60, intake 100–120
Participants: 85% overseas students from 45 different countries (40% Europe, 20% North and South America, 20% Asia, and 5% others)
Cost: Tuition fee: 22,500 Euros (approx. $23,560); estimated living expenses for a single person: 17,500 Euros (approx. $18,330)
Program director: Kai Peters
Accreditation: AMBA (British) EQUIS (European) AASCB (American)

Admissions

Admissions requirements: University degree; GMAT; 2 letters of recommendation; interview; questionnaire; work experience (average 2 years); proficiency in English
Applications deadline: June 15
Starting date: Mid-August
Application fee: 75 Euros (approx. $79)

Recruiting

Placement office: Preparing for job application, supports putting all elements into perspective company presentations
Number of companies recruiting: 135+
Examples of recruiting companies: Chrysler Europe, L'Oréal, Procter & Gamble, J. P. Morgan, KLM Royal Dutch Airlines, Philips Electronics

BRIEF DESCRIPTION OF THE SCHOOL

Rotterdam School of Management (RSM) actually started life as the Interuniversity Institute of Business Administration in 1970. After a brief spell of existence it was transferred to Delft where its two-year postgraduate course went from strength to strength. A restructuring of the Dutch university system brought it back to Rotterdam in the early 1980s to become the graduate school of Erasmus University, known as the Rotterdam School of Management.

The location of the school has inevitably played an important role in RSM's undeniably international slant. The Netherlands is a small country with few natural resources and a traditionally enterprising population that first started to look to international trade as a source of prosperity around the eleventh century, and has never looked back. This amazing little country has produced a disproportionately high number of multinational corporations, including Phillips Unilever, Heineken, and Shell, to name but a few. The city of Rotterdam epitomizes this tradition of international business in that it is the largest commercial port in the world, one of the reasons why many countries have established trade centers there. This "gateway to Europe" is also the economic, social, and cultural center of the Rijnmond region, the industrial heart of the Netherlands where more than a million people live. Anyone who is still not convinced that this constitutes an international environment should consider the fact that almost a quarter of the population of Rotterdam hold a foreign passport. Off-campus visitors find themselves immersed in an environment where nearly everyone speaks at least two languages, and where someone who speaks five is by no means unusual.

The strong influence of this international setting on RSM means that the school had already gone global while most other business schools were just starting to think about it. They are now at the stage where their academics are producing ground-breaking research in cross-cultural management and cultural norms and values, concepts which are integrated into the school's curriculum.

Entrepreneurship is another area of interest that is dear to many a Netherlander's heart, and this is duly reflected at RSM. The school believes that, far from being just a passing fancy among the business community, entrepreneurialism is a sustainable trend further boosted by new developments in information technologies, and it has expanded its portfolio of electives accord-ingly. Interestingly enough, the school has discovered that part-time MBAs are more likely to set up their own business than full-time MBAs, no doubt their research department will find the reason.

In addition to the full-time and part-time MBA programs, other programs at RSM include an International Executive MBA/MBI program and a doctorate program in Business Administration. The school also offers tailored, in-company programs for the public and private sectors, and action-learning "packages" combining lectures and case method with special assignments and discussions.

THE CAMPUS AND LIFE ON CAMPUS

Rotterdam is a shining example of postwar modernity in Europe. Lovers of modern architecture will marvel at the originality and style of the buildings in the city center and the numerous bridges across its many canals and rivers.

The city offers a wide range of arts with theaters, cinemas, and festivals. It is also a center for major sporting events. RSM students can discover the fun side of networking thanks to the school's International Business Club (IBC), which sponsors many extracurricular activities, such as balls, parties, seminars, lectures with guest speakers, and other MBA-orientated events.

RSM is located in a recently inaugurated building, complete with a new information technology center, on the Woudestein campus of Erasmus University within the city of Rotterdam. Other facilities located at the Woudestein include the auditorium, the university library, the Erasmus Computing Center, sports facilities, and most of the university administration services.

RSM has excellent computer facilities consisting of six computer labs with 200 personal computers complete with state-of-the-art access software. The library, or Business Information

Center as it is known, is well-equipped with reference material and provides students with access to external and CD-ROM databases.

Since there are no on-campus dormitories, the RSM Housing Office will assist students in finding suitable accommodations in Rotterdam. There are a number of housing complexes, some just a 10-minute walk from the school, which house the majority of the students during the MBA program. Others are a five-minute ride away for those who choose to adopt the most typical form of transport here: namely, the omnipresent bicycle. All admitted candidates receive detailed information about the housing options and prices.

THE PROGRAM

The 18-month full-time International MBA program aims to develop top international general managers with a solid knowledge and analytical competence in a wide range of functional disciplines.

Toward the end of August students lacking in statistical and mathematical backgrounds are required to attend refresher courses. All students attend an introduction program which comprises a mix of formal and informal gatherings aimed at familiarizing students with their new schedule and surroundings as well as at letting students, and their partners, get to know each other before the real onslaught of work begins.

The curriculum of the International MBA program in general management covers all major aspects of general management. The 13 core courses occupy approximately half of the total study hours and are concentrated during the first-year fall/winter semester so that students can start to have a good idea of which electives will suit them best. The spring semester moves on to project management and consulting skills workshops, and the summer is spent doing a three-month consulting project individually or in a team, under the guidance of an academic supervisor. In addition to selecting projects with an international focus, students are encouraged to work on a project in a company or in an operating unit based in a country other than their own.

The second year kicks off with fall electives and what the school describes as minicourses, starting off with a focus on business in Europe and then moving on to globalization. This semester is divided into two 7-week periods, each of which requires students to take on five elective courses and one minicourse. Alternatively students may be offered the opportunity to participate in an exchange program during these months (selection is made on a competitive basis) at one of RSM's many partner schools, situated throughout four continents. In January and February, the closing stages of the program, all students are back at the school to choose their preferred options from a series of two-week seminar-style course blocks, including entrepreneurial opportunities created by new information technologies, culture and strategy, and geopolitics and emerging markets. This part of the program also features recruitment activities, including on-campus presentations and interviews.

FACULTY, TEACHING, AND LEARNING PROCESSES

The faculty is composed of international professors and professionals from within the Rotterdam School of Management and Erasmus University, as well as visiting faculty from prestigious international universities, and consultants and managers active in different industries. The faculty is committed to a wide range of teaching methods, which are determined by the course material and their individual styles. Lectures, case studies, field trips, group work, management games, real-life projects, and independent work have a practical as well as analytical orientation, and are important in enhancing the learning process. Computing skills and increasing managerial and decision-making processes form a vital part of the program.

The atmosphere is friendly and informal. Students are especially enthusiastic about the hands-on project work and the international, multilingual student body. "The rewards in friendship, understanding, and experience in the industry overcame the inevitable barriers and pressure," we are told by Mario Weiss, a former student of the RSM International MBA program.

PLACEMENT

Career Planning is an integral part of the curriculum. At the start of the program each student receives the Career Management Guide, which contains information about services offered, guidelines for the job search process, information about interviewing and job offers.

The Career Planning Office has developed a number of career development activities, including training seminars and workshops in self-assessment, job search techniques, and résumé and cover letter writing.

FINANCIAL AID

Students are advised to explore all possible sources of funding in their own countries. Such sources could be national, such as ministries of education and foundations, or supranational organizations, such as the World Bank and regional development banks. The application package contains a list of possible financial assistance programs. Scholarship opportunities include the Hobsons MBA Scholarship open to application from all students, and the Mary Lugard MBA Scholarships. In addition there is a loan program for students from central and eastern Europe and central Asia.

5.
INSTITUTO DE EMPRESA

Contact:
Admissions Office
Phone:
(34) 91 568 9600
Fax: (34) 91 411 5503

INSTITUTO DE EMPRESA
María de Molina 13
28006 Madrid, Spain
Web site: www.ie.edu
E-mail: admissions@ie.edu

Program

Program ranked: International MBA.

Structure: 1 year (15 months) full-time; 6 periods, including an internship, an exchange program, the world reality seminar, and elective courses

Size of class: 110 admitted per year in two classes of 55 students each

Participants: Average age 27; 40% female, 60% male; 34% Spanish; 66% from overseas (29% South America, 37% rest of the world); 30 different nationalities

Costs: Course fees: 19,331 Euros (approx. $20,200); estimated living expenses for single person: 2,400,000 Ptas per year (approx. $15,100)

Program director: Manuel Bermejo

Accreditation: AEEDE (Spanish), AMBA (British), EQUIS (European)

Admissions

Admissions requirements: University degree; GMAT or admissions tests provided by the Instituto de Empresa; 3 references; fluency in English; students have an average of 3 years' working experience.

Application deadline: Late April

Starting date: September

Application fee: None

Recruiting

Placement office: Résumé database, recruitment events, career courses

Number of companies recruiting: 300+

Examples of recruiting companies: Andersen Consulting, General Electric, EFFEM, Hewlett-Packard, IBM, Repsol

BRIEF DESCRIPTION OF THE SCHOOL

The Instituto de Empresa (IE) was founded in 1973, and has since gained a reputation for excellence both in Europe and on the other side of the Atlantic. This dynamic school has gathered impetus at much the same rate as the Spanish economy, which is flourishing partly as a result of a stronger presence of many large Spanish corporations overseas, particularly due to the economic emergence of South America. IE has been quick to realize the importance of markets in South America, and it enjoys enviable relations on both corporate and institutional levels in that part of the world.

IE's international activities by no means stop there. Indeed, IE has strong links with the international business community, with prominent business leaders, such as Luciano Benetton, founder and CEO of the Benetton Group, and Peter Sutherland, chairman of Goldman Sachs International, on its advisory board. Collaboration from large corporations with IE projects is the norm—Hewlett-Packard, Microsoft, and Telefonica, for example, are currently collaborating with IE's information technology center in a joint venture to develop new information technologies that cater specifically to the needs of small- and medium-sized businesses. This initiative is just one example of IE's strategy for growth via the creation of several centers covering different areas of management, through which interested companies may channel their research activities in collaboration with the school.

Entrepreneurship is another main feature of IE's organizational culture (the literal translation of Instituto de Empresa into English is "Institute of Enterprise"). The school was founded by a group of entrepreneurs and claims to have pioneered the introduction of entrepreneurship as a core subject within the MBA program in Europe. One of the explicit objectives of its program is "to instill the entrepreneurial spirit among its students." The Department of Entrepreneurship supervises more than 250 business plans each year, and a significant proportion of its graduates set up their own business or contribute to new start-ups. The recently created Entrepreneurship Center is an innovative initiative designed to act as an interface between international business schools, potential investors, and entrepreneurs.

IE's portfolio of educational activities includes a wide array of programs in addition to the full-time and part-time MBA programs. Specialized master's degrees, such as a Master's in Corporate Legal Counseling and a Master's in Corporate Tax Counseling, are offered. The school's Management College, the unit responsible for senior executive education, also organizes a large number of open management programs and courses tailored for client corporations.

CAMPUS AND LIFE ON CAMPUS

IE is situated in the heart of Madrid's financial district. The main part of the school occupies several turn-of-the-century mansion-style buildings surrounded by a pleasant garden area where students often congregate to enjoy the warm climate. The buildings, while retaining a great deal of their original character, have been modernized to make room for the latest developments in new information technologies for use both in class and on an individual basis. All the lecture theaters are equipped with state-of-the-art multimedia equipment, and there is a library with access via Internet to all major business databases and journals. The large amount of syndicate rooms reflects the importance attached to teamwork here, and the Aula Magna is the scene of major conferences as well as social events. There is no on-campus accommodation as such, but IE provides an accommodation service that gives priority to overseas students. Rents are not exactly cheap, but prices are not as high as in London or Paris, for example.

Madrid is one of Europe's most vibrant capitals, combining a wealth of history in its architecture and traditions with stunning modernity. The lively cultural and social scene is in a league of its own. Art enthusiasts will marvel at the collections housed by the Prado and Thyssen Bornemiza museums, food lovers will become addicted to the thousands of tapas bars and restaurants in Madrid, and those who enjoy a night on the town will discover that New York is not the only city that never sleeps. Although the program does not leave much leisure time, it is worth taking the occasional break to wander around the city and experience its marvelous atmosphere, the result of a unique blend of Spanish and cosmopolitan culture.

THE PROGRAM

The IE International MBA program is bilingual, with classes in both English and Spanish. The first semester of the program is entirely in English in order to give foreign students a bit of breathing space to come to grips with Spanish, providing the opportunity to learn a language which is second only to English in geographic extension and increasingly used in the business world. The rest of the program is taught in both languages. The school provides intensive free Spanish classes for several months before the start of the program for those who want them. Students who undertake the Spanish course generally arrive with at least a beginner's knowledge of the language. The admissions department recommends that applicants who are in doubt about their level of Spanish should contact them for advice.

There is an optional preprogram focused on quantitative analysis for those for whom figures are not a strong point. The program itself is divided into six periods, the first three of which cover the major management disciplines, starting with the fundamentals and gradually moving on to more complex and integrated areas. These three periods comprise a total of 24 courses, each of which is followed by an assessment that will form part of the final grade. They also include a conference cycle with a number of lectures by leading managers about their respective companies and the business environment in general.

Period four is devoted to a remunerated corporate internship. Host companies are usually located via a joint effort between IE and the student, and internships may be undertaken either in Spain or overseas. Most of period five is taken up by the world reality seminar, an interdiscipli-

nary seminar that focuses mainly on international marketing, conducted by experts not only from IE but also from organizations and institutions from countries all over the world.

Period six consists exclusively of elective courses. Students select five or six electives from a list of around 35. The last two periods can be substituted by participation in an exchange program with one of IE's many foreign exchange partners in Europe and both North and South America.

FACULTY, TEACHING, AND LEARNING PROCESSES

The IE faculty roster includes some 73 full-time professors, more than 200 part-time faculty members and corporate speakers. The vast majority combine their teaching duties with extensive research activity and consultancy work. Teaching methods include the standards, such as case study analysis and the submission of reports and projects, as well as groundbreaking material in the form of creative role-playing and the innovative world reality seminar.

One of the program's core courses, entrepreneurial studies, fosters the development of initiative-building skills that are in such demand in today's executive market. This means that all students, either as individuals or within a team, have to develop a business start-up project, a significant proportion of which are converted into reality after graduation.

PLACEMENT

The Careers Management Department provides career advice and services for graduating students of all IE programs as well as alumni. The department organizes professional orientation sessions, conferences, and individual career counseling sessions throughout the year, and it publishes a curricula vitae book of graduating students each year which is distributed to over 2000 companies. Career advice workshops are designed to identify each student's preferences and offer guidance on professional development in different areas.

Over one thousand companies of varying shapes and sizes turn each year to IE's Careers Department for help in recruiting future executives from its varied programs. Many companies organize presentations, recruiting sessions, and interviews on campus using IE facilities. A large number of leading companies are based in Madrid and many of them are near the school, making for easy contact.

FINANCIAL AID

The IE foundation offers a range of scholarships and aid to students who have been accepted but find it particularly difficult to fund the program and related expenses. Scholarships are awarded on a basis of curriculum and personal circumstances.

The school has various agreements with other bodies, including the Spanish Agency for International Co-operation and several South American universities. IE also has a unique agreement with the Fulbright Commission for the funding of two scholarships for U.S. citizens which include tuition and living expenses.

6.
MANCHESTER
BUSINESS
SCHOOL

Contact:
Admissions Office
Phone:
(44) 161 275 7139
Fax:
(44) 161 275 6556

MANCHESTER BUSINESS SCHOOL
The University of Manchester
Booth Street West
GB-Manchester M15 6PB, United Kingdom
Web site: http://www.mbs.ac.uk
E-mail: mba@fs2.mbs.ac.uk

Program

Program ranked: MBA
Structure: 18 months full-time; 15 core courses and 5 electives; several projects/assignments
Size of class: 120–130 students for initial lectures, subsequently divided into two cohorts
Participants: Average age 28; 70% of student body is from overseas with an average of 5 years of professional experience
Costs: Tuition fees: 18,000 Pounds Sterling (approx. $29,027) for students from EU member countries; 21,000 Pounds Sterling (approx. $33,864) for students from non-EU countries (does not include introduction course or study trip); estimated living expenses for duration of course for a single person: 15,000 Pounds Sterling (approx. $24,190)
Program director: Andrew Stark
Accreditation: AMBA (British), EQUIS (European)

Admissions

Admissions requirements: Degree or professional qualification; minimum 3 years' experience in relevant post; test (or high GMAT score)
Applications deadline: June 30. Apply earlier to avoid disappointment, but there is a possibility of last-minute place
Starting date: September only
Application fee: 50 Pounds Sterling (approx. $80)

Recruiting

Placement office: Employer database; workshops in job research techniques, interview skills, résumé writing, and networking
Number of companies recruiting: About 80
Examples of recruiting companies: Citibank, AT Kearney, Andersen Consulting

BRIEF DESCRIPTION OF THE SCHOOL

Manchester Business School was founded in 1966 as the Faculty of Business Administration of the University of Manchester, but is now a self-contained and largely self-governing unit. Like London Business School, Manchester Business School was the "other" result of the Franks Report which recommended that Britain at that time desperately needed two new business schools, one in London and one in the north of England. It is interesting to note that these two business schools have consistently been the two top-ranking business schools in the UK. However, internal problems have taken their toll on the school's standing in recent years.

As well as the full-time and part-time MBA programs, the school offers more specialized programs: an MBA for lawyers, a public sector MBA, and a financial management MBA. In addition to the MBA programs, the school offers a master of philosophy and a master of business science; both focused mainly on research activities. There is also a Ph.D. program and a doctor of business administration (DBA).

The school's Business Development Center has recently launched an MBA in entrepreneurship for owner-managed and small- or medium-sized enterprises, the first fully fledged MBA of its kind in Europe. MBS's Business Development Center was created to provide executive training courses and foster research programs in the area of business development and expansion, aimed mainly at small- and medium-sized businesses or larger businesses seeking to run their departments on a quasi-autonomous basis.

Further programs and courses are designed and delivered by the school's Executive Center in partnership with major clients. The center also offers open programs, aimed at needs that many companies have in common, and is responsible for producing tailored in-company programs, as well as workshops and one-day seminars. Manchester is also known for its extensive research activity.

With 70 percent of its student body from outside the United Kingdom, including a large Asian contingent, Manchester is definitely international. The school encourages students to study one or more languages in its language center (typically French, German, Spanish, Italian, Japanese, and Chinese) and its exchange program is the largest in the world, allowing students a taste of working in a totally different environment. The European study program and the Asia Pacific program are opportunities for experiencing specific cultures firsthand. Take the example of student Nicola Stefani, who was in a work group with seven different nationalities, had an internship in the Netherlands, participated in an exchange program in the United States, then did an international business project in Brazil. And she is no exception!

MBS has a personal tutor system providing students with direct access to someone who can represent their views and listen to their personal concerns. The strong links that MBS enjoys with business and industry are reflected in a long list of corporate clients, both big and small. The school is one of few providing all of its students with host companies for consultancy projects, if necessary.

THE CAMPUS AND LIFE ON CAMPUS

The north of England is the cradle of the Industrial Revolution, and Manchester is studded with reminders of the era when it was the center of the cotton trade and the terminus of the Great Northern Shipping Canal. Anyone who takes a train ride to surrounding towns will experience a landscape that seems to have been taken directly from one of L. S. Lowry's haunting paintings.

The city of Manchester is the third largest city in England and the financial center of the north, where 80 of the *Financial Times* top 100 companies have offices or headquarters. A massive influx of immigrants during the 1950s and 1960s has resulted in a marked multiethnic flavor with a wealth of international restaurants, and even a small Chinatown. In addition, there are the traditional pubs, wine bars, cafés, and nightclubs, as well as more theaters than anywhere else in Britain outside London, and the outstanding Bridgewater Concert Hall. The airport, the largest outside London, provides easy access to cities throughout the world.

Manchester University has a sprawling campus and a visible presence in the city. Manchester Business School, although its students have access to all university facilities including its many and varied sporting and cultural venues, keeps much to itself in its own building. Building access is limited to participants of executive education programs. The site is pleasant and busy, yet relaxed with a bar, café, and restaurant, along with other facilities for the students' convenience.

The B-school has extensive, round-the-clock computer facilities complete with help desk, as well as the usual lecture halls, study and work rooms, and an extremely well-equipped library, reputedly one of the best of its kind in Europe.

On-campus accommodation is reserved exclusively for overseas participants. For those who prefer to live off campus, accommodations are available, although they may be lacking in desired amenities. Ask the school's student-friendly staff for advice on the best areas in which to live.

THE PROGRAM

The 18-month, full-time MBA is designed as an intensive, intrinsically hands-on learning experience. The school describes it as a 60-week program condensed into 18 months, comparable to a two-year program in the United States. Students are offered a foundation module before the main program begins. This four-week introduction is excellent for participants who have been out of school for some time.

The first two terms of the program cover 13 fundamental core courses, each of which comprises 30 hours of class contact time, equipping students with a solid working knowledge of the basics which will form the foundation on which to base more specialized studies in subsequent terms. These two terms also contain guidance on management and career development to help students make informed career decisions before selecting more specialized areas. The third term includes the student's first internal project, which is carried out within MBS using school material and under the guidance of a professor. Students must prove their readiness before the school permits them to solve a real problem in a host company. The external project immediately follows the internal project. Students are given a real-life situation demanding real solutions. These first three terms are "the diploma stage." The student must pass exams in order to go on to the second half of the program.

The second half provides more scope for specialization opportunities and a more personalized focus. The summer term offers the alternatives of an assessed internship, a lengthy dissertation, two elective courses, or a personal project and one elective. Although the school takes full responsibility for finding suitable projects for students through its many contacts, the student will be expected to play a part in helping to find a placement should he or she opt for the summer internship alternative. This is a popular choice as it gives students the opportunity to bolster their bank balances, which tend to be flagging at the mid-program stage.

The autumn term again offers four alternatives, giving students the choice of three electives plus an entrepreneur project, an international exchange program, a European study program, or an Asia Pacific study program. The student's choice is subject to availability; not everyone can go to the few places available in New York, for example. However, the school has a great many resources and disappointments are few. The winter term requires the student to deliver a lengthy international business project.

FACULTY, TEACHING, AND LEARNING PROCESSES

Almost all MBS faculty members have business and management experience, and 25 per cent are from overseas. They are encouraged to spend around one-fifth of their working hours on consultancy projects in order to bring up-to-date material and thinking into the classroom. Staff publications are evidence of dedicated research work.

The "Manchester method" places the emphasis squarely on learning through a practical, project-based approach. The school relies on some of the more traditional teaching methods such as lectures, case studies, tutorials, and group project work. Every course is subject to an assessment based on a minimum of two pieces of work in the form of examination case analyses, an essay, report, or group project.

Group work plays a key role following the theory that high-caliber and culturally varied students learn as much from each other as from professors and companies. The allocation of a personal tutor is part of a system of representation and feedback. If a student feels that he or she, or a work group, is failing in a particular area, then the personal tutor can be consulted before the problem gets too serious.

PLACEMENT

The Career Management and Alumni Center at Manchester Business School is dedicated to guiding the student toward making informed decisions and then helping him or her pursue them. Workshops run by internal experts and outside consultants provide instruction on how to write résumés, be successful in an interview, and make the most of networking, company research, and job search techniques. Students are also taught how to use the recruitment database and other information facilities to carry out company research and the job search itself. The summer internship is often the direct or indirect source of a job offer, providing the opportunity for both company and perspective employee to evaluate one another. MBA recruiter companies also visit the school. And, the school's recruitment curricula vitae, available in book form and on the Internet, constitutes yet another interface for employers and students.

All MBS graduates become part of an extensive alumni network, which prolongs their association with the school on both a professional and social level.

FINANCIAL AID

Scholarships are few. Sponsorship by companies is a main source of funding for the program, particularly the part-time version. AMBA (the Association of MBAs) can provide loans for those who manage to secure UK residency. For U.S. citizens, there is the MBA Loans Program, telephone 1-888-440-4622. The school code for Manchester is 012136.

IESE—INTERNATIONAL BUSINESS SCHOOL OF MANAGEMENT OF THE UNIVERSITY OF NAVARRA

7.
IESE

Avenida Pearson, 21
E-08034 Barcelona, Spain
Web site: http://www.iese.es
E-mail: MBAinfo@IESE.edu

Program

Program ranked: MBA
Structure: 2 years (21 months) full-time; 15 core courses in the first year; 1 core course and 14 elective courses in the second year; corporate internship at the end of the first year; Spanish language classes available throughout the program
Size of class: 220 students per year (3 sections of about 70 students each)
Participants: More than 46 nationalities (56% Spain, 21% rest of Europe, 15% Latin America, 6% North America, 2% rest of the world)
Costs: Tuition and virtually all course materials: 29,450 Euros (approx. $30,840) for the 2 years (A 10% nonrefundable deposit must be paid on acceptance to secure a place in the course.); estimated living expenses for a single person: 728 Euros per month (approx. $762)
Program director: Eduardo Martinez-Abascal
Accreditation: AEEDE (Spanish), AMBA (British), EQUIS (European)

Admissions

Admissions requirements: University degree; GMAT (average score 680); TOEFL (minimum 620); 2 references; work experience (average 3 years); fluency in English and Spanish at the time of graduation
Applications deadline: April 30
Starting date: October
Application fee: None

Contact:
Admissions Office
Phone:
(34) 93 253 42 00
Fax:
(34) 93 253 43 43

Recruiting

Placement office: On-campus presentations, electronic résumé book, interview preparation
Number of companies recruiting: 200+
Examples of recruiting companies: Andersen Consulting, Retevision, McKinsey and Co., PricewaterhouseCoopers, Société Générale de Banque, Chase Manhattan Bank.

BRIEF DESCRIPTION OF THE SCHOOL

The religious organization Opus Dei founded IESE in 1958 as the graduate business school of the University of Navarra, a prestigious private university in Spain. The school's main campus is in Barcelona, but it also has a small campus in Madrid, used mainly for executive education programs. IESE first offered its MBA in 1964, based on the same design as that of Harvard Business School.

One of IESE's long-standing policies has been to help set up schools in other parts of the world, such as Latin America, eastern Europe, and, most recently, China. These ventures were engineered by Professor Pedro Nueno, who is known throughout the European business school scene for his diplomatic abilities. Nueno has been instrumental in spinning the school's worldwide network of cooperative partners. In addition to numerous exchange programs for second-year MBA students with other B-schools all over the world, IESE currently offers several international executive programs in conjunction with other business schools, such as the University of Michigan and the China Europe Business School in Shanghai.

The school has made a determined effort to attract more applicants from eastern Europe, and thus enhance its international student body. The atmosphere at IESE is international with a distinct Spanish flavor. The MBA program is bilingual, equipping its participants to work in two of the most important languages in international business, English and Spanish. Spanish language classes are offered throughout the first year of the program.

One of IESE's distinguishing features may be a strong sense of identity that its members show toward their alma mater. The school, in turn, seems to be very active through its alumni network, which has delegations in different countries, and runs continuous education programs.

IESE is strong in financial management thanks to its International Center for Financial Research. Family business is another forte. The school has an endowed chair in family business along with seven other chairs in diverse management areas sponsored by Spanish companies.

There is a deeply rooted sense of tradition here, perhaps due partly to its religious affiliation, as well as a strong commitment to a humanistic approach to management education. "The students get a very clear feeling that they are not just going to deal with technical questions. We need to foster a sense of social responsibility," explains Professor Jordi Canals, a member of the school's board of directors. While the Catholic influence at the school is unmistakable, it is not overbearing—religion is not forced on the students.

In addition to the MBA, IESE's current academic offerings include an Executive MBA program, a doctoral program in business administration, and a range of management programs of varying length and content.

THE CAMPUS AND LIFE ON CAMPUS

Barcelona has undergone a major facelift over the last decade, largely due to its hosting the Olympic Games in 1992. It's a vibrant city with fascinating architecture, rich cultural opportunities, and an exciting nightlife. The city is well known in the fashion industry for its highly innovative sense of style, attracting a great deal of interest among top designers.

IESE is situated in the Pedralbes foothills, a wealthy residential area in uptown Barcelona. The school's attractive buildings offer fine views of the surrounding mountains and the Mediterranean. The first impression that the visitor receives is how still and well-ordered everything is. This orderliness, probably a result of the school's culture, suggests that everybody and everything has a place and a function.

The school is well-equipped where facilities are concerned. Lecture theaters are comfortable and the library, situated in one of the newest buildings on the campus, holds over 33,000 books and some 785 journals, along with access to online databases.

The school does not have halls of residence, but its accommodation service helps students find places nearby. Extracurricular activities are not exactly plentiful, but fortunately Barcelona has plenty to offer on that score.

THE PROGRAM

IESE's MBA program requires two years of study. The first year of the program is divided into three terms, each followed by exams. Classes can be taken entirely in English or entirely in Spanish. English speakers are given an intensive course in the Spanish language before the program begins. The first year covers the fundamental management disciplines, and it is much like that of an MBA program at an American business school. A typical day consists of three case discussions preceded by a group meeting. Curricular academic activities start at 8:15 a.m. and finish at 3:00 p.m.

The first year is followed by a corporate internship period lasting between 10 and 12 weeks. The internships are paid by the hiring companies and supervised by an IESE professor. Experience shows that internships are often an excellent source of job offers, as employers are able to see what graduates are capable of before committing themselves.

The second year of the program combines one core course and 14 electives from a sample list of more than 50. This year is intended to give the student a deeper and broader understanding of all management disciplines. Since IESE has an exchange program with 18 different business schools, the first term of the second year can be spent on an exchange program at a foreign school.

FACULTY, TEACHING, AND LEARNING PROCESSES

IESE's teaching faculty consists of 113 professors, many of whom combine their academic duties with consultancy work. The school also enjoys the participation of a significant number of foreign visiting professors who add to the international flavor of the teaching process. According to the opinion of IESE graduates, professors tend toward an open-door policy throughout the program, which makes for a more interactive learning experience.

The school emphasizes the use of the classical case method and teamwork and practices what it preaches by actively producing and using its own case studies. In addition, students from various backgrounds and nationalities learn from one another through team projects. Each team is allocated an academic adviser, and it meets on a daily basis to explore the members' views on cases before discussing them in a full-blown class situation.

PLACEMENT

The school maintains an active placement department. "We work closely with the students from the time of their entry into the program and develop a good relationship during the two years that they remain with us. We share their concerns, listen to their suggestions, and by the end of the two years, we have developed a relationship that has helped us to assess and treat them as individuals," says Patricia Ferrando, head of this department. Students are encouraged to use the Internet in their job search. All communication with students is made through e-mail; job offers and presentations on campus by companies are accessible through the network, and an electronic résumé book is available to recruiters through the school's Web site.

In 1998, the placement department was the source of employment for 81 percent of the students. The main recruiting sectors at IESE are consulting and financial services.

FINANCIAL AID

Most of the scholarships available are intended for European and South American applicants. However, the IESE Trust also awards some scholarships to applicants with an outstanding academic record, excellent professional experience, and personal merit, regardless of their nationality. In order to be eligible for these scholarships, candidates need to apply before

April 2. British applicants for IESE's MBA program are also eligible for the UK's AMBA (Association of MBAs) scholarship plan.

For loans, IESE participates in various programs, which include the Guaranteed Student Loan Program of the U.S. Department of Education (Code 021623 IESE-Universidad de Navarra), as well as the MBA Loans Program provided by the Graduate Management Admissions Council (GMAC: MBA Loans Processing Center, PO Box 64722, St. Paul, Minnesota 55164-0722, Phone: 800-366-6227).

8.

ISA HEC

ISA HEC School of Management
(Institut Supérieur des Affaires, École des Hautes
Études Commerciales)

1, rue de la Libération
F-78351 Jouy-en-Josas Cedex, France
Web site: http://www.hec.fr
E-mail: isadmission@hec.fr

Program

Program ranked: HEC MBA Program (ISA)

Type of course: 16 months full-time; academic year divided into two 8-month terms, the first one covering core management disciplines and the second providing 80 electives and the possibility of ending the course with either a major, a company consulting project, or an exchange program

Size of class: 250 (both September and January classes)

Participants: 20% foreign students from 32 different nationalities; average 4 years of professional experience with 10% of the students being young graduates

Costs: Program fees: 20,000 Euros (approx. $20,950); living expenses: 10,000 Euros (approx. $10,470)

Program director: Jean Loup Ardoin, Associate Dean HEC MBA Program (ISA)

Accreditation: AMBA (British), Chapitre (France), EQUIS (European)

Admissions

Admissions requirements: GMAT (average 640); TOEFL (if applicable) or TOEIC; references, university degree or equivalent, minimum 2 years work experience recommended but not mandatory, basic knowledge of French, and interview (which includes a 10-minute presentation)

Applications deadlines: May for September entry and November for January entry

Application fee: 68.6 Euros (approx. $72)

Recruiting

Placement office: Provides job-search workshops and seminars; contacts with alumni and companies; company presentations on campus

Number of companies recruiting: 300+

Examples of recruiting companies: Aerospatiale, Arthur Andersen, Bain & Company, BNP, General Electric, L'Oréal, Société Générale Des Eaux

Contact:
Admissions Office
Phone:
(33) 1 39 67 74 11
Fax:
(33) 1 39 67 74 65

BRIEF DESCRIPTION OF THE SCHOOL

HEC is certainly one of the places where the French "executive caste" is educated. A sample of its prominent alumni include Daniel Bernard, CEO of Carrefour, one of the largest retail distribution companies worldwide, recently merged with Promodés; Jean-Marie Laborde, CEO of Moët et Chandon, the illustrious champagne company; and Dominique Strauss-Kahn, the former French Minister of Economy and Industry. HEC was founded by the powerful Paris Chamber of Commerce in 1881 and has been consistently regarded as a premier European business schools.

Today the school has over 2000 full-time students undertaking a variety of programs and 3500 business executives enrolled in executive education seminars. Twenty percent of its students are from overseas, from over 30 different countries.

Therefore, ISA HEC's students are mostly French. They do, however, come from very varied educational and professional backgrounds. The fact that the environment has a markedly French flavor allows students from overseas to soak up a great deal of the French culture and mindset, with all its distinctive characteristics. On an academic level, students working together in study groups come into contact with different styles of thinking and problem solving on economic, financial, and legal issues, as well as on sales, distribution, marketing, and production.

For over 20 years, the school has extended its networks and forged links with the world's most prestigious institutions in order to offer its students an ever better choice and quality. To date, the school has concluded some 75 agreements with leading universities and business schools worldwide through different types of exchange. Two of the most recent initiatives are alliances with the American business school Amos Tuck and the Oxford-based Templeton College to develop joint projects in the field of new information technologies and management education.

ISA HEC's partner companies influence its strategy, teaching, and financial initiatives through permanent dialogue, joint decisions and actions, as well as their choice of projects to support. The school's alumni network comprises 20,000 alumni in over 50 countries.

The HEC foundation enjoys the collaboration of over 40 major companies, each of which supports HEC's ambitions and helps to promote the schools strategic orientation by promoting research programs in management science and encouraging international projects. The collaboration of these companies further strengthens the school's links with the corporate world in general.

THE CAMPUS AND LIFE ON CAMPUS

For many years the school was located in central Paris, but in 1964 it moved from downtown Paris to a campus, purposely built to be fairly self-contained, amid 250 acres of woodland near the historic Paris suburb of Jouy-en-Josas, not far from the world famous Versailles Palace. ISA HEC became the first French Business School with a "real" campus outside of Paris. Nevertheless, its proximity to the "City of Light" lets students enjoy the magnificence of this city.

The school offers on-campus accommodation: 1400 single rooms and 50 apartments reserved for married couples. In addition there are tutorial rooms, a sports hall, sports fields, amphitheaters, a library of over 60,000 books and 650 periodicals, and more than 1200 network computers. The fully equipped computer rooms and the students' bedrooms are connected to the ISA HEC local area network. The campus network provides e-mail service, access to various internal and external databases, cases cited by the professors and used in classes, and the library database.

The Students' Association also organizes a full slate of sporting events (using their superlative sporting facilities) and cultural events, such as the annual gala party (which attracts ISA HEC alumni from around the world as well as professors, administrators, and current participants); the European MBA sports tournament; art exhibitions; visits to Paris theaters and operas; international dinners; and conferences. This particularly sociable business school has over 60 different associations and clubs focusing on areas like languages, music, weekend activities, gastronomy, sports, computers, journalism, as well as a wide variety of clubs in specific professional sectors like banking and finance, civil engineering and environment, international affairs, law, health, consulting, multimedia, etc.

THE PROGRAM

The bilingual French/English MBA program was created in 1969. Its academic year is divided into two terms: mid-September through mid-February and mid-February through mid-June (exchange students can arrange to take their finals in April).

The 16-month MBA program is focused on general management skills and knowledge during the first two semesters. The second part of the curriculum addresses each participant's career objective with specialized areas of concentration offering more than 80 electives and three different tracks. Students may specialize in one field (major), such as entrepreneurship, international finance, or management consulting. Alternatively they may do a company consulting project or participate in an exchange program. The International Exchange Program includes agreements with universities in Europe (7 schools), North America (13), Asia (4), Canada (4), South America (4), Australia (1), and Israel (1).

Participants may choose to enter either the French-speaking or the English-speaking section of the program. In each section classes are identical, but they are taught in either English or French during the first four months of the curriculum. Thus, participants enjoy a progressive period of adaptation to "bilingualism."

After this introductory period, courses are taught in equal proportion in French and English. All participants will therefore acquire more than an operational fluency in both languages by graduation. Even though knowledge of French is not an entry requirement, participants must show a minimum knowledge of French to gain admission. In addition to French and English, the school offers classes in eight other languages.

FACULTY, TEACHING, AND LEARNING PROCESSES

ISA HEC's 106 permanent MBA faculty members are highly qualified and hold close ties with the business world through research, consulting, and executive programs. The school also has 70 part-time faculty and some 35 visiting professors from schools like Harvard, Stanford, and Cornell. Teaching methods include case-based teaching, interactive teaching in small groups, as well as teamwork.

There are more than 100 full-time faculty members involved in different programs, including courses overseas at Cambridge, Michigan, Duke, London Business School, etc. The teaching staff has published 160 books in the last 10 years.

PLACEMENT

The Career Development Office provides job-search workshops and seminars, counseling, an extensive documentation center, contacts with the alumni network, and privileged contacts with the businesses that work in close collaboration with ISA HEC. Each year it publishes and distributes a book containing the résumés of all MBA students.

FINANCIAL AID

ISA HEC offers a wide range of scholarship possibilities, depending on which group applicants belong to. Participants who have worked in France are eligible for all types of financing as part of their company training program. ISA HEC's AMBA accreditation allows UK citizens to use the bank financing arrangements set up by the AMBA.

U.S. residents and citizens are eligible for federal and state guaranteed student loans: ISA's code number is 022934.

9.
ASHRIDGE MANAGEMENT COLLEGE

Contact:
Admissions Office
Phone:
(44) 1442 841143
Fax:
(44) 1442 841144

ASHRIDGE MANAGEMENT COLLEGE

Berkhamsted
GB-Hertfordshire HP4 1NS, United Kingdom
Web site: www.ashridge.org.uk
E-mail: info@ashridge.org.uk

Program

Program ranked: MBA

Structure: 10 months, modular; four 4-week modules plus a study week; 12 core courses, no electives as such; project assignments plus a consultancy project

Size of class: Maximum 30 students

Participants: Average age 34, but 45 is not unusual; average work experience 12 years; 50% of student body is from overseas

Costs: Tuition fees: 20,500 Pounds Sterling (approx. $33,060) (includes on-campus meals and refreshments) plus 6000 Pounds Sterling (approx. $9675) for project support from Ashridge tutor or consultant plus value added tax at current rate; estimated living expenses for duration of course for a single person: 10,000 Pounds Sterling (approx. $16,125)

Program director: Stephen Robinson

Accreditation: AMBA (British), EQUIS (European)

Admissions

Admissions requirements: Degree or professional qualification; minimum 5 years' experience in relevant post; admissions test (or high GMAT score)

Applications deadline: October

Starting date: January intake only

Application fee: None

Recruiting

Placement office: Not in evidence, relies more on alumni network

Number of companies recruiting: N/A

Examples of recruiting companies: N/A

BRIEF DESCRIPTION OF THE SCHOOL

Ashridge Management Center came into being in 1959 as the result of an act of Parliament, and remains an independent, nonprofit educational organization. Its founders included directors from Guinness, Shell, and Unilever, which helps explain the practical content of its programs.

Every fiber of Ashridge's framework favors a practical hands-on approach. Ashridge seems to eschew things academic and is run by a chief executive officer rather than a dean. For years Ashridge concentrated on consulting services and short courses for business people. The executive MBA program was first introduced 10 years ago, based on the wide variety of expertise gained over the years and designed to break away from the traditional MBA model. Other programs include a wide-ranging selection of four-day open programs, a master's program in organization consulting, a diploma in general management, and an enormous quantity of tailor-made programs. These account for half of the school's executive education activities and eight million Pounds Sterling of its annual income.

Ashridge Online is a relatively new development involving an online teaching system that is one of the most advanced of its kind. It offers 10 to 20 hours of online learning through integrated case studies and interactive exercises for managers, along with links to external resources.

The accent at Ashridge is on management, be it of the general or top-level variety. The school is renowned for its management consulting services rendered to some 60 international clients each year. The services specialize in corporate level strategy, strategic styles, and the changing relationship between business and society.

Ashridge is currently seeking the right to grant its own degrees, no mean feat in Britain where public universities have all but a monopoly over this particular area. The plan is to apply for monotechnic status, thereby enabling the school to award degrees in a sole subject.

Personalized attention is one of the main characteristics that set Ashridge apart from its counterparts. With a maximum of 30 students to each class, professors, who maintain an open-door policy and provide mentor-style tutoring, can lavish attention on program participants. Ashridge is also known for unusual teaching methods, and students can expect the unexpected.

Another feature that affords the school its high ranking is the way it strives to create an international environment. One of the admission criteria is that part of a candidate's experience must have been gained in an international context. The range of nationalities among both students and teaching faculty is broad.

The emphasis that the school places on project assignments, together with high costs, tend to attract participants with more years' experience (an average of 12 years) than other MBA programs. This means that learning is accelerated as it isn't necessary to wade through so much groundwork before branching out into more specialized directions.

THE CAMPUS AND LIFE ON CAMPUS

No visitor could fail to be impressed by the sheer elegance and historical value of Ashridge's campus, situated in the kind of surroundings that William Blake was thinking about when he wrote about "England's green and pleasant land." Born and bred city dwellers may suffer a few withdrawal symptoms as they alight from the train after the 30-minute ride from London Euston to Berkhamsted, but only the most hardened will not be charmed by this small town.

Six miles from the town, after a ride through leafy glades and rolling fields, the visitor gets a first glimpse of Ashridge. The expression "steeped in history" must surely have been coined here. The original building was actually a monastery, its claim to fame being that King Edward I held parliament there in 1290–1291. Through the centuries the building had a rich and colorful history, and more associations with royalty. When the eighth Earl of Bridgewater was forced to sell the estate and mansion to an educational trust in 1923, the academic community gained a national treasure.

The reception area, from which a magnificent stone-lined gallery can be seen, reveals how this beautiful building has been restored and maintained to exceptionally high standards. The visitor will probably be invited to have tea or coffee in "the white room," reminiscent of a gentlemen's country club with its high backed chairs and enormous windows overlooking an English country estate garden. City slickers and society animals may well feel out of place here, but for those whose aim is to buy a Bentley rather than a Ferrari with their expected raise in salary, this is as idyllic as it gets.

Unfortunately most of the working day is not spent in the main building. Most accommodations, lecture theaters, rooms, and resources are located in a modern extension built for the school. The new area, while limited in space due to building regulations governing historically sensitive sites, is pleasant as well as practical. Learning facilities include a unique virtual resource learning center, open 24 hours a day, and excellent computer and video facilities. As for leisure facilities, students can wind down by working out in a well-equipped fitness center or simply taking a stroll in the school's magnificent gardens.

On-campus accommodation consists of comfortable, self-contained study rooms, which are usually rented on a full-board basis at prices that are reasonable considering the surroundings. Ashridge has won several awards for its catering facilities. It is possible to rent or share off-campus rooms and/or apartments (except for one of the four-week long modules, when all students are required to live on campus). Due to the proximity to London, housing prices are high.

THE PROGRAM

The content of Ashridge's MBA program is in keeping with the school's approach to executive education. Apart from the usual core subjects, the learning process is based on undertaking 12 assignments throughout the program, each one involving a live issue in one of the school's participating organizations. But the real lifeblood of the program is the "live consultancy project,"

pioneered by Ashridge and much copied on the other side of the Atlantic, which consists of tackling a real problem in a real business under the close guidance of an Ashridge professor or consultant. Although the school makes every effort to help self-sponsored students find companies willing to let them tackle a particular problem in the form of a major consultancy project, the students are also expected to play their part in finding a host company. Companies pay students quite well for their efforts, but there is a 6000 Pounds Sterling (approx. $9675) charge to cover the fees of the professor-cum-top-level consultant who oversees the entire project.

The program is divided into four intensive four-week modules, all with what the school calls "assignment and project milestone dates," so students will find themselves living with one foot on campus and the other in the real world. In addition to the four modules there is an "international study week" with four assignment deadline dates.

Ten major themes are another integrated element of the program: issues in the global business environment, strategic leadership, personal values and development, analytical processes, communication skills, business and society, and implementing change. The idea behind this is to get away from functional blocks and to concentrate on individual and organizational performance. This aversion to functional blocks gives the program enough flexibility to cater to individual needs, allowing the student to specialize or reinforce weak areas. At the beginning of the course there is a diagnostic session based on psychometric testing, after which students and faculty get together to design specific learning processes to strengthen weak areas and promote maximum feedback.

So-called soft skills are taken seriously, with leadership at the top of the list. Students are equipped to develop a capacity to influence, build teams, handle one-on-one situations, and encourage creativity and innovation.

FACULTY, TEACHING, AND LEARNING PROCESSES

The school's full-time and part-time faculty is smaller in number than the average top-notch European business school. As can be expected, practically all members of the faculty do consulting, both for the school and on a private basis, which means that they are kept abreast of changing trends that are in turn brought into the classroom.

At Ashridge they tell us that, "You don't analyze a remote case study with 20/20 hindsight, you put a living organization under the microscope and find out how well the theories and models stand up. You take real problems and see how far the frameworks can take you in finding solutions." Hence the emphasis on real assignments and a final consulting report as a way to learn how to deal with real problems in real companies.

The fact that the program brings together mature people with experience gained in different countries, functions, and organizational cultures means that students will learn almost as much from each other as from professors and host companies. With such a rich blend of backgrounds someone nearly always has an interesting personal anecdote to add to class discussions.

A typical feature of the program involves bringing in actors to re-create given situations. One example is the media-handling weekend, during which students work with journalists from the BBC to prepare news broadcast, all part of learning about crisis management.

Unusual forms of training are the norm here—blackboard and chalk are definitely out. Ice-breaking tends to be done with a sledgehammer. Take the occasion when Ashridge used pop singers to instruct members of two groups of managers, who were having problems working together, to sing duets with each other. Ashridge is also one of the few business schools in the world with its own "outdoor training" facilities. Couch potatoes be warned!

PLACEMENT

Not one of Ashridge's strong points. A good 50 percent of Ashridge MBA students are sponsored by their organizations so their needs are covered. As for self-sponsored students, the school relies on the widespread reputation of its program. Graduates report that the school's belief in itself is well-founded and organizations are usually suitably impressed. The school includes career development as a research area in its center for management and organization learning, as well as offering an online learning module under the label of "Self-managed Career Development." Students are obviously expected to use their initiative when it comes to searching for that plum job. The school does, however, do its bit by maintaining an active alumni network, always useful when it comes to finding that vital contact.

FINANCIAL AID

Again, while company-sponsored students are sitting pretty, others find themselves faced with a major outlay in course fees and living expenses. Although this may be somewhat relieved by payment for the consultancy project [the average fee is over 11,000 Pounds Sterling (approx. $17,739)], it doesn't lighten the load that much. The best advice is to start looking for a major loan the moment a decision is taken.

Two scholarships, covering 50 percent of the program fee, are awarded each year to self-funding students who intend to use their MBA year to start their own business. Candidates who wish to apply for this scholarship have to submit an essay illustrating how they think an MBA at Ashridge is going to contribute toward their project.

10.
SDA BOCCONI

Contact:
Admissions Office
Phone:
(39) 02 5836
3204/3287/
3281/3298
Fax:
(39) 02 5836 3275

SDA BOCCONI—SCUOLA DI DIREZIONE AZIENDALE
DELL'UNIVERSITÀ LUIGI BOCCONI

School of Management
Master's Division—UCI
Via Balilla 16–18
I-20136 Milano, Italy
Web site: www.sda.uni-bocconi.it
E-mail: admissions@sda.uni-bocconi.ita

Program

Program ranked: Bilingual MBA (Italian, English)
Structure: 16 months full-time.
Size of class: 65 (total intake 130)
Participants: 49% aged between 28–30; 45% international students; 36% with 3–4 years of working experience
Costs: 19,110 Euros (approx. $20,000); living expenses about 2,000,000 Lira per month (approx. $1080)
Program director: Mario Mazzoleni
Accreditation: ASFOR (Italian), AMBA (British), EQUIS (European)

Admissions

Admissions requirements: Undergraduate degree; 2 years' professional experience strongly recommended; GMAT or equivalent test in Italian at the school; 2 reference letters; TOEFL or certificate testifying the knowledge of Italian; interview
Applications deadline: No later than April 30
Starting date: September
Application fee: 77.5 Euros (approx. $81)

Recruiting

Placement office: Services for career goals, company presentations, contacts to companies, network of companies
Number of companies recruiting: 121
Examples of recruiting companies: Ford, L'Oréal, Procter & Gamble

BRIEF DESCRIPTION OF THE SCHOOL

The Scuola di Direzione Aziendale (SDA) Bocconi is the graduate arm of Milan's Bocconi University. The university itself was founded in 1902 with a view to specializing in the teaching of economics, business, and social sciences. The SDA was set up in 1971, and quickly became Italy's top business school. In addition to offering MBA programs it carries out 800 management development seminars for 10,000 managers each year, mostly Italian.

Being Italy's only high-profile international business school, SDA has pushed hard to set up exchange programs and links with a large number of leading business schools scattered across the globe. Examples include Johnson Graduate School of Management at Cornell University, London Business School, Manchester Business School, and the Rotterdam School of Management.

The school is one of the participants of PRIME (Program for International Managers in Europe), a joint venture of six European business schools, including Rotterdam and Groupe HEC. The objective of the program is to train highfliers who are aiming for positions involving international responsibilities.

As well as being able to provide a sound academic foundation, Bocconi enjoys privileged relations with the Italian business community, which are two of the reasons that its graduates can probably boast the best multinational-based job offers in Italy.

THE CAMPUS AND LIFE ON CAMPUS

Spending part of one's life—albeit only a brief part—in a country like Italy entails immersing oneself in two cultures: the sunny, artistic, joyous Mediterranean culture and the rational, efficient, dynamic middle-European one.

Milan is in the heart of Italy's main industrial and commercial region, with easy access to the Alps, the Riviera, and all the main cultural centers of Italy, and Bocconi is bang in the center of it. Milan offers numerous cultural opportunities, such as art in all its forms, theater, and concerts, including the famous La Scala. The Italians have a well-earned reputation for representing the epitomy of style and chic (it's a close competition between Milan and Paris for this particular honor), which could explain one of their great national pastimes that every foreign visitor initially scoffs at and then ends up doing themselves—i.e., people watching. It could also

explain why one of the specializations available on this program is that of fashion and design. Given that the tough program will not leave participants the amount of free time needed to appreciate this cultural hotbed, it is recommended that, if humanly possible, participants spend some time here after the completion of the program.

Applicants interested in sports will be pleased to hear that SDA Bocconi is involved in organized sports activities, e.g., MBA sports contests with other European MBA schools.

On a more relevant note, at least academically speaking, the MBA program is held in a pleasant building, renovated in a functional style which makes it difficult to imagine that it was once a convent school. It has 10 modern classrooms, all furnished with multimedia equipment, and 50 special group work areas. In addition the division offers a language laboratory and has a network of personal computers. There is no on-campus accommodation as such, although the school helps students find apartments. SDA has a service which offers a list of accommodation possibilities and even helps find roommates.

THE PROGRAM

The first part of the program focuses on the development of analytical knowledge and basic management skills. The second part deals with the integration of knowledge and advanced management skills. The second half of the program, which offers an excellent range of electives, allows students to work on company field projects, either individually or in groups,

The program extends over 16 months (from September to December of the following year), offering 13 core courses and varied electives. Ten months are dedicated to classroom activity in two separate language sections (Italian and English) with a common curriculum divided into five phases: prelude, pillars, functional management, general management, and itineraries. An excellent opportunity to learn the beautiful Italian language, but don't let the romantic in you prevent you from considering the sad fact that its use is limited to its country of origin.

The so-called prelude is a phase of individual learning, achieved by studying the teaching materials supplied by SDA Bocconi before the start of the program. The pillars are the structural elements of the course, equipping participants with the basic techniques they will need for the following phases of the program. Students must pass tests before proceeding to the next phase. The functional management phase focuses on the technical concepts associated with the various functional areas of companies. Students receive individual consulting to help them choose their study paths for the final part of the program. Progress to the general management phase depends on an assessment of participants' skills evaluated on the basis of their classroom performance and on tests administered at the end of the single courses.

General management is the phase in which students integrate the various functions examined in the previous phase. This closes with individual and group tests focusing on the interfunctional aspects of management. In the itineraries phase (i.e., electives) students are invited to broaden their knowledge and test their managerial skills through a combination of in-company projects, courses, and workshops. This phase includes the opportunity to specialize in both conventional and more unusual areas of study. One particularly interesting option is the aforementioned focus on fashion and design, which aims to enable graduates to act as an interface between designers, market needs, and the management of company resources. In this phase both English and Italian are used interchangeably.

Another feature of this program is the horizons program, which gives students the chance to get to know more about leading personalities of the world of science, industry, culture, information, and entertainment. Opinions are subject to debate between participants and protagonists as real business world meets academia.

FACULTY, TEACHING, AND LEARNING PROCESS

The MBA's teaching faculty includes over 100 teaching and research staff of SDA Bocconi as well as visiting professors from Italian and foreign universities and business schools. In fact, SDA Bocconi organizes more than 500 management education courses annually, an extra guarantee of the continuous updating of its faculty.

The teaching method is an interactive process whereby participants gradually acquire tools and skills. In addition to lectures and individual study, strong emphasis is given to group work, meetings with guest speakers, case discussions, computer simulations, and other interactive techniques.

Again, there is the familiar pattern of exchange of information within teams and between study teams, in addition to instruction provided by professors. The school places a great deal of emphasis on interaction between participants and between teachers and colleagues from varying cultural backgrounds.

PLACEMENT

Through its recruiting and career management activity, the school offers participants opportunities to meet companies. The school publishes a book containing curricula vitae in both Italian and English that is made available to companies. Training sessions and seminars are offered to help students manage their contacts with prospective employers more effectively and to help them improve their oral and written self-presentation skills for optimum performance in job interviews.

FINANCIAL AID

A number of scholarships fully or partially covering tuition fees are offered by sponsoring companies and organizations. Scholarships are awarded on the basis of admission test results and other criteria as specified from year to year by the sponsoring entity. Participants are encouraged to seek out the numerous opportunities available in all countries, such as the sponsorship of the company that employs (or will employ) them or scholarships offered by private foundations, international organizations, or local governments. In most countries, banks offer citizens preferential loans to finance postgraduate education. Admission to the MBA program is independent of the possible awarding of a scholarship.

11.
CRANFIELD SCHOOL OF MANAGEMENT

Contact:
Admissions Office
Phone:
(44) 1234 754431
Fax:
(44) 1234 752439

CRANFIELD SCHOOL OF MANAGEMENT

Cranfield
GB-Bedford MK43 OAL, United Kingdom
Web site: http://www.cranfield.ac.uk/som
E-mail: p.hayes@cranfield.ac.uk

Program
Program ranked: MBA
Structure: 1 year (4 terms) full-time; 16 core courses, approx. 12 electives, several projects
Size of class: Maximum 50 students
Participants: Average age 31; almost 40% from overseas; average of 9 years of relevant work experience in all sectors of business
Costs: Tuition fees: 18,500 Pounds Sterling (approx. $29,834) (includes free loan of laptop); estimated living expenses for duration of course for a single person: 10,000 Pounds Sterling (approx. $16,125)
Program director: John Mapes
Accreditation: AMBA (British), EQUIS (European)

Admissions
Admissions requirements: Degree or professional qualifications; minimum 5 years' experience in relevant post; admissions test (or high GMAT score)
Applications deadline: No final date for admissions but best to apply before July
Starting date: September and January
Application fee: None

Recruiting
Placement office: Network of contacts through business and social events; bulletin information on jobs; résumé database; broad-based source for MBA employment
Number of companies recruiting: 80+
Examples of recruiting companies: Lily Industries, KPMG, Andersen Consulting

BRIEF DESCRIPTION OF THE SCHOOL

Cranfield was founded in 1946 as the first postgraduate College of Aeronautics, and built up a solid reputation for expertise in management, advanced technology, and applied science. In 1967 the school created its School of Management as a department within the college, just a year before the college was given university status.

Like Ashridge, Cranfield offers a wide variety of executive development seminars. Over 6000 senior managers attend the school's executive development programs each year. Apart from the full-time and part-time MBAs (a modular MBA is in the pipeline), which are among the longest-standing in Europe, the school also offers a master of science in project management, logistics and supply change management, and transport management.

The school claims the highest number of contact teaching hours of any UK business school and places strong emphasis on individual development. "The Cranfield experience" is the result of a combination of high-achievers, an open-door policy, an interactive learning process and constantly updated research amid a strong sense of community. A 1996 graduate noted, "From day one, everyone was brought into the Cranfield culture: students from the previous year organized and facilitated the orientation week. This made it crystal clear that we were not there to be taught, but to learn actively."

The school reinforces its international environment by strongly encouraging acquiring a second and preferably a third language. Regular classes are available at the school's language training center in French, German, and Spanish. Russian, Japanese, and Mandarin are offered according to student demand.

A selection of 77 elective courses makes for a high level of flexibility within the program, allowing students to pursue areas of particular interest in far greater depth and develop a truly customized program. The four-term structure also allows extra time to further consolidate areas in which the student has opted to specialize. Cranfield has long-standing contacts with the corporate world which have been strengthened through numerous consultancy projects undertaken by its students.

THE CAMPUS AND LIFE ON CAMPUS

The campus is located between the two largest cities in England, London and Birmingham, on the edge of an area known as Milton Keynes. A 1964 master plan to designate 9000 hectares (22,000 acres) in the English countryside for development of a new town resulted in the creation of Milton Keynes. The emphasis was to create a balance between housing and employment so as to avoid large numbers of people having to commute to work.

The planned town is distinguished by an impressive system of parks, futuristic buildings, and the Peace Pagoda, a symbol of marked Asian influx to the area. The Cranfield campus is about a 25-minute ride from the Milton Keynes train station, through an area noted for interesting old towns and villages with characteristic thatched cottages.

The campus, situated on the site of a World War II airfield with many of the original barrack-style buildings, is not especially striking. Glen Miller admirers take note—the famous band leader broadcast his 1940's swing music throughout the world from this airfield, and concerts of his music are still a feature of the area's lively culture scene. The management school is housed mainly in additions constructed during the 1960s and 1970s, unfortunately not a golden era of British architecture. Fortunately, communal gardens lend a pleasant touch of green to the campus.

Although Cranfield's location does not lend itself to an active social life, students tend to form close, long-lasting working and personal relationships which make for a pleasant and productive year. The school actively encourages the involvement of partners and children in all extracurricular activities.

On-campus leisure facilities include a gym, squash, badminton, and tennis courts. Hobby pilots can take advantage of the university's own airfield. The campus is a self-contained community with its own bank, post office, bookshop, general store, and social club. There is an on-campus playgroup for small children.

On-campus accommodation is plentiful and pleasant, available for both singles and families. Reasonably priced housing is available in surrounding villages. The University Housing Office provides assistance for both, and there is also an information service that puts MBA students who wish to share in contact with others. A car is almost essential, or at least a valid driver's license. Public transport is practically nonexistent, slow, and exorbitantly expensive.

THE PROGRAM

As one of the longest-standing MBA programs in Europe, the Cranfield full-time MBA enjoys a solid reputation. It is an intensive 12-month program divided into four terms that cover much the same ground as the traditional two-year, U.S.-style programs.

Technophobes and those whose last clash with mathematics was in high school will be interested to know that the school offers short, optional, preprogram math and information management skills courses. These are followed by a compulsory orientation week run by MBA students from previous years.

The core subjects covered during terms one and two are designed to equip the student with the fundamentals of all the disciplines and show how key functional areas are interrelated. Terms three and four deal with the few remaining core courses, including the business start-up course which takes the form of a "business game" that teaches students how to draw up a business plan. International business law is also covered, but the second half of the program centers mainly on the 12 or so electives selected by students from a range of some 77 topics. Students may opt to carry out either a major consultancy project or several shorter ones to replace part of their electives. Although the school will assist in organizing consultancy projects, students are expected to use their own initiative in finding host organizations. Fortunately Cranfield's reputation makes this task easier as the school enjoys a high level of confidence and trust among many companies.

There is an exchange program option during the second half of the full-time MBA that gives students the opportunity to spend time in a different culture, language permitting. This is particularly valuable for those students who intend to work in a multinational company.

FACULTY, TEACHING, AND LEARNING PROCESSES

Cranfield's faculty consists of some 90 permanent staff and 40 visiting professors and lecturers. The school values its professors' experience in commerce and industry, considered essential to provide a good blend of practical and academic expertise.

A wide variety of teaching methods is employed, from lectures to case studies to role-playing exercises. The television room is the scene of many a prickly situation at the office, simulated by professional actors and complete with the typical explosive mix of emotions and interests. One such scene may be the delicate task of telling an employee that he is to be let go. During the crisis management exercise, teams take the role of a board of directors dealing with a frenzied media in the wake of a major corporate incident. Guests from the world of communications play the role of hard-nosed journalists.

Philippe Schmitt, who graduated in 1992, said, "Cranfield is not just about acquiring specialist knowledge and a sound background in management, but it is also about learning to cope with pressure, and developing your leadership and teamwork skills."

PLACEMENT

Career advice and counseling are readily available for full-time MBA students. An annual register of graduates seeking employment is circulated among some 3000 companies. Students are offered advice on how to channel their efforts into making the right choice and achieving their goals during a series of career development lectures and information evenings during term two. The MBA program career office offers support to students who have preferred to wait until the end of the program to begin their search for a new job.

The school also maintains an active alumni organization, the Cranfield Management Association. The association organizes business and social events throughout the year to keep its members in contact with each other as their careers develop, and publishes *The Career Moves Bulletin* twice a month with info provided by the recruitment specialists who form part of its executive recruitment service.

FINANCIAL AID

A limited number of scholarships are available for exceptional students. Scholarships include Fulbright awards for MBA programs, open to North American citizens with a minimum of 3.5 GPA on their bachelor's degree. For further details and application forms contact the Institute of International Education, 809 United Nations Plaza, New York, NY 10017-3580. The Cranfield MBA is also registered under the U.S. Department of Education, Office of Secondary Education, (No. 01049300). Loans for the overseas student are somewhat scarce. Permanent residents of the United Kingdom can apply for the AMBA business school loan scheme. Others must organize their own funding.

12.
NIJENRODE UNIVERSITY

NIJENRODE UNIVERSITY—THE NETHERLANDS BUSINESS
SCHOOL

Straatweg 25
NL-3621 Breukelen, Netherlands
Web site: http://www.nijenrode.nl
E-mail: mba@nijenrode.nl

Program

Program ranked: International MBA
Structure: 13 months full-time; 6 blocks containing over 20 core
courses and 3 electives plus the possibility of either a project/thesis
or a financial management major and a further 3-month module
to obtain a double degree
Size of class: 60 students per class
Participants: Average age, 27.5 years; average work experience, 4.5 years;
68% international students, 16 different nationalities
Costs: Tuition fee: 18,151 Euros (approx. $19,000); double degree
tuition fee: 19,058 Euros (approx. $19,953); estimated average liv-
ing expenses, including health insurance and course materials:
12,340 Euros (approx. $12,913)
Program director: Karel Samsom, Associate Dean MBA Programs
Accreditation: AMBA (British), EQUIS (European)

Admissions

Admissions requirements: University degree; minimum 2 years experi-
ence; TOEFL (for nonnative English speakers); GMAT; 2 refer-
ences; personal interview
Applications deadline: Rolling basis
Starting date: August
Application fee: 68 Euros (approx. $71)

Recruiting

Placement office: Personal advice, job opening postings, résumé books,
career skills and case workshops, company presentations on cam-
pus, career fairs
Number of companies recruiting: 100
Examples of recruiting companies: ABN-AMRO Bank, General Electric,
ING Bank, Philips, Lucent Technologies

Contact:
Admissions Office
Phone:
(31) 346 291 607
Fax: (31) 346 250 595

BRIEF DESCRIPTION OF THE SCHOOL

Nijenrode was established in 1946 as the first business school actually
financed by the business community. The initiative came from the
then-top executives of internationally prestigious companies such as

AKZO, KLM, Philips, Shell, and Unilever. The founding fathers foresaw a growing need for internationally oriented business people who regard entrepreneurship as a profession. They wanted to enrich the Dutch educational scene with an institution which could train talented and internationally oriented people who would help rebuild the national postwar economy. In 1982 Nijenrode acquired full university status and remains the only private university in The Netherlands and one of the top business schools in Europe.

Today Nijenrode provides a course structure for both students and executives. The school has a strong reputation in management programs enhanced by its close ties with the national and international business communities.

The international MBA is a full-time, 13-month program that aims to develop globally minded business leaders and managers, who possess the specific skills essential for success in the twenty-first century. Students are put in situations that closely simulate the realities of management. They learn to make important decisions under time constraints, often with limited information.

Nijenrode students can complete the program by choosing a project/thesis or a financial management major. The school also offers a double degree (see the program description below).

Nijenrode is a pioneer in the provision of information services via the Internet. The school has two internationally acclaimed Web sites. One of the sites provides general information about the university's programs, forthcoming events, faculty, facilities, and the campus, while the other is packed with resources for business and economics.

THE CAMPUS AND LIFE ON CAMPUS

The campus is situated on the Nyenrode family estate in the town of Breukelen about 22 kilo-meters southeast of Amsterdam. The estate even has a thirteen-century castle, which now accommodates several administrative departments.

At the heart of the campus is Nijenrode's library that is used by corporate clients and alumni, as well as current students. The school has state-of-the-art computing services available 24 hours a day. Computers are also installed in the small conference rooms that are available for group meetings and discussions. Full multimedia facilities in all classrooms support a wide range of teaching techniques, enabling professors and students to use personal computers that are linked to professional presentation media, audiovisual equipment, and computer simulation facilities.

The Nijenrode computer network also provides the student with quick and easy access to newspaper and magazine articles and to dissertation extracts from dedicated databases throughout the world. The home page offers full text research papers from Nijenrode and other economic and business faculties.

Young and international best describe the campus atmosphere at Nijenrode. The average age of the students is 27.5 years, and 68 percent of the student body come from more than 16 different countries. Every class is a one-of-a-kind experience providing participants with an unlimited source of multicultural knowledge.

Nijenrode's location lets students enjoy the city life of nearby Amsterdam with its museums, historical sites, magnificent architecture, superb landscapes, and extravagant nightlife. Although living costs in The Netherlands are relatively inexpensive, most students live on campus as it is both convenient and reasonable.

THE PROGRAM

The MBA program, all taught in English, provides thorough grounding in the fundamental areas of marketing, finance, accounting, and operations management; it focuses on developing the ability to communicate, motivate, and lead people.

Students are involved in an intensive study program throughout the year, combining stress situations, group work, competition, grading, presentations, lectures, cases, workshops, seminars, and heavy demands on time.

The core courses in a wide range of subjects are part of an overall six-block curriculum.

The final portion of the Nijenrode MBA may involve either a project/thesis or a three-month financial management major.

The project/thesis is a company sponsored research and consulting assignment that provides an excellent stepping stone to employment after the MBA. The financial management major is an alternative for the project/thesis which permits students to focus on either controlling or treasury. Graduates of this major qualify for jobs as controller, treasurer, financial analyst, or portfolio manager in (investment) banking or for jobs in general management and consultancy.

With Nijenrode's double degree program, students can earn both the MBA and the DRS (Dutch equivalent of a master of science in management). After completing the regular 13-month MBA program, selected students obtain the DRS degree after three additional months of study, so that in just 16 months they earn two degrees.

FACULTY, TEACHING, AND LEARNING PROCESSES

Nijenrode's teaching philosophy is geared to developing globally minded business leaders and managers who can respond and adapt to fluctuating trends in the business world. Faculty members are experienced in coaching mature graduate students with substantial business experience. The faculty and staff work closely with students, both in and outside the classroom, establishing a partnership that is beneficial to both. The capstone thesis project is the culmination of this joint venture, with faculty and staff supervising projects and collaborating with students on this important undertaking. Interaction and assessment are key ingredients. Self-assessment and assessment by peers, the faculty, and the business community are all features of the program.

In combination with the curriculum, a variety of different teaching methods are used including: lectures, case discussions, group and individual presentations, computer simulations, consultancy projects, role-playing, and guest speaker presentations

This emphasis on teamwork enables students to learn about others, the tendencies of cultures, and the dynamics of group enterprises. This intensive learning experience yields strong friendships that develop into valuable international networks.

PLACEMENT

Nijenrode's Career Services' Office (CSO) plays an active role in helping students to clarify their career objectives and match their talent with the right companies.

CSO helps with self-assessments, résumé and cover letters, and interview preparation. Among the services offered are:

- *Résumé book:* Students' curricula vitae will be part of the official class résumé book, which is distributed in December.
- *Career skills and case workshops:* Several workshops are scheduled throughout the year to cover the various topics of networking, self-marketing, writing résumés and cover letters, and how to perform in an interview and negotiate contracts. In addition, consultants will conduct workshops in order to sharpen case analysis skills for interviews.
- *Career fairs:* At the campus career fairs students have the opportunity to meet with a variety of international companies

and their representatives for one-stop shopping on campus.

- *Alumni forums:* Alumni forums give the student the chance to pose questions, socialize, and network with Nijenrode alumni.
- *A business partnership for recruiting:* Each year top multinational companies attend Nijenrode to present their firms to the class and conduct recruiting sessions.

FINANCIAL AID

Most MBA students fund their MBA education through a combination of savings and loans. Regrettably, the university does not offer financial assistance in the form of scholarships or assistantships. To avoid disappointment, it is suggested that the student explore all possible sources of funding in his or her home country well ahead of time.

13.
GSBA ZURICH

GSBA ZURICH—GRADUATE SCHOOL OF BUSINESS ADMINISTRATION, ZURICH

Schützengasse 4/Bahnhofstrasse
Postfach 6584
CH-8023 Zurich, Switzerland
Web site: http://www.gsba.ch
E-mail: gsba@pop.spectraweb.ch

Program

Program ranked: Executive dual degree MBA of GSBA, Zurich/SUNY, Albany

Structure: 2 to 4 years part-time; six 2-week modules, each on a core area of business administration plus thesis paper at the end of the program; 1–2 modules spent at SUNY, Albany

Size of class: 250 total

Participants: 60% German, 35% Swiss (mainly Swiss-German), 5% Austrian, Asian, American

Costs: 48,000 Swiss Francs (approx. $30,000)

Program director: Dr. Albert Stähli (Dean)

Accreditation: SUNY, Albany, MBA is AACSB-accredited

Admissions

Admissions requirements: GMAT 550 minimum; TOEFL 550 minimum; 5 years' management experience; 3 references from employers; bachelor's or master's degree; fluency in German and English

Application deadline: Rolling admissions

Starting date: Students start with the next module after being admitted

Application fee: 150 Swiss Francs (approx. $100)

Recruiting

Few events organized for recruiting companies (Students are executives and settle their career matters directly and personally, in a typical Swiss manner.)

Contact:
Admissions Office
Phone:
(41) 1 211 60 68
Fax: (41) 1 221 09 84

BRIEF DESCRIPTION OF THE SCHOOL

Founded in 1985 as the MBA-awarding arm of the Swiss Oekreal Foundation, the GSBA Zurich is located close to both Germany and Austria, thus serving the entire German-speaking market, where it has developed to become one of the leading business schools.

Since college and graduate school education is free in Germany, Switzerland, and Austria, mainly mid-career executives are willing to take the time and spend the money to go for an MBA. They realize that their conventional law, engineering, or scientific degrees will not help them become effective managers in a global world. GSBA Zurich targets managers with five or more years' management experience who live in central Europe.

The school's executive MBA program with six 2-week modules is ideal for time-pressed managers. It allows them to fly into Zurich from Germany, for example, work day and night on their respective full-time modules, return home, and come back for the next module. In theory, they can complete the modules on their vacation time.

Indeed, the MBA program does not have time to cover basics. This is the task of the school's executive bachelor of business administration (BBA) program to which more than 90 percent of all MBA applicants are admitted before they are allowed to enter the MBA program. The BBA is more like the first year of an American two-year MBA program, covering the basics of business administration.

The modules are scheduled too far apart to justify staying in Zurich just to work on an MBA. However, students, like the faculty, could fly in just for the two-week modules, getting an intense international and executive-level MBA while staying in their careers. The flexible structure involving rolling admissions and a duration of between two and four years, gives students the opportunity of adjusting their MBA to their career schedules.

GSBA Zurich is noted for its manager-friendly modular program structure and its own *"Living Case Study"* method, which utilizes a live case with a continuing supply of new data and events. The executive MBA program is offered jointly with SUNY, Albany. The entire faculty at GSBA Zurich comes from other schools throughout America and Europe.

The school, which is essentially a German-American school, has a unique team-teaching approach for its modules. Normally a German-speaking professor teaches his sessions in German; his American counterpart teaches in English. Thus there is a strong balance between continental and American business concepts.

Overall the GSBA Zurich program is much like a series of executive development courses combined into a degree program. Most students are over 35 years of age and expect to work at an accordingly high level within their MBA program.

Matthias Klein, a GSBA Zurich graduate and an asset manager in Frankfurt summarizes: "On the one hand I learned a lot about strategic management, but on the other, I learned a lot from working alongside high potentials with backgrounds very different from mine." Faculty members also benefit from the advanced level of their students, who keep them in touch with the business world.

THE CAMPUS AND LIFE ON CAMPUS

GSBA has a new main campus on Lake Zurich and a facility in downtown Zurich.

Participants have virtually no time to see or experience Zurich. They work at the school most days and nights during the two-week modules, attending classes and working-group sessions and preparing for class. Students live in nearby hotels.

THE PROGRAM

The GSBA Zurich program consists of six 2-week modules, each covering one area of business administration. Normally participants take up to three modules per year. Each module is preceded by a three-month preparatory period during which participants read texts and papers at home. Before beginning the module, each participant must pass a "pretest," determining whether he or she has a sufficient level of knowledge to begin the module.

Two of the six modules can be taken at SUNY in Albany, New York; the other four in Zurich. The faculty for many of the modules is from SUNY Albany, and graduates receive MBA degrees from both schools.

Participants are graded on their performance in classroom discussions, their presentation at the end of each module, and on final exams. All participants complete a final thesis. Most often the thesis topic pertains to a problem or task of the participant's employer. If so, the employer has a role in evaluating it and gets to keep the end product. This policy boosts the school's popularity among employers. However, most participants are self-sponsored; that is, companies do not pay their way. "They want to be flexible to change jobs after getting their MBAs," says Dean Albert Stähli.

Guest lecturers (normally CEOs and specialists in the respective fields covered by the modules) are invited to speak to the students during the program.

FACULTY, TEACHING, AND LEARNING PROCESSES

The school uses faculty from other institutions for the duration of the modules, a concept also used by the Helsinki School of Economics. GSBA Zurich is proud to point out that its relations with visiting professors are long-standing. It has used largely the same faculty for most of the past 8 to 10 years. There are 12 members in the European faculty and 22 in the American faculty, most of whom are full professors at their home institutions.

Each module is team-taught by two faculty members—normally a European and an American professor. This ensures that participants get the best of both worlds. Teaching draws on conventional as well as live case studies. The live case studies focus on current corporate and economic situations that continue to develop in the course of the module and the MBA program. Companies covered in the live cases supply GSBA Zurich with a constant flow of updated information, which participants and professors weave into the case and classroom work.

Classes are limited in size (normally 30 to 40 students)—far below the 60 to 80 student classrooms at some other business schools in Europe. Professors take time for the students. As two professors teach each module, the student/faculty ratio is among the best in Europe.

The school researches and writes its own cases. The emphasis is mainly on teaching executive-level degree programs. The learning process takes place in class and in the working groups, the latter considered the real focal point of the participants' learning experience.

PLACEMENT

GSBA Zurich has no placement services since its participants are employed and are generally at a senior level. The school has an alumni organization that is actively supported by its several hundred members.

Surveys by GSBA Zurich show that graduates do quite well. Prior to their MBA at the school, 42 percent of the participants were top or general managers, 25 percent were department or group heads, and 17 percent held professional-level jobs. After completing their MBA, 68 percent were top or general managers, only 8 percent were department heads, and 6 percent still held professional positions. Thus, the MBA promoted a substantial proportion of department heads and professionals into top management positions. The salary development showed that while 51 percent earned more than 10,000 Swiss Francs (approx. $6530) per month prior to their MBA, 75 percent were in this category after graduating, and 92 percent earned more than 9000 Swiss Francs (approx. $5880) per month after graduating.

FINANCIAL AID

Most participants pay the 48,000 Swiss Francs ($30,000) total tuition fee themselves. Other costs vary according to the distance of travel and hotel quality, but range from $8000 to $15,000 total. No scholarships are available. Financing by befriended banks is available.

14. WARWICK BUSINESS SCHOOL

WARWICK BUSINESS SCHOOL

University of Warwick
GB-Coventry, CV4 7AL, United Kingdom
Web site: http://www.wbs.warwick.ac.uk
E-mail: fmbain@wbs.warwick.ac.uk

Program

Program ranked: MBA
Structure: 1 year full-time; 11 core courses, 9 electives plus consultancy project
Size of class: Maximum 60 students
Participants: Average age 29; 50% of student body from overseas; average of 5 years' professional experience
Costs: Tuition fees: 17,000 Pounds Sterling (approx. $27,415); estimated living expenses for duration of course for a single person 10,000 Pounds Sterling (approx. $16,126)
Program director: Peter Doyle
Accreditation: AACSB (American), AMBA (British)

Admissions

Admissions requirements: Degree or professional qualifications; minimum 3 years' experience in relevant post; admissions test (or good GMAT score); candidates who do not meet requirements not necessarily excluded, limited exceptions made
Applications deadline: June 30
Starting date: September only
Application fee: 40 Pounds Sterling (approx. $64)

Recruiting

Placement office: Career manager, MBA profile book, networking events.
Number of companies recruiting: 50+
Examples of recruiting companies: IBM Consulting, Ford, Andersen Consulting

Contact:
Admissions Office
Phone:
(44) 1203 523922
Fax:
(44) 1203 523922

BRIEF DESCRIPTION OF THE SCHOOL

The University of Warwick was established in the mid-1960s in the Midlands, one of the most industrial regions in Britain, so it is hardly surprising that business and engineering were its leading departments from the beginning. Warwick Business School was thus created with ready-made links to industry.

The school is one of the largest in Europe and offers an array of master's programs, undergraduate courses, and research projects, plus a doctoral program and numerous executive development courses, both general and tailor-made. Apart from the original full-time, 12-month MBA program, the school also offers a modular study version, an evening study version, and a surprisingly successful distance-learning MBA. MBA modules are also taught in Hong Kong, Brussels, and Toulouse, and distance-learning partners are found in equally far-flung places such as Singapore, Sweden, and Greece. Specialist master's courses include master of science degrees in economics and finance, financial mathematics, management science and operational research, and industrial relations plus a master of arts degree in organization studies.

Warwick Business School's fortes are marketing and strategic management, finance, organizational behavior, and industrial relations. Information systems strategy is the main interest of the school's dean, Bob Galliers, who has written two books and numerous articles on the subject. He is editor in chief of the *Journal of Strategic Information Systems* and is coeditor of the *International Information* book series published by McGraw-Hill.

The MBA program at Warwick is research-driven with emphasis on innovation. The school's research has a 5A rating for international and national excellence from the 1996 assessment of the Higher Education Funding Council, a highly respected body responsible for gauging quality in UK business schools. The school has managed to forge strong links with the industrial sector through its research and development centers, as well as through the consultancy projects carried out by its graduates.

The accent is also on internationalism, with about 50 percent of the student body from overseas; many from Asia. MBA students are given the opportunity to carry out a three-month project overseas, and the school maintains links with businesses and institutions from an impressive number of countries all over the world.

THE CAMPUS AND LIFE ON CAMPUS

Warwick Business School is not actually in Warwick. The campus is in the county of Warwickshire and fairly near the city itself, but far closer—just four miles—to the city of Coventry, which also has its own university. Unlike the historical city of Warwick, Coventry is an industrial city, which had to be practically rebuilt after air strikes during World War II, its multiethnic community being due to the massive influx of Asian immigrants during the city's rebirth in the aftermath of the Blitz. The city offers a variety of leisure and cultural activities, including the Coventry Jazz Festival held in August, and surrounding areas provide a wealth of architectural history with castles (Kenilworth and the magnificent Warwick Castle) and historical cities and towns (Warwick and Stratford-upon-Avon, the birthplace of William Shakespeare).

The four miles that separate Coventry from Warwick University are enough to transport the visitor into another world. The ride will take you right into the Warwickshire countryside and onto the campus, which is spread out amid 200 hectares (490 acres) of landscaped greenery. It is self-contained with banks, a bookshop, health center, post office, hairdresser, small supermarket, bars and restaurants, as well as its own art gallery, two cinemas, and a concert hall. As with most British universities, both indoor and outdoor sports facilities are excellent, giving students the opportunity to practice just about every sport imaginable from athletic track events to croquet. Although all the basics are available here, life can be a bit claustrophobic as in any all-student community. The campus is well linked by bus with Coventry and nearby Leamington Spa, but a car could make life easier and more interesting for those times when you need to get away from academia and return to the real world.

While the Business School forms an integral part of this modern university and its campus, the MBA program has its own building, well-equipped with amphitheater style lecture halls and numerous areas for group work, as well as excellent computer facilities.

On-campus accommodation is modern and practical, set in well-planned surroundings. On-campus accommodation for the exclusive use of postgraduates is also available. Off-campus accommodation is readily available and prices in the Midlands of Britain are fairly reasonable. For those with small children, the university has a nursery on campus.

The airport of the nearby city of Birmingham provides fairly good international access, and London Euston is 75 minutes from Coventry by train.

THE PROGRAM

The one-year, full-time MBA program kicks off with a mandatory introductory course, a one-week module that explains how to profit most from the program with particular emphasis on working in teams, communication skills, and how to use computing and library resources.

The program itself is divided equally among the 11 core subjects and numerous electives, all built around four underlying themes— internationalization, integration, learning and innovation, and implementation.

Term One comprises seven core courses and the "Director's Forum." The latter is an initiative whereby the directors of leading worldwide companies present key management issues of the twenty-first century.

During the second term students follow two further core courses, including the recent addition managing the international organization, an intensive one-week module covering international strategic issues such as managing across

different cultures, international strategic planning, and international negotiating processes. Students then choose 5 electives from a list of 10.

After obtaining a solid knowledge of key business processes during the first and second terms, students move on to the third term for the last of the core courses and to study four more of their chosen areas of specialization in greater depth. These electives are from a list of 18, which vary from year to year and are presented as intensive one-week modules. This term also offers students the opportunity to take either an introductory or advanced course in French, Japanese, Spanish, German, Mandarin, or Italian.

The final term, or project term, runs through July, August, and September. It is dedicated exclusively to producing the management consultancy project. Although the school will give assistance in finding suitable projects, students are encouraged to search for their own, partly to take the onus off the school, but also as a practice in initiative and to make sure that their project meets their personal needs and aspirations.

FACULTY, TEACHING, AND LEARNING PROCESSES

Warwick has scored high marks in official surveys for its overall standard of teaching. It has more than 100 full-time teachers and more than 60 research faculty, a large number of whom are top-level consultants to government and industry. In addition to its own staff, the school often brings in senior managers and other key figures from the business community to speak. The strong emphasis on research activities means that course material often incorporates not only current issues but also emerging concepts of management.

Teaching methods include case studies, lectures, and seminars, but Warwick has been quick to adopt more recent techniques such as computer-based learning, simulations, and business games. Like many other schools, it relies on the caliber and variety of nationalities of its students, as well as its teachers, to stimulate a constant exchange of ideas and experience.

The objective of Warwick's MBA is to equip managers with the confidence needed for a place in a continually changing, cross-cultural business environment. As one student said, "On top of giving you the necessary management knowledge and skills, the course aims at developing high motivation and fighting spirits. . . . Major multinational companies were looking for high profile MBAs who could quickly and easily adapt to different cultural environments."

PLACEMENT

The Career Management Department at Warwick has a dual role. First, it helps students to identify their career choice during the career development module in term two. Then, on completion of the course, it acts as a bridge between students and the business world. The school has its own career manager working with the full-time MBA program team to strengthen employer liaisons and to offer one-to-one counseling. The department also issues an annual MBA profile book containing the curricula vitae of all MBA graduates, which is distributed to management consultants, the banking sector, and multinational organizations. One in five students receives an offer of employment from the sponsor of his or her consultancy project.

This support continues well into the student's subsequent career. The Alumni Association helps to maintain the contacts made during the program and to expand them further through the organization of social and professional events. Members of the association are also kept up-to-date on the results of Warwick's latest research projects in the form of publications and academic reports.

FINANCIAL AID

Some 90 percent of those who opt for the full-time MBA program at Warwick are self-funded; the majority probably rely on a loan to cover at least part of the cost of the program and living expenses. The school offers four scholarships of 4500 Pounds Sterling (approx. $7257) each; one is for a public sector employee; two are for women (one UK and one overseas); and one is for a North American. The final selection of scholarship recipients is based on an essay submitted after formal acceptance.

Warwick is included in the AMBA loan plan, but this is only available to UK-based students. Overseas students are advised to contact the British consul or consulate in their country of origin.

15.
E. M. LYON

E. M. Lyon—École de Management Lyon

23 Avenue Guy de Collongue
BP 174,
F-69132 Ecully Cedex, France
Web site: http://www.em-lyon.com
E-mail: cesmamba@em-lyon.com

Program

Program ranked: CESMA MBA
Structure: One-year, full-time; 12 core courses, varying number of electives, projects; internship or exchange program
Size of class: 60
Participants: Average age 30; average experience 7 years; 33% female; 45% from overseas.
Costs: Tuition fee: 15,400 Euros (approx. $16,130) payable in installments; living expenses are around 50,000 French Francs (approx. $8000)
Program director: Judith Ryder
Accreditation: AMBA (British), Chapitre (France), EQUIS (European)

Admissions

Admissions requirements: Good degree; GMAT or TAGE-MAGE (French equivalent of GMAT); the TOEFL or an in-house test; proven work experience (rare exceptions for young graduates with strong entrepreneurial potential and international background)
Applications deadline: June
Starting date: September
Application fee: Enrollment and selection procedures: 100 Euros (approx. $105)

Recruiting

Placement office: Presentations, interview practice, alumni network job offers
Number of companies recruiting: 100+
Examples of recruiting companies: General Electric, Procter & Gamble, Hewlett-Packard, Suchard, L'Oréal

Contact:
Admissions Office
Phone:
(33) 4 78 33 78 65
Fax:
(33) 4 78 33 77 55

BRIEF DESCRIPTION OF THE SCHOOL

Groupe ESC Lyon, as it was then called, was founded in 1872 by some local businessmen at the Lyon Chamber of Commerce and Industry, making it one of the oldest business schools not only in France but also in Europe. E. M. Lyon is what is known in France as a *grande école,* a prestigious title bestowed on France's better higher education establishments, particularly in the engineering field. Having done very nicely over the last 125 years the school is now in the throes of a five-year development plan aimed at promoting lifelong learning, fostering a spirit of entrepreneurship among its students, and consolidating its European identity as opposed to appearing to be exclusively French.

The European model that the school envisions, is one that takes into account humanistic values, long-term thinking, and the need to accommodate social values and benefits as well as economic results.

The school has always placed great emphasis on things entrepreneurial, probably a throw back to its founders; the aim of its "CESMA MBA" program is to develop successful entrepreneur-manager profiles and encourage initiative and self-development in an atmosphere where students examine who they are and what they want to do. The CESMA part of the MBA title is merely a historical touch referring to the official name of the MBA when it was first started 28 years ago by the French for Center of Management Training and is not intended to give any particular impression.

On the international side, E. M. Lyon has built up an extensive list of partners scattered around the globe. Lyon was the first French school to set up a double degree. There are now two double-degree programs (with Cranfield School of Management in the United Kingdom and the University of Belgrano in Argentina) and many more double-degree agreements. The school has exchange agreements with 60 universities and business schools, including Carnegie Mellon University in Pittsburgh, HEC-Montreal, ESADE in Barcelona, Lancaster University in the United Kingdom, Waseda University in Tokyo, and Monash MT Eliza Business School in Australia.

Apart from the full-time and part-time CESMA MBA program, E. M. Lyon offers open programs, tailor-made programs, and entrepreneur programs to some 4500 executives each year.

THE CAMPUS AND LIFE ON CAMPUS

E. M. Lyon is situated in a pleasant 18-acre park in Ecully, just a 10-minute drive from the center of Lyon, a bustling city of 1.2 million. Just two hours by train from both Paris and Geneva, Lyon has an exceptional European location bordered by the Alps to the east, the Burgundy vineyards to the north, and the Mediterranean to the south.

Lyon, center of the second most important region in France after Paris, has a long tradition as a business center which facilitated ties between the north and the south of Europe. Many firms that now operate worldwide were created and continue to grow in the region, both in industry and in services.

Schedule permitting, Lyon is good place to explore, its historical center being on UNESCO's list of world heritage sites. The city has impressive Roman ruins (theaters), a Renaissance quarter (Old Lyon), museums, and monuments, not to mention a reputation for being the source of some of France's finest cuisine.

E. M. Lyon shares its modern style campus with other higher education establishments including an engineering school and École des Arts Culinaires. Apart from having access to the campus' sports facilities, restaurant, cafes, and language center, E. M. Lyon's share of the campus includes an "espace entrepreneurs," where students can meet and work on business start-up projects together. There is a recently inaugurated library and access to information technology equipment. Most classrooms are connected to the Internet.

Up to 350 students are provided with accommodation in two modern facilities located on the campus. Student apartments are equipped with telephone, access to the Internet, and all other standard facilities.

THE PROGRAM

The CESMA MBA program is bilingual, offering participants the option of taking the first-term core courses in either French or English, thus giving foreign students time to brush up on their French, if needs be, before the difficult task of attending classes in a foreign language begins. The general structure of the program combines core courses, concentrating on basic international management skills and key company functions, with multidisciplinary courses and seminars, concentrating on strategic issues facing companies today.

The program consists of three main components. The first part of the program comprises the 12 foundation courses and is known as the "competencies" phase. This is followed by the electives (the student can choose to what extent he or she wishes to specialize), which may be undertaken at Lyon or at one of its many exchange partners abroad, the so-called individualization phase. The program is interspersed with five interfunctional courses and a total of nine seminars and workshops, which comprise the "vision" component.

Students who do not participate in an exchange program may choose between a company placement, a range of in-company projects offered both in France and elsewhere, an individual project, or an entrepreneurial project. The entrepreneurial project is often carried out in small groups, and offers an opportunity for investing in a business start-up, a takeover, or a development project. The individual project offers an opportunity to discover new careers, positions, or domains within companies and to refine a career plan. For non-French participants, both of these options constitute an excellent opportunity to learn about a different market and develop a new network of contacts. For par-

ticipants intending to change careers at the end of the program, the project offers a period for structured reflection, matching personal aspirations to the realities of the job market.

FACULTY, TEACHING, AND LEARNING PROCESSES

Lyon's 105-strong full-time faculty is backed up by a large number of part-time professors, including practicing executives who bring live issues into the classroom.

The school recently set up its own research center to provide it with direct access to new expertise, basing its foundations on long-term partnerships with firms, the idea being that this will ensure the quality and continuity of research. It will also give the school the opportunity to practice what they preach to their students, that is, to further develop their own personal style and skills. The school believes that while it is important for decisions to be made based on information, personal development plays a key role in innovation; accordingly, approximately 20 percent of the contact time is spent teaching the student how to know what they want.

There is a strong emphasis on teamwork making for plenty of intercultural exchanges. All participants have the opportunity to work on a project that they define in line with their professional ambitions. This method encourages the development of realistic yet ambitious objectives.

PLACEMENT

Counselors from the E. M. Lyon Careers and Orientation Department offer individualized support and advice to participants in planning their career and in their search for employment. Each year, the school's career office receives notices for more than 4000 job openings.

More than 100 European firms and European subsidiaries of international companies visit E. M. Lyon each year to give presentations and to recruit potential employees among the students. These sessions act as an interface between students and companies, permitting professionals to present perspectives in their sector and the realities of their profession.

In addition to activities undertaken by the career office, E. M. Lyon's Alumni Association claims a network of 9500 graduates throughout the world in 83 countries.

FINANCIAL AID

CESMA MBA participants residing in France benefit from preferential rates for bank loans, provided that a currently employed French resident agrees to guarantee the loan. These loans can be arranged for those not residing in France under the same conditions.

Non-French participants who do not have that level of contact in France are advised to seek funding for their studies in their country of origin. A certain number of scholarships may be available by contacting the French embassy in the relevant country.

Participants who have worked in France can request a *Congé Individuel de Formation* (individual training leave) which enables them to receive all or part of their established salary, and, occasionally, payment to cover the costs of the program. Requests for this kind of funding are examined individually and should be initiated several months before the beginning of the program.

E. M. Lyon may occasionally be able to provide assistance in the form of loans or grants after examination of the candidate's request.

16.
HENLEY MANAGEMENT COLLEGE

Contact:
Admissions Office
Phone:
(44) 1491 571454
Fax:
(44) 1491 418861

HENLEY MANAGEMENT COLLEGE
Greenlands, Henley-on-Thames
GB-Oxford RG9 3AU
Web site: www.henleymc.ac.uk
E-mail: mba@henleymc.ac.uk

Program
Program ranked: MBA
Structure: 12 months (approx.) modular; four 4-week residential modules, divided into three parts; varying number of electives; dissertation; includes international study week
Size of class: Approx. 30
Participants: Middle managers; female 15%; average age 33
Cost: Tuition fee: 16,500 Pounds Sterling (approx. $26,607); living expenses vary according to how the student organizes his or her stay (on a permanent or modular basis)
Program director: Maureen George
Accreditation: AMBA (British)

Admissions
Admission requirements: Bachelor's degree (or equivalent), 3 years' relevant working experience, relevant academic or business references, TOEFL, GMAT, interview
Application deadline: Rolling basis
Starting date: May
Application fee: 30 Pounds Sterling (approx. $49)

Recruiting
Placement office: Most students sponsored by organizations; no career management services

BRIEF DESCRIPTION OF THE SCHOOL

Henley Management College was founded in 1945 by a group of business leaders as a private educational institution for training managers in the skills needed to pull Britain out of the postwar era. The school has been pioneering new techniques in executive development and management education for more than 50 years, one of the latest being a virtual business school which was launched in December 1998 in partnership with Ernst and Young.

Henley first offered an MBA program in 1974 under the aegis of Brunel University, a full-time MBA being taught at the Brunel University campus until Henley was finally granted the power to award its own degree programs in 1997. Having, over the years, started to offer part-time, modular, and distance-learning versions, Henley decided recently to concentrate on the modular version of its MBA and its full-time program disappeared.

The school's distance-learning program has attracted a great deal of admiration and its reputation has spread like wildfire. This program now boasts learners in as many as 90 countries, which has served to increase the school's already large number of worldwide partner institutions. True to its reputation for being at the forefront in information technology (IT), one of Henley's distance-learning MBAs offers a unique IT program aimed at highfliers in the accounting field. It uses laptops and video conferencing to connect learners with fellow students and professors.

The school's focus on IT is also evident in its Future Work Forum, an initiative that was first set up in 1992 to provide a meeting point for individuals or organizations with innovative ideas for working using IT.

Henley offers a wide range of executive development programs and enjoys a leading position in the corporate program field. The Henley Research Center fosters the development of expertise in particular areas of management that relate closely to teaching and research interests. As well as assignments commissioned by organizations, the center carries out research sponsored by national and international agencies, and it offers both organizations and individual managers the opportunity to carry out interdisciplinary research into issues of strategic importance.

THE CAMPUS AND LIFE ON CAMPUS

The main campus of Henley Management College is located in the south of England at the appropriately named Greenlands, amid 30 acres of parkland on the banks of the river Thames.

Greenlands is midway between Henley-on-Thames and Marlow, about an hour's drive from London.

The location is marvelous, on a bend of the River Thames, near to where the area's famous regatta is held. Housed in a beautiful nineteenth century stately home, this school is definitely a place for those who hanker after a bygone age of grace (and for those who would have loved to have starred in *Room With a View*). The campus offers an impressive range of leisure facilities, including a fitness center with a bar/lounge area and an outdoor heated swimming pool. For those who like to practice sport at a more leisurely rate, croquet and snooker are but two examples of a wide variety of activities available on campus.

With regard to academic facilities, the campus also fares well with a well-stocked library, syndicate rooms with networked computers, closed-circuit television, photocopying facilities, and an information technology center.

The campus has extensive accommodation facilities which are pressed into use for all residential programs, including the modular MBA. Accommodation between modules could be tricky and expensive, except for students who choose to come and go from home, but this time could also be used for other purposes, academic or otherwise.

THE PROGRAM

The modular MBA has a May intake only and is oriented toward general management, with a strong international focus. Modular programs are designed to permit managers to undertake an MBA without having to be away from the organization for too long, the idea being that students only have to spend four weeks at a time away from their corporate responsibilities.

Henley's three-part MBA program is designed to integrate management topics through team teaching and to develop strategic decision-making skills. The first part covers foundations of management, managing information, and managing people. The second part stays with management skills, but this time it covers marketing, performance, and financial resources. The third part moves on to strategic direction and business transformation, covering areas that encompass organizational trends for the twenty-first century. This final part of the program also permits students to specialize via electives, culminating in a dissertation on an area and issue selected by the student.

An international management week comprises a weeklong trip based at "partner" centers in cities such as Grenoble, St Petersburg, Barcelona, Amsterdam, and Brussels. Study focuses on issues relating to managing business across national boundaries and the impact of international management in a national context.

Course work is subject to continuous assessment throughout the program, encompassing presentations, projects, company visit analysis, and group and individual work. All assignments, examinations, projects, and dissertations are subject to assessment throughout the program. There are examinations at the end of parts one and two, each one consisting of one or more case studies. Assessment is based not only on the coherence of answers but also on creativity and practicality of recommendations.

FACULTY, TEACHING, AND LEARNING PROCESSES

There are 50 full-time faculty members at Henley complemented by some 60 associate faculty and a network of almost 400 part-time tutors worldwide. Almost all faculty members have practical management experience.

The school promotes self-managed learning. Its intensive program requires considerable commitment and self-motivation. Learning takes place in small, international and multidisciplinary work groups.

Learning from the Henley MBA courses can be applied directly to the workplace, ensuring direct relevance for MBA students and employers alike. Each course has an assignment which tests the students' ability to apply the concepts they have learned to a real situation. In most cases, this can be their own organization or one with which they are familiar.

PLACEMENT

Because the vast majority of participants of Henley's executive training programs are sponsored by companies, formal careers advice is lacking. Most students hold middle or senior management positions and are looking to enhance their careers rather than bring about a drastic change. As with any MBA program, however, it is an excellent starting point for boosting network contacts. Students who opt to join the Henley Alumni Association are included in a yearbook and are invited to intend networking events at the college and around the United Kingdom.

On completion of a course at Henley, graduates automatically form part of The Henley International Alumni Network, whose members currently amount to some 10,000 around the world. Formal national alumni groups operate in 20 countries, including a virtual group in the United States, and informal groups are to be found in many more places.

FINANCIAL AID

Scholarships are practically nonexistent here as most students are sponsored by their organizations or are expected to fund themselves.

The school does form part of a business school loan plan, operated by two of the UK's major banks, which would cover the cost of course fees at a favorable rate of interest. To qualify, applicants should be under 40 years of age and intend to continue working in the United Kingdom upon completion of the stud-

ies. It would be reasonable to expect that the bank would want some kind of guarantor in the form of a UK resident, so it may be a better idea for overseas students to look for loans nearer home.

17.
THE JUDGE INSTITUTE

Contact:
Admissions Office
Phone:
(44) 1223 337051
Fax:
(44) 1223 339581

The Judge Institute—University of Cambridge

Judge Institute of Management Studies
Trumpington Street
GB-Cambridge CB2 1AG, United Kingdom
Web site: http://www.jims.cam.ac.uk/mba
E-mail: jims-mba-enquiries@lists.cam.ac.uk

Program

Program ranked: MBA
Structure: 1-year, full-time; core courses from October to mid-April culminating in a consulting project; elective courses and a dissertation between April and September
Size of class: 80 (plenary sessions; divided into groups of 15–20 in some courses)
Participants: Roughly 20% from Britain, 20% from Asia, and 20% from North America; nearly one-third studied a science field in their first degrees; roughly 30% worked in banking and finance before starting the MBA
Costs: 20,000–21,500 Pounds Sterling (approx. $32,250–$34,670)
Program director: G. Walsham
Accreditation: AMBA (British)

Admissions

Admissions requirements: University degree; GMAT; work experience; TOEFL if first language not English
Application deadline: None, rolling admissions (May recommended)
Starting date: September, October
Application fee: None

Recruiting

Placement office: Prepares students for interviews, arranges individual meetings with employers, and publishes profile book of graduates
Number of companies recruiting: 100
Examples of recruiting companies: McKinsey, Goldman Sachs, Procter & Gamble

BRIEF DESCRIPTION OF THE SCHOOL

Although Cambridge possesses an 800-year university tradition, its MBA program is one the newest in the world, launched in 1991. And although the university is among the large institutions of higher learning in Europe with 15,000 students, the MBA program has not grown beyond 80 students and intends to remain small.

The Judge Institute managers have done a good job of transferring the image and tradition of Cambridge University to their school. This was partly accomplished by thoroughly integrating Judge into the university. Most students are accommodated in the 300 or so colleges and are part of the famous Oxbridge tutoring system. They enjoy the full status of Cambridge students, may use all university facilities, attend classes in other departments, and later are automatically part of the worldwide alumni network.

In addition, Judge has quickly established itself in the business school world with a large and strong faculty, newly renovated facilities, plenty of funds sponsored from admirers of Cambridge, and scholarships from such reputable firms as McKinsey. The corporate world likes recruiting Judge graduates as much as it does hiring Cambridge grads from other colleges and departments. As a Judge student you feel the school has been around as long as Cambridge itself, everything has a finished feeling.

Yet even Cambridge underwent some development. Before the shortened, one-year MBA program was introduced, the MBA was several years long—too long for students with several years work experience.

Perhaps the most distinguishing feature of Judge is how the school successfully reconciles the old and the new in its MBA program. Teaching in small classes with the most modern equipment and providing numerous guest lecturers from the executive ranks of global corporations are combined with learning in a highly traditional setting. Students enjoy the beautiful architecture of the colleges and the Old World ambiance of Cambridge.

Cambridge is largely a technical university. Bill Gates selected Cambridge for a large grant for long-term research. Britain's version of Silicon Valley is located around the town and school. The majority of Judge students have an engineering background—more than at most other business schools.

Another particular feature of Judge is its modern approach to teaching. Judge claims that "there is very little traditional lecturing." Classes are small because there are 30 full-time faculty for only 80 students. The program involves a lot of work in small student groups, in up-to-date computer labs. There are visits to companies plus a practical dissertation at the end of the program. Courses cut across departmental lines incorporating elements of technical management with philosophy and skills. Enterprise, or entrepreneurship, studies are being pushed since the Margaret Thatcher Foundation donated two million Pounds Sterling (approx. $2.5 million) to the school to set up the Margaret Thatcher Professorship of Enterprise Studies.

This ties in to Cambridge's penchant to ensure that students have as much contact with the corporate world as possible. Cambridge is only an hour by train from London's center and thus it is easy for students to do business and for business leaders from all over the world to fly in and give guest presentations at Judge. Cambridge MBA students automatically become student members of the Institute of Management, the United Kingdom's main professional body for managers, which also provides additional access to library, research, and professional facilities.

THE CAMPUS AND LIFE ON CAMPUS

Judge's main facility is a completely rebuilt industrial building near the center of the city with an impressive lawn and atrium area just inside the school. The building was opened by the Queen in 1996 and contains everything a modern business school should, such as a library, teaching rooms, a dedicated MBA study area, and a large common room. In addition, students have access to the university's extensive facilities, including modern language labs, libraries, and the Graduate Union, with its support services (e.g., printing), which is situated next to Judge and is something of a center of student life at Cambridge.

However, MBA students benefit from the old system of being part of the college system of learning and living. The university consists of 31 colleges, the oldest, Peterhouse, was founded in 1284. Some, like Trinity, harbor nearly 1000 students; others like Lucy Cavendish, have fewer than 100. All MBA students belong both to a college and department (Judge for MBA students). Two-thirds are fortunate enough to actually live in a college. Once an application to Judge is successful, the school applies to a college for the student. Not all students can live directly in a college but the colleges also have rooms in hostels and buildings around the city. The life within the college is an important educational experience. The colleges are separate foundations and elect their own faculty members. MBA students living there find that this is a mind-expanding intellectual experience as they find themselves discussing and debating management issues with students from all disciplines, such as law, philosophy, and physics.

In addition, despite the grueling schedule at Judge, students find time to enjoy some of the advantages of Cambridge or nearby London. Cambridge offers theater, movies, pubs, rowing on the river, and bookshops that are open late. Students may attend lectures and events at other departments and schools. Due to its global reputation, Cambridge is international, with students, faculty, managers, and a host of other personalities from around the world on the scene.

There are almost half as many nationalities as there are students in the MBA program, which statistically means two or so students from one country only. In fact, in a recent class 22 percent were British, 21 percent East Asian, 19 percent North American, 15 percent Latin American, 11 percent European, and 6 percent Australian or New Zealanders. Their average age was 29 and they had an average of 5.5 years of work experience, the range of work experience being between 2 and 13 years. The science bias of Cambridge is evident when looking at students' academic backgrounds before coming to Judge: 31 percent completed degrees in a scientific field, 29 percent in business or accounting, 25 percent in economics or finance, 8 percent in law or politics, and 8 percent in the arts or humanities.

Engineers came from all sectors. Earning an MBA gives them the necessary management know-how to get promoted in managerial jobs instead of remaining in specialized positions.

DESCRIPTION OF THE PROGRAM

The five "phases" of the Judge MBA progress from core courses to individual study and research, culminating in a 16,000-word dissertation on a topic jointly selected by students and faculty. The first phase begins two months before the actual academic year and is only required of entrants who need more background in economics, statistics, financial accounting, and computing.

The actual program begins with phase two, which takes an interdisciplinary approach to business administration. The course Management Practice, for example, is described as a "bridge between the conceptual models and analytic techniques." The course discusses the nature of leadership and how to work effectively within groups. At the end students complete an integrative project which involves small teams working on a new venture idea.

Similarly, phase three contains more core courses and two integrative projects, one of cross-functional management simulation (a business game) and the other a company-based consulting project. Students work for a month in a company in small groups analyzing problems and developing solutions. The final two phases are dedicated to electives and researching and writing the dissertation.

In addition to the one-year, full-time MBA, Judge also offers a two-year "sandwich" variant, which covers the same material over a longer period of time for students with career and perhaps family commitments. Roughly one-fifth of Judge students take advantage of this form of MBA study at Judge.

FACULTY, TEACHING, AND LEARNING PROCESSES

Although Judge employs more than 30 faculty members, not all are concerned only with teaching 80 MBA students. They may be responsible for other undergraduate, master's, and Ph.D. programs. Even so, the student/faculty ratio is good; Cambridge claims that some classes have only 5 to 12 students.

Cambridge considers its faculty to be one of its major assets. Most are drawn from other colleges. In addition to the faculty, prominent guest speakers lecture frequently at Judge. Martin Sorrell, CEO of WPP, the worldwide advertising group; Euan Baird, CEO of Schlumberger; and Sir Geoffrey Chandler, Chairman of Amnesty International, are typical examples from a long list of guest lecturers at Judge.

PLACEMENT

Judge has its own career advising service, which prefers an individual approach to matching up graduates and employers. While the office does put out a profile book of graduates, it does not organize large recruitment or career days.

It does emphasize preparing students well for interviews and testing by potential employers. It offers individual advice, help in writing cover letters and résumés, and practice in interview techniques. It circulates lists with company vacancies, conducts psychometric testing, and maintains links to alumni organizations. In addition, students can look for a job on their own, for example, by speaking with guest lecturers, who are often unofficially looking for promising personnel for their companies. The large Cambridge alumni association may also be of help, as well as the subgroup to the general alumni association, Cambridge Alumni in Management (CaiM), which was set up just for Judge graduates. It puts out a membership directory and a newsletter and organizes events in which Judge students may take part.

In any case, most students are looking for a new start after finishing their MBAs. Only about 10 percent are sponsored by their employers. Although the number varies, about 100 companies recruit or regularly sponsor students at Judge, including many global blue chips such as British Petroleum, Citibank, Goldman Sachs, Shell Oil, and even the U.S. Customs Service.

FINANCIAL AID

Judge's excellent connections to the corporate world have opened the door to several scholarship opportunities. McKinsey & Co, the worldwide consulting firm, awards scholarships of 15,000 Pounds Sterling (approx. $24,190) each to deserving students with between two and six years' experience and the right to work in the United Kingdom. McKinsey may offer the recipients a job if they perform well in the program.

Students with at least three years experience in the hospitality or tourism industries may be eligible for the Browns Restaurant Scholarships. American applicants with a grade point average of 3.5 or more in their first degrees may have chances at a Fulbright Scholarship. The British Council awards scholarships to foreign students.

ADMISSIONS AND CONTACT INFORMATION

There is no admissions deadline; that is, applications may be submitted any time. However, the criteria for admission are tough to fulfill: a high grade point average (3.2) in your first degree, several years of work experience (the average is over five years), a top GMAT (average is over 600), and fluency in English demonstrated in a TOEFL score over 600 if your native language is not English. Qualified students are often invited to personal interviews on campus or by alumni closer to the applicant's home. Of those invited to an interview, roughly 70 percent are admitted.

**18.
ESADE**

ESADE—Escuela Superior de Administración y Dirección de Empresas

Información y Admisiones, Programa MBA Full Time
Av. Pedralbes 60-62
E-08034 Barcelona, Spain
Web site: www.esade.es
E-mail: info@esade.es

Program
Program ranked: MBA
Structure: 2 years, full-time, divided into 3 periods; last period comprises a varying number of elective courses or an internship abroad; student exchange program also available
Size of class: 125 per intake (distributed in 3 sections)
Participants: 80% Spanish, 15% Latin American, 5% other nationalities
Costs: Tuition fee: 4,600,000 Pesetas (approx. $28,750); living expenses: 95,000 Pesetas per month (approx. $594)
Program director: Josep Rucabado
Accreditation: AEEDE (Spanish), AMBA (British), EQUIS (European)

Admissions
Admissions requirements: University degree; GMAT or school's admission test in Spanish; personal interview; fluency in English or Spanish
Applications deadline: Rolling basis
Starting date: September
Application fee: $100

Recruiting
Placement office: Provides diverse services to students, personal advice, company presentations on campus, résumé book
Number of companies recruiting: 150+
Examples of recruiting companies: Andersen Consulting, Arthur D. Little, Marks & Spencer, PriceWaterhouseCoopers, Seat (Volkswagen Group)

Contact:
Admissions Office
Phone:
(34) 93 280 29 95
Fax:
(34) 93 495 20 77

BRIEF DESCRIPTION OF THE SCHOOL

ESADE was founded in 1958 as an institution of the Society of Jesus, the well-known religious order of the Catholic church, and joined the Ramon Llull University of Barcelona as a federated member in 1992.

The Jesuits have been one of the most active organizations in education for almost four centuries and one of the most influential organizations within the Catholic church. They have an important network of universities worldwide, from Keio University in Japan to Georgetown University in the United States. As part of this network, ESADE enjoys the rich heritage of Jesuit educational centers, combining a humanistic approach with top quality studies. The fact that the school belongs to a religious organization is not perceptible. It is a founding member of CEMS, the Community of European Management Schools, a visible network of European and international universities that works toward the creation of a common university degree in management.

ESADE offers undergraduate programs in business, law, and foreign languages, as well as its MBA program and a significant number of open programs for executives and training programs tailored for corporate clients.

The school offers a unique five-year undergraduate/graduate program in which participants obtain the bachelor's in business and the MBA. The full-time MBA is available as a separate program for those who have not followed the combined five-year program. The school also offers a part-time MBA, a Ph.D. in management sciences, and a diverse range of continuous education programs on executive development, public management, and tourism.

As ESADE's undergraduate programs in business and law are at the forefront, the atmosphere in the school is quite "junior" compared to that of many other MBA schools. Since all of the undergraduate students in the combined bachelor's/MBA program join the regular participants in the full-time MBA, the overall profile of the MBA class is low in terms of professional, academic, and life-experiences background. For these reasons, although the school is international in outlook, ESADE is less an international institution than IESE (Barcelona) or Instituto de Empresa (Madrid).

Nonetheless ESADE's student exchange network is impressive, including student exchange programs with institutions in 20 countries such as ISA HEC in Paris, Stern School of Business in New York, Manchester Business School, and the Australian School of Management in Sydney.

THE CAMPUS AND LIFE ON CAMPUS

ESADE is situated in Barcelona, the home of the 1992 Olympic games whose metropolitan area has a population of around 4.6 million. This city on the Mediterranean coast is located in northeast Spain very close to the French border. It's a pleasant and lively city with beautiful parks and a surrounding countryside providing excellent opportunities for outdoor activities, both in the nearby Pyrenean mountains and on the Mediterranean coast. Cultural and entertainment offers are also outstanding. Barcelona is Europe-oriented with an important international business community.

The ESADE campus is located in a residential area close to some of the city's university campuses. It consists of three buildings, including a multimedia center with six computer lab rooms and an impressive library.

There is no on-campus accommodation, so most of students share apartments. The school provides information on housing possibilities in student's residence halls and flats to rent in the nearby area. The ESADE atmosphere is similar to that of a university with a mixture of students enrolled in different degree programs sharing facilities. A students' association for MBA participants, Club Master, organizes different social, cultural, and sports activities to help students get to know one another. The club is especially beneficial to international students, helping them to integrate into the program.

THE PROGRAM

Students can opt for a Spanish or English version and are split into three streams: two Spanish and one English. Participants have to be fluent in both languages by the end of the program no matter which version they chose at the beginning. There is the possibility of changing from the Spanish to the English version or vice versa at the end of the first year. Language training at ESADE is excellent. Its language school has the latest equipment, and most language professors are native. Those students fully fluent in both English and Spanish may opt for French or German classes.

The program is divided into three phases. The first phase, which covers the first semester of the course, aims at unifying the participants' management knowledge and working methods. In phase two participants get into the core of the program by analyzing the major business disciplines.

The final phase of the program involves specialization in either a management field or business sector. The possibility to specialize in a business sector is unique, including the following: hospital management, business taxation, public management, and international management. Students who decide to take international management combine regular classes at the school with a three-month internship in a company based in a country different from their country of origin.

Participants in the MBA program can choose among more than 40 schools for their exchange period. If you opt for this alternative, you cannot do the specialization phase at ESADE, but instead spend a three- or six-month period taking the elective courses at a foreign school.

The program includes a company internship period between the first and second year. The careers management department of the school coordinates job positions received from companies in order to find the most suitable placement for participants.

FACULTY, TEACHING, AND LEARNING PROCESSES

ESADE's faculty is large due to the multiple academic offerings of different undergraduate and postgraduate programs and the fact that the university comprises three schools. Its 169 full-time and 248 part-time professors make the school's faculty population one of the largest by European standards.

A significant number of research projects by professors relate to Catalonian business because of the school's connections with numerous private and public institutions of the region. Many are sponsors for the research studies as sponsors.

Participants in the MBA program are assigned to a group on arrival and work with that group for the first year. A significant percentage of the program's workload is based on group projects, such as the business project that students develop under the supervision of a professor. Although case study methodology is most common, many subjects include other teaching techniques, such as business simulation and lectures given by top executives from a wide range of companies and industries.

PLACEMENT

The ESADE Placement Department provides services to graduates of the different programs offered at the university, including young graduates of the school's five-year combined undergraduate/graduate programs in business and law, MBA full-time graduates, participants in executive development programs, and alumni. The placement service handles more than 1500 job applications annually and arranges 600 business internships. In addition, it organizes corporate presentations on campus, makes preselection of candidates, and publishes an annual book with the résumés of students in the final year of their program.

There is also a database with information on jobs available that can be accessed from all the computers of the school and a monthly newsletter which includes job opportunities and is sent to all members of the school's alumni association.

FINANCIAL AID

The school has signed different agreements with financial institutions to facilitate students' access to study loans. These loans are only available for those students who come from the European Union or hold a residence visa in any of the EU countries. The school arranges the whole procedure with the financial institution. ESADE does not offer scholarships to MBA candidates.

19.
IMPERIAL COLLEGE MANAGEMENT SCHOOL

Contact:
Admissions Office
Phone:
(44) 171 594 9205
Fax:
(44) 171 823 7685

IMPERIAL COLLEGE MANAGEMENT SCHOOL

Full-Time MBA Admissions
53 Prince's Gate
GB-London SW7 2PG, United Kingdom
Web site: www.ms.ic.ac.uk
E-mail: m.school@ic.ac.uk

Program

Program ranked: Full-time MBA
Structure: 1 year, full-time; 3 terms: the first concentrates mainly on core subjects, the second on a specialization, and the third on electives and an individual project
Size of class: 150
Participants: Average age 29; 42% from the United Kingdom, up to 30 nationalities represented; over 3 years' work experience
Costs: Tuition: 13,500 Pounds Sterling (approx. $21,770); costs for off-campus housing: 8000 Pounds Sterling (approx. $12,900)
Program director: Roger Betts
Accreditation: AMBA (British)

Admissions

Admissions requirements: University degree; 2 years' work experience (minimum); GMAT (550 min.); TOEFL (for non-English speakers)
Application deadline: End of July
Starting date: October
Application fee: None

Recruiting

Placement office: Workshops for students, counseling, corporate visits
Number of companies recruiting: 50
Examples of recruiting companies: Andersen Consulting, PricewaterhouseCoopers, Smithkline Beecham

BRIEF DESCRIPTION OF THE SCHOOL

Imperial College Management School is a relatively new addition (founded in 1987) to the Imperial College of Science, Technology and Medicine, one of Britain's premiere institutions for educating engineers and scientists. The Imperial College of Science belongs to the University of London and is its largest college. As such, like other "new" UK MBA programs (e.g., Cambridge's MBA), the Management College of Imperial benefits from the reputation and facilities of its mother institutions. Imperial College as a whole has consistently been rated among the 10 very best

UK universities by *The Times,* perhaps the United Kingdom's best-established university ranking.

"The day I got accepted on the Imperial MBA Program I was ecstatic, excited, and scared. Why? Because I was accepted into one of the most prestigious institutions in the world," says Irshad Mowjee, a recent student in the Management College's full-time MBA program. And indeed the Management School has established its own merits. It too has done well in rankings and has established itself as a center of entrepreneurial study and research in the United Kingdom and internationally. It recently won an award for the best business plan.

The school's location in central London is within walking distance from many of London's cultural attractions and is a selling point for many students, although the tough one-year program is not likely to leave much time for extracurricular activities.

In addition to the full-time MBA, the school offers a part-time executive MBA, a master of science in finance, and an advanced certificate in health management. Its MBA is bigger than most with 150 students admitted each year.

Perhaps one of the most distinguishing features of the school is its dean, David Norburn, an experienced business school manager and the entrepreneurial father of the school. He not only recruited excellent faculty and optimized the curriculum, but also established the school's reputation as a center in several areas. One is the area of entrepreneurship. He attracted top faculty and in 1998 Imperial took first place in the European Business Plan competition, organized by INSEAD and London Business School. Dean Norburn's engaging style has also helped bring corporate recruiters and contacts to the school.

Imperial would certainly appear to have taken the fast track toward establishing a reputation as one of Britain's major business schools. According to the *MBA Career Guide International* (PCG International, London, 1996), Imperial is among the United Kingdom's top five business schools, together with London Business School, Manchester, Cranfield, and Warwick. And, in a recent survey and ranking in the *Financial Times* (1998), Imperial ranked top in the world as "best value for money." The school is accredited by the UK program accreditation agency AMBA. In 1994 the school was awarded an "excellent" grade following the visit of the Higher Education Funding Council of England's Quality Assessment Team, and in 1995 the school was appointed as the major provider of the civil service public sector MBA in competing against 16 other British business schools.

THE CAMPUS AND LIFE ON CAMPUS

Imperial does not have a "campus" in the American or Oxbridge sense with green parks and large social and recreation areas. The school's building is in Kensington, an attractive part of central London, well known for its museums, Hyde Park, and Harrod's, the "best department store in the world." Within walking distance are the Royal Albert Hall, Royal College of Art, Natural History Museum, and Victoria and Albert Museum. Across the street is the Science Museum, and sports facilities are located just around the corner.

Consistent with its location in a major global center of business and culture, the student body is highly international. Over 50 percent are from outside the United Kingdom and from roughly 30 countries. Typical for many UK business schools, including Manchester Business School, is the large proportion (over 30 percent at Imperial) of Asian students. Fifteen percent come from other European countries and only 3 percent from the Americas. A large proportion of the student body (32 percent) has only 2 years of work experience; 29 percent, 3 to 5 years; 26 percent, 6 to 10 years, and 13 percent, 11 years.

DESCRIPTION OF THE PROGRAM

The merits of the Imperial program are its brevity and clear structure. The first term, the autumn term which lasts from October to December, concentrates on classical core courses. The spring term starts in January and lasts until March, and includes exams of the core courses, further core courses, and a full assortment of six specialization areas, including entrepreneurship and innovation, project management, health management, finance, competing strategically through services, and public sector management. Few schools offer such a large variety of specialization courses. The third and final term, the summer term, involves more exams of the courses of the preceding term plus "options," and the final project. Options are electives such as legal framework of business, business and the environment, business ethics, and capacity planning.

The final project continues to mid-September and thus wraps up the entire program. While it focuses on a specific company and/or market, its emphasis is on research more than consulting. It does involve working with corporations and writing a final thesis paper that must be satisfactorily presented.

FACULTY, TEACHING, AND LEARNING PROCESSES

The workload is heavy, but normal for an MBA. The program involves classroom sessions, group work with other students, plus individual homework and research. The school has a clear policy of assessment and grading students' work, relying more on exams than mere class participation. The three elements of the program are core subjects, options and electives, and the project. Students must do well in each of these areas; that is, good work in one cannot compensate for poor work in another. The specialization areas are, however, weighted very heavily.

The Association of Business Schools (UK) rates teaching at the school as "excellent." The staff is large (40 full-time, including 11 professors), with roughly as many part-time lecturers and visiting professors. The staff teaches not only the full-time, one-year MBA but also the executive MBA and other programs. The school's mother institution, Imperial College, has an excellent reputation in terms of faculty—a fact likely to rub off on the management school. Imperial can claim 44 Fellows of the Royal Society and four Nobel laureates among its faculty. The management school has come a long way in this respect, and includes world authorities in entrepreneurship, innovation, and finance.

PLACEMENT

The Career Service offers a fairly wide variety of services including a careers room, personal marketing workshops, personal career planning workshops, career presentations, career counseling, and meetings between students and potential employers. According to *Which MBA?* of the Economist Intelligence Service, student satisfaction with this service is not high (62 percent out of 100 percent). However, this does not necessarily mean the service is poor. It may be that expectations are inordinately high.

The average starting salary for management school graduates was 40,000 Pounds Sterling (approx. $64,500) with 50 companies recruiting on campus. The major recruiters are consulting and auditing firms, such as Andersen and PricewaterhouseCoopers, which is due in part to the program's strong quantitative emphasis and Imperial's strong reputation among consulting companies. Many of the school's faculty are consultants and are actively encouraged to pursue their consulting activities by the school's director.

FINANCIAL AID

While the School gives students advice on where to locate financial aid, it does not provide its own funds in the forms of scholarships, special loans, or other grants. Students are expected to finance tuition fees themselves.

20.
HELSINKI
SCHOOL OF
ECONOMICS
AND BUSINESS
ADMINIS-
TRATION

Contact:
Admissions Office
Phone:
(358) 9-4313 8696
Fax:
(358) 9-4313 8613

HELSINKI SCHOOL OF ECONOMICS AND BUSINESS
ADMINISTRATION

International Center
P.O. Box 1210
FIN-00101 Helsinki, Finland
Web site: www.hkkk.fi/mbafi
E-mail: mbafi@hkkk.fi

Program

Program ranked: International MBA

Structure: 1 year, full-time; 12 core modules, 9 electives, a semester at another business school, a business project or case study; taught in two-week course modules, three major specializations; program carried out at two campuses

Size of class: 60–80 annually

Costs: EU students: 65,000 Finnish Marks (approx. $11,450); non-EU students: 85,000 Finnish Marks (approx. $15,000) in tuition; roughly $1500 for books and material

Program director: Jyrki Wallenius, Associate Dean

Accreditation: AMBA (British), EQUIS (European)

Admissions

Admissions requirements: University degree; GMAT, TOEFL (over 550) or English fluency; relevant work experience; 3 recommendations

Applications deadline: Mid-September

Starting date: January (preparatory courses)

Application fee: None

Recruiting

Placement office: Résumé database, recruitment events, business fair, career courses

Number of companies recruiting: 130

Examples of recruiting companies: Coca-Cola, Hewlett-Packard, Microsoft, Nokia

BRIEF DESCRIPTION OF THE SCHOOL

The Helsinki School of Economics is the most prominent of Nordic business schools, situated just one mile from the city center. The school was founded by a group of businesspeople in 1911, and now prides itself on fostering sustainable development and promoting high ethical standards.

The capital of Finland has always acted as a bridge between the West and Russia and the entire eastern region. Thus, despite its northern latitude location, business and commerce have played an essential role in the city of Helsinki's history—far more than most Europeans and North Americans realize. Finland considers itself one of the worlds communication superpowers, a belief that has been backed up in a recent worldwide country survey in which Finland was recently ranked third for overall competitiveness, largely due to its research and development activities in the fields of technology and communication. The school has recently created a Center for Markets in Transition, aimed at developing research and offering programs in these fields. Not surprisingly, then, one of its star pupils is Mauro Montanaro, director of strategy and business planning at Nokia, one Finland's proudest claims to corporate fame. JOKO Executive Education Ltd. is another of the School's pet projects, the aim of which is to convert academia's latest achievements into innovative training programs. JOKO is an integral part of the school, offering both open and customized company programs for managerial development needs.

The global distribution of Helsinki's academic partners is impressive, including such schools as Manchester Business School, University of Michigan, International University of Japan, Asian Institute of Technology, Indian Institute of Management, Norwegian School of Management, University of Adelaide (Australia), and Hochschule St. Gallen (Switzerland).

The school has recently converted its two-year program, created in 1983, into a new intensive one-year MBA program consisting of 12 core courses and 9 electives. There is also a new part-time evening and weekend option, of two or three years, for students who want to continue working (presumably in Helsinki) while they study. All these programs are delivered entirely in English.

THE CAMPUS AND LIFE ON CAMPUS

Students applying to Helsinki have a choice of two campuses, one in Helsinki itself and the other in Mikkeli, 230 kilometers (143 miles) from this Scandinavian capital. Joseph Valacich, a visiting professor from Washington State University, says, "Small class sizes and first-rate computing facilities create a very favorable learning environment . . . in Mikkeli." The differences between the two campuses lie in the specializations available, faculty, and facilities. In Helsinki students can specialize in finance and international business, while in Mekkeli they specialize in digital technology management, the computer facilities there being superior to those on the Helsinki campus.

The Helsinki School of Economics campus is not a single integrated facility, its departments and different parts of the school being scattered all over the city. The MBA program in Helsinki, however, takes place entirely in the International Center, a new facility with its own café, recreation facility, instruction rooms, and a new computing center.

Participants in the school have access to one of the largest libraries on business and economics topics in Scandinavia with more than 200,000 books, 1600 periodicals and 40 CD-ROM databases.

The program manages to entice students from some 20 countries, although this figure may vary from year to year. Thirty percent are women, 29 is the average age, and students have an average of five years' work experience. Most have a business and economics background (44 percent), followed by engineering (20 percent), other sciences (20 percent), and liberal arts (8 percent).

The school does not offer on-campus housing, but does help in locating it in a tight housing market. It claims that students do not need cars and that the public transport system is passenger-friendly. For the benefit of those who do not realize just how far north Finland is, go prepared for the bitterly cold winter, but also for marvelously long and fresh summer days. Visitors will not fail to be impressed by the Scandanavians who are light years ahead of the rest of the world where environmental awareness is concerned. This is a place for people with a love of nature and the sea, but not in the beach-lovers sense of the word.

THE PROGRAM

The School's MBA program was conceived as a general management MBA, including a similar range of core and elective courses as most other programs, but with a few innovative twists. From the beginning the program was different from others because it employed only "borrowed" faculty, more than 80 of them from all over the world. Thus the school was quickly able to boast a top international faculty without having to recruit its own full-time professors and invest heavily. The advantage for students is that the teaching faculty as a whole are likely to be better than if the school had to recruit and pay professors on a full-time basis, but this method can give rise to lack of coordination between professors that hardly see each other.

Of the 12 core courses, 8 are taught during the first semester, a fairly typical system designed to familiarize the student with basic management skills before selecting the areas they wish to specialize in. Helsinki offers specializations during subsequent semesters in international business, finance and digital technology management. Digital technology management consists of learning about computers, systems integration, and assorted technologies, as well as how to integrate these into corporate management—a specialization similar to that offered by the Rotterdam School of Management. The aim in all three cases is to complement the solid base of general management knowledge and skills, rather than eclipsing it.

The second half of the program includes a semester abroad. During the final part of the program, students carry out a consulting proj-

ect and write a case study themselves. The consulting project is fairly typical in that the school brings students and sponsoring companies together, and students "sell themselves" to faculty and company representatives with a view to obtaining a particular project.

Note that technophobes and anyone who is a bit nervous about working with figures can kick off with a noncredited preparatory program and business mathematics course before the official start of the program.

FACULTY, TEACHING, AND LEARNING PROCESSES

The large international faculty comprises professors brought in a visiting basis from leading businesses around the world.

The arrangement of sequential course modules means that courses are not held parallel to each other, but rather in sequence, the idea being that this prevents faculty from having to take expensive, semester-long sabbaticals from their home institutions. At Helsinki the faculty teach two-week, full-time modules in succession. The obvious drawback is that students are not really integrating different courses during a semester, but concentrate instead on just one field at a time. When one module is over, a new one starts, and it's a case of hoping that the previous one is not so forgotten that the student can't see how it is interrelated to subsequent areas.

A closer look at this arrangement reveals another potential snag. The school lists more than 80 visiting faculty, yet only 21 course modules are required for graduation, including 9 electives (out of a total of 40). It may not be easy for faculty to identify themselves with the school or fully integrate their courses into the program, making it difficult for every piece of the puzzle to fall into place to form a single program. The school emphasizes that faculty use "their own approaches," which on the one hand could provide a rich diversity of class material but could also be somewhat chaotic.

Helsinki students are introduced in stages to writing cases. They first take a course in case writing, then they research and write up the case—a good, integrating exercise which helps demonstrate what students have learned in their MBA studies.

PLACEMENT

The Career Services Center offers the usual services to students, such as organizing events involving recruiters and writing bulletins and providing résumé services. The center was set up in 1991 and claims to have longstanding relations with a list of international blue-chip companies. It is not clear whether the European, global, or only Finnish branches of companies such as Coca-Cola and Hewlett-Packard actually recruit at Helsinki.

FINANCIAL AID

MBA students, be they Finnish or foreign, may be eligible for state-guaranteed loans, but only if they have lived in Finland for the two years preceding their MBA studies. Note that grants from Finnish companies are scarce. Finnish foundations are legally hindered in providing foreign students with support.

SUCCESS STORIES: INTERVIEWS WITH GRADUATES OF EUROPEAN BUSINESS SCHOOLS

European MBA grads enjoy worldwide career opportunities.

What would my career be like if I had an MBA from a top European school? What are the possibilities? How would I view the world? What types of people hold European MBA degrees? What are their views of business issues?

We could have tried to impress readers by interviewing only chairmen of European or global blue chips who earned their MBAs at INSEAD or London Business School. Instead we selected graduates in various industries at different stages of their climb up the career ladder. This gives a better view of the numerous paths you can pursue with a European (or perhaps any) MBA. Those with MBAs are not only investment bankers or consultants in boring gray suits and dark red ties. They are also entrepreneurial managers like Fernando Barnuevo of J.P. Morgan on Wall Street and Aric Austin at MTV in London. Both have worked in numerous countries and think their MBA studies were crucial in their current careers.

Instead of quoting many alumni on lots of topics, we thought it best to talk to fewer alumni on limited topics. Thus, we interview only four individuals, but each personally and in depth. We ask questions related to the "why" behind their actions. We hope this will give you a better feel for what could await after you complete an MBA at a top European B-school.

Aric Austin
Head of Ad Sales, Strategic Planning and Commercial Operations
MTV Networks, Europe, London

MBA from Rotterdam School of Management

Born in Spain, raised in Munich, Germany, with a bachelor's degree from the University of Virginia, the American Aric Austin worked in the United States, Japan, and Australia before doing an international MBA in Rotterdam. He entered the media business at MTV Europe—not a typical industry for MBAs, building and systematizing the company's marketing and advertising business in just four years.

What do you do at MTV?

My job was practically newly created for me and matched the strategic direction in which MTV was moving. In this, I coordinate airtime sales Europewide, write marketing and management reports, coordinate between the numerous European offices of MTV, and compile budgets and forecasts. It is not a "typical" MBA job, but it requires the management skills and business knowledge which I learned during my MBA studies at Rotterdam.

What did you do before studying in Rotterdam?

I was born in Spain, raised in Munich, went to high school and college (University of Virginia) in the USA. I then taught English in Japan, worked in Australia, and ran the service department of a car dealership in the States. My parents are American, and I just got a British passport. As such I was predestined for a multifaceted life and career path.

Why did you decide to go for an MBA and why did you choose Rotterdam?

I started thinking about doing an MBA when I was working in the States. I wanted to expand my management skills and knowledge to open up a larger number of career opportunities worldwide. I was a generalist and I wanted to remain a generalist—able to do many things in many places. I believed that the MBA was a kind of overall management and skills qualification.

Why Rotterdam? I looked at most of the top European schools, but few offered such a broad and international education as Rotterdam. I wanted to study on the European continent and the program had to be very international. But the choices were limited. Germany does not really have a business school culture, and I don't speak any of the Romance languages, which eliminated France, Spain, and Italy. The two-year program at Rotterdam allowed me time to learn enough about all management fields. Other programs were too short but, like the Rotterdam program, have student bodies from all over the world.

Tell us about your MBA studies.

The Rotterdam MBA program lasts nearly two years, which is a necessary period of time to acquire a broad business education. For me, learning the actual management disciplines, such as finance, marketing, human resources, etc., took a back seat to the "softer" human skills. Rotterdam put you in a group with other students from all over the world. In these groups you had to work on case studies and projects. You had to learn to reconcile different cultures and ways of thinking. This taught you the people skills you need for a global career. It also gave me contacts with capable people from all over the world.

Where would you recommend doing an MBA, in Europe or the USA?
You should do an MBA in a place where you are not from. If you are European, go to the States or Asia. If you're American, make the step to study in Europe or Asia. Europe is particularly international, which American schools are not. Some American schools claim that they offer internationally oriented MBA studies. Yet here the cases are mostly American and the orientation is very national. However, if you're European or Asian, go to the States. There is no doubt that the USA is currently the business leader in the world. Learning the American way of business is useful for those who have not been exposed to it.

Do you think that European schools will become stronger trendsetters than the American schools?
Globalization will get more people thinking about doing their MBAs in Europe. Globalization is not a temporary trend but a phenomenon which will grow in momentum. Also, the image and perception of the quality of European business schools have undergone a lot of change over recent years. Five to ten years ago, doing a European MBA was something of a novelty. The European schools have done a lot in recent years to promote themselves and improve their programs. Many are accredited and most are listed in guides and books which applicants to MBA programs regularly consult. They are now taken much more seriously.

How did you come to work for MTV after completing your MBA?
Toward the end of my MBA studies, I was recruited by a London-based consulting firm specializing in the steel and aircraft industries. After eight months I left because it was too specialized and confining. I did not feel that I could apply enough of my skills there, that I could create and build up something at the firm.

I began looking for something in the media business. Most firms asked for specialized media experience instead of looking at my overall skills. The job-securing process at MTV was fairly arduous. I started interviewing with MTV in August and only received a job offer the following April. A member of the top management needed a right hand to build, systematize, and coordinate the Europewide marketing and sales activities. Still, I had to put a lot of effort into convincing MTV that I was right for the job. I stuck to it, though. I knew it was what I wanted at the time. The job would give me the opportunity to create something, to be creative in a generally dynamic and successful company. I was not disappointed. The job at MTV has been rewarding. The company is vibrant but much more professional and organized now than when I started here four years ago.

Which guidelines do you follow in hiring people?
I look at who you are, what you've done, and whether you have interesting skills and ideas. I don't focus that much on whether the applicant

> "Globalization will get more people thinking about doing their MBAs in Europe."

has specialized skills in the media business. I think that too many companies limit their potential by looking for specialized knowledge rather than more general skills and abilities. This is too short-sighted and inward-looking. It hinders their growth potential and creativity.

How is your Rotterdam education helping your current work?
The MBA not only taught me a lot about marketing and business principles, which I use in my reports and forecasting for MTV, more importantly, it taught me how to understand and deal with different cultures from a business standpoint. I can better understand the priorities of the MTV office in Italy as opposed to the one in Germany. If you travel around the world a lot and grow up in different places, you only learn about the cultural differences of countries and mentalities in a social setting. Through my MBA, I understand what these differences entail in business terms.

Are you in touch with the school or the contacts you made during your MBA?
When I recently changed my e-mail address, a friend of mine looked at the list of people I sent my message to. He was amazed because there were people from all over the world and from all walks of life. Certainly I stay in touch with some people more than others, but in essence the teaching method at Rotterdam fused people together in a common and very tough learning experience. Indeed, I think that the education at Rotterdam may be different than at comparable American schools; less cut-throat and more cooperative and mutually supportive.

What do you want to do next in your career?
My time at MTV has been very productive for both sides. MTV has become much more professional and strategic than when I first started here four years ago. I feel I have made a contribution and soon it may be time to move on to something totally new, utilizing different skills of mine, possibly in a different place. I'm playing with the idea of doing something entrepreneurial perhaps in the Internet area. However, Internet is something of a bandwagon on which many people seem to be jumping. Probably, for every person who has made a million in this field, there are 50 who have lost everything. I want to take time to explore new ideas in new locations. I think the entrepreneurial area is where I will head next. The worst thing would be to be 60 or 70 and say "I wish I had done that back then." It's better to try and fail, than to never have tried. Not trying something is a certain failure.

How could your MBA help you in an entrepreneurial venture?
Business knowledge and contacts will help the most. However, when I studied at Rotterdam the school did not sufficiently address the entre-

> "The MBA . . . taught me how to understand and deal with different cultures . . . "

preneurship area. I think that Rotterdam has remedied this weakness in the meantime. In general, Europe has been behind in entrepreneurial activity. There is a fear here of taking risks and the service sectors—especially in Germany—are underdeveloped. Now Europe is moving toward becoming more entrepreneurial. This may be a good opportunity for entrepreneurs to start up in Europe. There's less competition in Europe, especially in Germany. If I set up a service business in the USA, I might not be successful because the entire economy is so service-oriented. In Germany I might be number one with the same idea.

What do you advise MBA graduates to do in planning their careers?
Make sure that your job matches your skills and inclinations. Do not fall into the trap of just going to McKinsey or another "typical" MBA recruiting business, just because it's the easy way. This will not give you the job satisfaction you actually could achieve. I would be willing to bet that many—if not most—of the people in such jobs are not that happy with them. Take time to examine what your abilities and aims are, and find a job, employer, and career that fits them.

Fernando Barnuevo
Managing Director
J.P. Morgan Equities Inc., New York

MBA from Instituto de Empresa, Madrid

The Instituto de Empresa MBA helped Barnuevo reach the top levels of Wall Street.

From the Spanish farmlands to the pinnacle of world finance on three continents. The Spaniard Fernando Barnuevo is Managing Director of J.P. Morgan Equities Inc. at the company's world headquarters on Wall Street, a position he reached after only 11 years at the company. Barnuevo completed his MBA at the Instituto de Empresa in Madrid, which brought him to J.P. Morgan in Madrid, then in Latin America, San Francisco, and finally New York.

What led you to do an MBA?
As a university graduate with a law degree I had wanted to work for one of the best investment banks in the world. J.P. Morgan was definitely among the best and they only hired MBAs. So getting the job I wanted was an important initial motivation for attending business school. The real benefit of the MBA to my life and career was that it turned me from a somewhat romantic conqueror into a focused and pragmatic businessman.

Was the MBA simply a means to getting the job you wanted?
Initially probably yes. But the MBA changed my life in many ways. Working in classes and on case studies helped me learn from the mistakes of others before I started my career as an investment banker. It

taught me how to focus on essentials and become an entrepreneur even in a large organization like J.P. Morgan.

Did the MBA give you an entrepreneurial spirit or did you already have some of that characteristic?

From childhood on I possessed something of an entrepreneurial spirit. My father was a farmer. The career perspective he had was to increase the size, efficiency, and effectiveness of his farm, which he did with an entrepreneurial spirit. I was convinced that any career I would pursue should enable me to unfold the same entrepreneurial spirit.

What made you chose the business school you did, the Instituto de Empresa?

As soon as I realized that I needed an MBA for a career in a top investment bank, I started comparing schools. Friends recommended IE to me. I was impressed by the entrepreneurial spirit of the people at IE and by their "hunger" for success. IE was a relatively new school then. It was in something of an infant stage—full of energy and enthusiasm. That attracted me. I found that the other leading business schools in Europe didn't have the same mix of hunger and entrepreneurial spirit combined with learning rigor. IE was founded by business executives and entrepreneurs, and I think that to this day imbues its faculty and students with these characteristics.

Have you been in touch with your alma mater and do you know if it is still that way?

I recently received a CV from an IE graduate, which was the only one I ever received from a graduate of this institution. I normally receive polished CVs from Harvard, Yale, Stanford people. They all look very similar and seem to want to fit into a mold. But the CV from the IE person was different. He communicated the same entrepreneurial and individualistic spirit that I remember from IE. I've been in touch with the school and it has grown to be one of the biggest and most successful B-schools in Europe. But the people there are still modest, hungry for business, and full of entrepreneurial spirit.

As a manager and recruiter of MBAs, what are you looking for in a job applicant?

I don't look that much at which school an applicant went to as much as many may think. In this business we try to look at who you are, not so much where you went. I don't think a school can fundamentally change who you are. It mainly highlights good characteristics you already have and brings out weaknesses so you know what to work on and improve. The problem with the cookie-cut graduates from many top schools is that we as employers can't assess your weaknesses and thus we don't

> "I normally receive polished CVs from Harvard, Yale people. But the CV from the IE person was different."

know what risk we are taking in hiring you. The real person's personality seems to be somewhat hidden. In addition, many Harvard-type graduates tend to be overconfident. Especially in the equities business, overconfidence leads to expensive mistakes.

Where should someone study for an MBA? In Europe or the USA?

The geography is less important. If you're a creative person but terribly disorganized, go to a school stressing organization, such as Harvard. Go to a school which brings out and helps you overcome your personal weaknesses. In any case, being exposed to a lot of diversity is also important in your studies. And the European programs bring together people from all over the world, exposing you to diversity.

What are the main overall benefits of an MBA?

Helping you avoid making mistakes. The advantage of working in MBA classes and on case studies is that you see what mistakes others have made and you can avoid making them. Making mistakes later in your career is normally more costly and time-consuming. At good business schools you learn that the world is full of very smart and capable people. Thus you learn never to lower your guard and not be overconfident. There's always someone with a better idea and who has had your good ideas before you did.

"The MBA helps you avoid mistakes."

Were you ever overconfident?

Before going to business school, I had my own retail clothes business. Our formula for success was doing the exact opposite of what our competitors did. Pale colors and boring clothing were in at that time. We used bright colors and differently cut clothing. The business took off. We became overconfident and always did the opposite of what everyone else did. We became overconfident and then designed clothing the market didn't go for. The business went downhill, and I lost a lot of money learning that lesson.

Could you have been successful without an MBA?

Yes, but it would most likely have taken me longer. Without an MBA, you make more mistakes and have to learn a lot on the job. The MBA gives you a head start in business.

When should someone go for an MBA? Right after college or later in life?

After spending a few years on the job first and then going for an MBA, you can benefit most from an MBA. This pre-MBA business experience allows you to learn more about your strengths and weaknesses. During your MBA studies, you can better focus on building on your strengths and overcoming your weaknesses.

Really learning is a lifelong process which lasts either until you die or give up your business. The MBA gives you the tools to really start this learning process.

> "... you are likely to automatically make money."

What are the overall elements of success?
Coordination, hunger, focus, fear, and listening to others. Many of the most successful executives at J.P. Morgan do a very good job of listening to others. In our society there is too much talking and hearing, and too little actual listening. I recently went on vacation to Tibet with my family. I was struck by how people in that culture could listen. They love to listen and thereby learn more quickly.

What does it take to be successful in equities?
A lot of common sense, a long-term view of things, a view for essentials, and a hunger for success. The basic principle is that banking is a peoples' business and is based on trust. Listen a lot to what people have to say, and you are likely to make the right decisions. I am wary of people who go for an MBA only to make money. If you concentrate on the business you're in and on being good about what you are doing, you are likely to automatically make money. If you are only after money, you will lose friends, your perspective, and many other things that make life worth living.

Marcus Bernhardt
Director of Radisson/SAS Hotels Belgium, France, Italy, and Luxembourg; Director of the Radisson/SAS Brussels

MBA from the GSBA Zurich

As the European hotel scene increasingly becomes a matter of the large international chains and big business, and less a matter of private hotels, professional managers like Marcus Bernhardt are beginning to quickly rise to the top of the international hierarchies. Bernhardt, a Swiss citizen, had already been highly successful in the grand hotels of Switzerland before doing an MBA, but wanted a greater management challenge. He completed an executive, modular MBA at the GSBA Zurich to acquire a complete view of management, which he could then later apply to the international operations at Radisson/SAS. He quickly advanced within the Radisson organization and is now in charge of 13 large hotels in four countries, 1200 people, and $180 million in annual sales.

What are your current responsibilities at Radisson/SAS?
I am responsible for 13 hotels in four countries, and I am director of our hotel in Brussels city center, our "flagship" hotel, so to speak. Both jobs involve the entire span of management tasks, from marketing to strategic and financial planning. I report to the European president within Radisson/SAS.

What did you do before joining Radisson/SAS and where does your MBA fit in?
I initially completed a business education and later added studies at the Hotel Schools of Luzern and Cornell University. At 26 I was named director of a large grand hotel in Switzerland and soon thereafter moved into that organization's board of directors in charge of four hotels. However, I did not want to stop there but wanted to acquire a more generalistic education to enable me to fill other management positions possibly in other business sectors. However, I did not want to interrupt my career for one or two years for a full-time MBA. Thus, I attended the GSBA Zurich, which offered an executive part-time MBA.

What were your experiences at business school?
A key element was the excellent quality and level of the other program participants. The student body was very high level—all successful managers, not entry-level people. Some came from companies in charge of thousands of people, others were from smaller firms. Their divergent backgrounds meant that a high variety of thoughts and concepts flowed into class discussions and small group work. I'm regularly in touch with many alumni to this day, exchanging ideas and concepts. The professors were from the United States and Europe. It was amazing what they were able to bring across in class. The cases and materials were accordingly international. Very importantly, the program covered all fields of business administration from an *executive* viewpoint. An important topic was business reengineering, which remains immediately applicable to what I have to do in my business today.

What happened after business school?
I graduated from the GSBA Zurich in 1996 and since then have enjoyed a rapid expansion of my responsibilities. Although headhunters approached me with offers while at Zurich, I came to Radisson/SAS via personal contacts. Radisson/SAS told me that despite my background and education, that I would have to prove myself before they could give me international responsibility. Thus, I first became director of the Brussels Radisson/SAS, a flagship hotel. Thereafter I was charged with creating and integrating an international organization of hotels in Belgium, France, Italy, and Luxembourg. This organization did not even

> "The professors were from the United States and Europe."

fully exist when I started. One of my jobs was to put together marketing, IT, controlling, and other functions for this hotel group—a challenging exercise with which my MBA studies helped me a lot. They had given me the necessary know-how in all these areas.

Are there many people like you in the European hotel business?
From the 120 to 130 hotel directors in our organization, I know of only two who have MBAs. If I compare this with our organization in the United States, most—if not all—directors and managers have MBAs. Most of the directors of private hotels—even large private hotels—have advanced through the classic career route, through the kitchen, beverage, and other hotel areas, perhaps having attended hotel schools. I also fear that there still are hotel directors who do not really know their bottom lines and certainly do not manage their hotel along modern lines of business administration. But I think this is changing. In our business in Europe there are a lot of mergers and acquisitions going on which require a more highly qualified management. Plus, our clients are themselves businesspeople with top backgrounds who expect hotel management by professionals for professionals. The MBA is likely to sooner or later become the standard in the hotel business in Europe as well. It is a highly dynamic business; an international business.

What qualities do you think are particular to MBAs?
I can only speak for the hotel industry in Europe. I think that MBAs know how to work in a context of tough number crunching, of international business, and are braver in making difficult decisions. In the huge changes in our business in this time, managers must be good at people management, making the right decisions quickly and implementing far-reaching changes. These qualities are perhaps more important for managers in our business today than typical hotel-related knowledge such as knowing the culinary side of the business thoroughly.

Another important point is the people management abilities you acquire with an MBA. Human resource directors sit next to the president's office, like the financial or marketing managers. If you hire the wrong people, particularly at a higher level, this will cost your firm a fortune. Not only does it involve high severance payments but it means undoing all of his or her mistakes within the organization—mistakes which may weaken the company for a long time to come. The success or failure of a company depends on the quality of the managers and employees. I value human resources highly and meet once a week with my human resources manager. In a people business like the hotel business, guests notice if there are personnel problems within the organization.

" . . . MBAs . . . are braver in making difficult decisions."

Would you sponsor employees for an MBA?

If they were directors, yes. However, department heads in our business probably lack sufficient background, particularly in finance. In addition, they may not be fluent in English.

Does an MBA make sense for managers of smaller organizations, that is, smaller hotels?

I *can* recommend an MBA even to directors of "smaller" hotels with 500 to 700 rooms. The MBA allows you to work better under pressure and improves how you communicate with your CEO. You speak the same business language, at the same level. Even so, the MBA is not a sufficient condition for being successful. One should not think that it is sufficient to study a lot and hang up diplomas on your office walls. The right personality, background, and the ability to translate what you have learned into practical results are what count in the final analysis.

Gemma Harman
Associate
A.T. Kearney, London

MBA from Manchester Business School

Her career sounds as if it were already complete before she even started her MBA studies. In four years she had already worked in Germany and the United States in the aluminum and steel business, in marketing for British Airways in London and Germany, for the ad firm Saatchi & Saatchi in London, and for United Utilities on change management. She did her undergraduate work in business at the University of Münster in Germany and the University of Manchester. During her MBA studies she spent a term in Melbourne, consulting with corporations all over Asia and Australia.

" . . . I work on internal projects such as e-commerce, branding, and business school recruitment initiatives."

Describe your current job at ATK.

As an associate, my job entails working across many industries, ranging from aerospace, automotive, telecommunications to retail, and thus signifies a steep learning curve during each new project I work on. All project challenges and opportunities are different and demand 110 percent effort.

In terms of experience to date, I have been involved in a variety of projects ranging from process redesign, media communication, marketing strategy, global logistics to corporate strategy. In addition, I work on internal projects such as e-commerce, branding, and business school recruitment initiatives.

What is your professional background? What did you do before going to Manchester for your MBA?

My background is highly diverse and multifunctional, which is one of the reasons consulting suits me. I have worked in Germany, the United Kingdom, the United States, Italy, and Australia for Hoogovens Aluminium, British Steel, British Airways, Saatchi & Saatchi, and United Utilities.

Where and what did you study before doing your MBA?

After working in Germany for some time I began a degree at the Westfalische Wilhelms University in Münster. Recognizing that I needed a more international business approach and faster turnaround time in studying to remain competitive with European counterparts of my age, I transferred to UMIST School of Management, where I graduated with a first-class honors degree in management sciences.

How does studying in Germany compare with the United Kingdom?

Initially I had to register for many courses that I either did not wish to do or did not need in order to begin studying what I really wanted. I felt that this emphasis extended the study period unnecessarily. I saw many students graduate as late as 27 or 28 but without significant work experience or a focused degree. I felt that graduating at such a late age was a disadvantage in terms of employment attractiveness compared to international management students graduating earlier and having on average five years work experience by the time students graduate in Germany.

In addition, I sat in lecture halls with many hundreds of students with the professor often totally inaccessible. This situation created a large status gap between students and professors and did not lend itself to a truly two-way interactive learning environment.

In contrast, studying at UMIST School of Management brought me into direct contact with professors who were on the forefront of their fields. Many professors were also consultants or had worked for blue-chip companies, which brought the learning environment alive. Real contact and networks with the outside business world is highly important when studying subject matter such as management science—you just cannot rely on pure theory.

In addition, class sizes were much smaller and the academic levels very high. Students were given more choice concerning what and how they wished to study.

Why did you decide to do an MBA?

The MBA is an interdisciplinary and practical degree that seemed to fit my interests and plans to go into consulting. I believe I had already gained a sound understanding and experience in management through my combined previous experience and academic study—the MBA fur-

> "Many professors were also consultants or had worked for blue-chip companies . . ."

ther develops project skills and knowledge in less explored management areas in a practical method. The MBA enables you to work effectively in practical and functional areas through a series of "real" projects, such as the entrepreneurial project. In essence, it is ideal for something as broad and interdisciplinary as consulting.

How did the entrepreneurial project work?

The project was very exciting and insightful. It involved teams developing a complete business plan and strategy for an entirely new company or activity. Organizations who contacted the school requesting "consultants" were either those interested in developing small business units or small- to medium-sized firms that wanted to overhaul or redesign their businesses. My specific project involved establishing an entirely unique retail organization from a concept on paper. My team worked on the project for two to three months, doing research, strategic, and implementation work.

Another project was the "International Business Project" which came at the end of the 18-month MBA program. Here too, blue-chip companies invited students to put forward proposals to win an assignment. Student teams competed among themselves to win assignments. This project lasted three months and was a true consulting experience. It allowed students to gain a real insight into the world of consulting plus gain the opportunity of working closely with international CEOs and other senior management levels.

Do you think that an MBA qualifies you better for consulting than for other jobs in business?

The MBA can be regarded as a preparatory degree for a career in consultancy. Firstly, it prepares you to become fluent and gain an expertise in all business functions. Secondly, it reflects the pressure, constant challenge, heavy workload, and need to excel in any piece of work you undertake. As a result, it gives you great insights.

Do you think 18 months are necessary for an MBA, or is the shorter 11-month variant of the MBA at schools such as Insead sufficient?

The pace at MBS was very fast and the workload heavy. Shorter programs, such as INSEAD, are fine if you want to simply get the theoretical side of the MBA over with. However, I feel the extra months allow students to truly get value out of their MBA—putting what they learned into practice. I believe the variety of practical projects to be indispensable management training, teaching you skills you cannot learn in a purely theoretical environment. In addition, the longer program means that you can also enjoy an international business school exchange. I went to the Melbourne Business School and also worked at the same time gaining even more cross-cultural management experience.

"I went to the Melbourne Business School and also worked at the same time . . . "

Do you have any recommendations to prospective MBA students?
Any student who wishes to pursue an international management career should seriously consider an MBA. The outcome is beneficial regardless of the journey students pursue thereafter. It equips the student in terms of (1) international project management skills, (2) experience working with highly diverse, multicultural business professionals, (3) understanding of all major business functions ranging from corporate finance to e-commerce strategy, and (4) building an international network that will remain invaluable even after the MBA is long finished.

THE 10 EUROPEAN RUNNERS-UP

THE IDEA OF RUNNERS-UP

Runners-up are MBA programs which almost made it into this ranking, or might have made it if other criteria had been used, or those that show so much promise they are likely to be included in future rankings by the author or other institutions. The point of a runners-up section is to signal to both applicants and schools that these MBA programs are strong and deserve probably the same consideration as the programs included in the ranking. It should also encourage runner-up schools to continue their good work.

Runners-up have made good impressions in many different ways. They are not ranked among one another, and within our alphabetic list there are no "stronger" or "weaker" runners-up. The criteria which influenced selection include:

HOW THE RUNNERS-UP WERE SELECTED

- The mother institution, normally a university, is particularly reputed.
- The program curriculum is innovative, yet it may be too new to be in the top 20.
- The faculty members are excellent.
- The student body and number of alumni are increasing and are bound to reach a "critical mass" soon.

Why aren't these programs in the ranking? They have few, if any, alumni. Neither faculty nor administration has had the opportunity to establish a track record. Most have new and unproven programs. Although the programs may appear good in theory, it would be unfair to rank them next to those with established performance records. This applies to schools such as Oxford's Said and Koblenz's joint program with Kellogg. The Oxford school belongs to one of the world's most reputable universities, received 20 million pounds sterling from the Oxford alumnus Said, but in this sensitive stage of its development, it lost its first dean (John Kay resigned) and has no permanent quarters yet. The Koblenz executive MBA program began just a few years ago and enrolls only 60 students. Koblenz as a first-degree-awarding institution is well reputed in Germany as well as among its numerous partner institutions with which it maintains student exchange relationships. The school received a large grant from the German industrialist and entrepreneur Otto Beisheim and named itself after him. With the help of these funds the school moved into permanent quarters in a suburb of Koblenz.

Other runners-up have established very good programs but they just did not make it into this ranking. They might appear in other rankings, or their mother institutions may be included in major institutional rankings or otherwise be evaluated positively and convincingly.

Each runner-up is commented on briefly with mention of interesting developments and strengths of the program or the institution.

CITY UNIVERSITY BUSINESS SCHOOL

Frobisher Crescent
Barbican Centre
EC2Y 8HB London, United Kingdom
Web site: www.city.ac.uk/cubs/
E-mail: cubs-postgrad@city.ac.uk

Program

Program ranked: MBA
Structure: 12 months full-time; program has 4 key elements: (1) required core management program; (2) specialist modules (general and strategic management, electronic business, finance, human resources and management, international business, management of technology, and marketing); (3) a set of elective courses; (4) a 3-month business project
Size of class: 133 intake per year
Participants: Average age, 30; average work experience, 6.3 years; men/women ratio, 64 to 36; international students, 65 percent
Costs: 15,000 Pounds Sterling (approx. $24,190)
Program director: Carol Vielba
Accreditation: AMBA (British)

Admissions

Admissions Requirements: University degree, GPA, or appropriate professional qualifications, or at least 6 years of relevant business experience; minimum of 3 years' experience; score of at least 550 in the GMAT; 2 references; for non-native English speakers: TOEFL (min. 540) or IELTS (min. 6.5) or Cambridge Certificate of Proficiency (min. C)
Applications deadline: May 31
Starting date: Late September
Application fee: 45 Pounds Sterling (approx. $73)

Recruiting

Placement office: Full support service throughout the program, including job search and career orientation

---

CITY
UNIVERSITY
BUSINESS
SCHOOL

Contact:
Admissions Office
Phone:
(44) 171 477 8606
Fax:
(44) 171 477 8898

EAP

EAP—European School of Management

6 avenue de la Porte de Champerret
F-75838 Paris Cedex 17, France
Web site: www.eap.fr
E-mail: drouach@eap.net

Program

Program ranked: MBA

Structure: 12 months full-time; the program, taught in English, is divided into 4 learning blocks: building your confidence with business; shaping the international future of your business; confronting the challenges of the international arena; international consultancy project

Participants are required to take French throughout the year they spend in Paris. The program includes seminars at EAP centers in Berlin, Madrid, or Oxford for reinforcement of European management

Size of class: Maximum 35

Participants: 16 different nationalities, mostly from European countries; average age, 31; average work experience, 7 years

Costs: 19,056 Euros ($19,950); the consulting project at the final stage of the program earns students an average of 5335 Euros ($5590)

Program director: Daniel Rouach

Accreditation: AMBA (British), Chapitre (France), EQUIS (European)

Admissions

Admissions requirements: Undergraduate degree; GMAT; TOEFL for non-native speakers; minimum 3 years of relevant professional experience; 2 letters of recommendation; interviews and completed application forms

Applications deadline: October 15

Starting date: January

Application fee: 91 Euros ($95)

Recruiting

Placement office: Careers seminars, personal advice, résumé book, electronic curricula vitae database, presentations on campus

Number of companies recruiting: 100+

Examples of recruiting companies: Arthur D. Little, Pricewaterhouse-Coopers, Johnson & Johnson

Contact:
Admissions Office
Phone:
(33) 1 440 93386
Fax:
(33) 1 440 93335

ESSEC

ESSEC—École Supérieure des Sciences Economiques et Commerciales

Avenue Bernard Hirsch
BP 105
F- 95021 Cergy-Pontoise Cédex, France
Web site: www.essec.fr
E-mail: guibilato@edu.essec.fr

Program

Program ranked: MBA
Structure: Full-time, 2-year program; first part intended for students from the French école system; second part mixes these students and other French and foreign students; students choose from 200 different courses, including foreign language and humanities; English courses available
Size of class: 500 per intake
Participants: Average age, 21; 40 different nationalities
Costs: 6602 Euros per year (approx. $6912)
Program director: Christian Koenig
Accreditation: AACSB (American), AMBA (British), Chapitre (France)

Admissions

Admissions requirements: GMAT or TAGE/MAGE, French or English proficiency test, personal interview, letters of recommendation, work experience
Applications deadline: April
Starting date: October
Application fee: 150 Euros (approx. $157)

Recruiting

Placement office: Personal advice, seminars on job searching, interview workshops, résumé book, company presentations, campus career fair
Number of companies recruiting: 250+
Examples of recruiting companies: BNP, L'Oréal, LVMH, Cartier, Société Générale

Contact:
Admissions Office
Phone:
(33) 1 34 43 31 37 /
34 43 30 84
Fax:
(33) 1 34 43 30 01

SAID BUSINESS SCHOOL

SAID BUSINESS SCHOOL—UNIVERSITY OF OXFORD

The Radcliffe Infirmary
Woodstock Road
Oxford OX2 6HE, UK
Web site: www.sbs.ox.ac.uk
E-mail: info@sbs.ox.ac.uk

Program

Program ranked: MBA

Structure: 12 months, full-time; divided into 4 terms; during first term there are sessions on improving group and leadership processes, during which data analysis and computing are introduced; in the second term integrative sessions on business functions continue with tutorial work and an emphasis on global business; the third term provides the opportunity for specialization while continuing studies in international business; the summer term is dedicated to a business project that takes place overseas

Size of class: 65

Participants: Students in the last course represented 22 different nationalities; average age, 27; average GMAT score, 652; average work experience, 5 years

Costs: Tuition, 16,000 Pounds Sterling (approx. $25,760); college fees, 2130 Pounds Sterling (approx. $3430); estimated living expenses, 11,000 Pounds Sterling (approx. $17,710)

Program director: Richard Whittington

Accreditation: AMBA (British)

Admissions

Admissions requirements: Degree (GPA of 3.5 or its equivalent); TOEFL (600) or IELTS (7.5) for non-native English speakers; GMAT (normally over 620); 3 references; a sample of written work of 1000–2000 words, with details of work experience (minimum 2 years); applicant interviews

Applications deadline: Rolling basis

Starting date: Early October

Application fee: 60 Pounds Sterling (approx. $97)

Recruiting

Placement office: Personal advice, resume book, job interviews on campus

Number of companies recruiting: 50+

Examples of recruiting companies: McKinsey, Bain & Co., Andersen Consulting

Contact:
Admissions Office
Phone:
(44) 1865 228470
Fax:
(44) 1865 228471

STRATHCLYDE
GRADUATE
BUSINESS
SCHOOL

Contact:
Admissions Office
Phone:
(44) 141 553 6000
Fax:
(44) 141 552 8851/
2501

STRATHCLYDE GRADUATE BUSINESS SCHOOL

199 Cathedral Street
Glasgow
G4 0QU Scotland, UK
Web site: www.strath.ac.uk
E-mail: admisions@sgbs.strath.ac.uk

Program

Program ranked: MBA

Structure: 12 months, full-time; 36 months, part-time; based on a 4-stage approach: stage 1, business foundations, designed to bring participants from a wide range of work, academic, and cultural backgrounds to common level of business and management understanding; stage 2, management, participants choose a set of management optional courses; stage 3, specialization courses or generalist approach; stage 4, project

Size of class: 100 per intake

Participants: Average work experience, 9 years; students from 30 different countries (30% from United Kingdom)

Costs: Full-time, 11,300 Pounds Sterling (approx. $18,220); part-time, 9200 Pounds Sterling (approx. $14,835); on-campus accommodation, 2400 Pounds Sterling (approx. $3870)

Program director: Chris Huxham

Accreditation: AMBA (British)

Admission

Admissions requirements: Minimum 3 years' experience; GMAT (min. 550), TOEFL (min 600); 2 letters of reference; completed application forms

Applications deadline: None

Starting date: September

Application fee: None

Recruiting

Placement office: Career facilitator available to help participants with their professional development and to assist in finding jobs after graduation

UNIVERSITY
COLLEGE
DUBLIN

UNIVERSITY COLLEGE DUBLIN—THE MICHAEL SMURFIT GRADUATE SCHOOL OF BUSINESS

Carysfort Avenue. Blackrock
Dublin, Ireland
Web site: www.ucd.ie/gsb/
E-mail: padmin@blackrock.ucd.ie

Program

Program ranked: MBA
Structure: 12 months full-time; operates on a semester basis with a 3-tier progression: (1) foundation level in the principal business functions of marketing, production, human resources, finance, law, and management; (2) corporate level of business strategy, business integration, and overall managing resources of the business; (3) major applied research project in area of business selected by participants
Size of class: 40 students per class
Participants: Average age, 31; average work experience, 5 to 7 years; country of origin, 88% European, 6% North American, and 6% other.
Costs: Full-time, 7500 Pounds Sterling ($12,100); part-time, 8500 Pounds Sterling (approx. $13,700)
Program director: Kenneth Meates
Accreditation: AMBA (British)

Admissions

Admissions requirements: University degree or equivalent professional qualification; 3 to 5 years' business experience; acceptable score in all sections of the GMAT (average 575); English fluency; TOEFL for non-English native speakers; 2 references; interview, whenever possible; emphasis placed on a candidate's objectives, commitment, and ability to function as a team member
Applications deadline: For initial acceptance period: March 31; applications accepted on an ongoing basis subject to availability of spaces
Starting date: Early September
Application fee: 20 Pounds Sterling (approx. $33)

Recruiting

Placement office: Extensive services
Number of companies recruiting: 50+
Examples of recruiting companies: Oracle, Bank of Ireland, Deloitte & Touche

Contact:
Admissions Office
Phone:
(353) 1 706 8934
Fax:
(353) 1 283 1911

UNIVERSITY OF EDINBURGH MANAGEMENT SCHOOL

UNIVERSITY OF EDINBURGH MANAGEMENT SCHOOL

7 Bristol Square
Edinburgh EH8 9AL, UK
Web site: www.ems.ed.ac.uk
E-mail: management.school@ed.ac.uk

Contact:
Admissions Office
Phone:
(44) 131 650 6339
Fax:
(44) 131 650 8077

Program
Program ranked: MBA
Structure: 12 months, full-time; introductory week for study and career orientation; first term focuses on core subjects in main company functions; in second and third terms, students take compulsory course in strategic management and choose 4 elective courses from a selection of 50; running parallel is a program consisting of communication and presentation skills, languages, and outdoor development opportunities; there is a consultancy project at this stage; students produce a dissertation during the final term
Size of class: 100 per intake
Participants: 7 years' average work experience; 33 different nationalities (37% British Isles; 25% the Americas)
Costs: 9300 Pounds Sterling (approx. $15,000) for EU citizens; 9900 Pounds Sterling (approx. $15,960) for non-EU citizens
Program director: Richard Kerley
Accreditation: AMBA (British)

Admissions
Admissions requirements: Candidates are generally required to have a good degree or equivalent qualification plus a minimum of 2 years' work experience; 2 references; evidence of academic qualifications; GMAT test score (preferred); ELTS (6.5); TOEFL (580)
Applications deadline: August/September
Starting date: October
Application fee: None

Recruiting
Placement office: Career management advisor based on site; linked to the university careers office; personal guidance and counseling
Number of companies recruiting: 170
Examples of recruiting companies: Andersen Consulting, The Royal Bank of Scotland, Glaxo Wellcome

UNIVERSITY OF NOTTINGHAM

THE UNIVERSITY OF NOTTINGHAM

Business School
Jubilee Campus
Nottingham NG7 2RD
United Kingdom
Web site: www.nottingham.ac.uk/unbs
E-mail: MBA@nottingham.ac.uk

Program

Program ranked: General International MBA

Structure: 12 months full-time study divided into six core modules and six elective modules. Of the elective modules, up to two modules may be in other area-specific MBA programs offered by the school (e.g., financial MBA). Elective modules include Japanese Institutions, Entrepreneurship and Financial Fraud and Misconduct, to mention only a very few. Program involves group and individual projects.

Size of class: 100

Participants: 70% are foreign students, mostly from the EU

Costs: Tuition fee, 11,000 Pounds Sterling ($17,500); living expenses, 2000–2500 Pounds Sterling ($3200–$4000)

Program director: Ian Gow (School Director)

Accreditation: AMBA

Admissions

Admissions requirements: Good first degree, 3 years professional experience or more, GMAT, TOEFL (for non-English natives)

Applications deadline: None, but early application suggested

Starting date: Late September

Application fee: None

Recruiting

Placement office: Yes

Number of companies recruiting: 50+

Examples of recruiting companies: British Telecom, The Boots Company, and various international banks

WHU KOBLENZ—OTTO BEISHEIM GRADUATE SCHOOL OF MANAGEMENT

Burgplatz
D-56179 Vallendar, Germany
Web site: www.whu-koblenz.de
E-mail: mba@whu-koblenz.de

WHU KOBLENZ

Contact:
Admissions Office
Phone:
(49) 261 6509 331/
332
Fax:
(49) 261 6509 329

Program

Program ranked: Executive MBA (in conjunction with J. L. Kellogg Graduate School of Management)

Structure: 24 months part-time; program content tailored to the needs of the participants and their companies and institutions; emphasis on (1) behavior in learning organizations, (2) international management, (3) managing groups of cooperating firms for international competitiveness

Size of class: 40 approx.

Participants: All have a university degree; at least 3 years of practical experience; and come from industrial firms, financial institutions, and service industries

Costs: 24,542 Euros ($25,700) for the 2-year program

Program director: Horst Albach

Accreditation: EQUIS (European)

Admissions

Admissions requirements: Completed application form, 2 letters of recommendation, a letter from the applicant's firm, university transcripts, TOEFL, and an interview

Applications deadline: End of May

Starting date: August 31

Application fee: None

Recruiting

Placement office: Most students sponsored by their companies; the placement office provides careers advice and access to German companies

VIENNA UNIVERSITY OF ECONOMICS AND BUSINESS ADMINIS-TRATION

WIRTSCHAFTSUNIVERSITÄT WIEN—VIENNA UNIVERSITY OF ECONOMICS AND BUSINESS ADMINISTRATION

International MBA
Augasse 2-6
A-1090 Wien, Austria
Web site: www.wu-wien.ac.at/inst/imba/
E-mail: IMBA@wu-wien.ac.at

Program

Program ranked: International MBA WU-Wien (in conjunction with the University of South Carolina)

Structure: 14 months full-time; divided into two 7-month periods; the first in Vienna includes cross-cultural and communication skills, foundations of international business, management of the global enterprise; in the second at the University of South Carolina participants enroll in 4 graduate-level elective courses in business administration and economics, as well as the capstone course, strategy and policy in the global business enterprise; all students must participate in the summer management consultancy project

Size of class: 50

Participants: Primarily from western and eastern Europe and North America; average age, 28; average work experience, 3 years

Costs: $25,000 tuition; $13,000 estimated living expenses

Program director: Wilhelm Brunner

Accreditation: AACSB through University of South Carolina

Admissions

Admissions requirements: Bachelor's degree or equivalent; 2 years of full-time work; GMAT; TOEFL; 2 letters of recommendation; certified official transcripts in English from every university attended; statement of career objectives; résumé

Applications deadline: November 1

Starting date: May

Application fee: None

Recruiting

Placement office: Personal advice, careers seminars, recruiting on campus

Number of companies recruiting: 150+

Examples of recruiting companies: Henkel, Nestlé, Unilever, Ernst & Young

Contact:
Admissions Office
Phone:
(43) 1 31336 4327/
5311
Fax:
(43) 1 31336 768

BY THE NUMBERS

ADMISSION REQUIRE- MENTS

TOP 20 SCHOOL	APPLICATION FORM	GMAT	TOEFL	LETTERS OF REFERENCE	YEARS' EXPERIENCE
Ashridge	Yes	Yes	Yes	None	5
SDA Bocconi	Yes	Yes	Yes	2	2
Cranfield	Yes	Yes	Yes	None	5
E. M. Lyon	Yes	Yes	Yes	None	Relevant
ESADE	Yes	Yes	Yes	Yes	Relevant
GSBA Zurich	Yes	550	550	3	5
Helsinki	Yes	Yes	550	Yes	3
Henley	Yes	Yes	Yes	Yes	3
Instituto de Empresa	Yes	Yes	Yes	3	3
IESE	Yes	680	620	2	3
IMD	Yes	Yes	Yes	3	3
Imperial College	Yes	550	Yes	None	2
INSEAD	Yes	680	620	2	3
ISA HEC	Yes	640	Yes	Yes	2
Judge Institute	Yes	Yes	Yes	None	Relevant
London Business School	Yes	680	600	Yes	3
Manchester	Yes	Yes	Yes	None	3
Nijenrode	Yes	Yes	Yes	Yes	2
Rotterdam	Yes	Yes	Yes	2	2
Warwick	Yes	Yes	Yes	None	3

BREAKDOWN BY GENDER

TOP 20 SCHOOL	PERCENTAGE MEN	PERCENTAGE WOMEN
Ashridge	71	29
SDA Bocconi	73	27
Cranfield	80	20
E. M. Lyon	80	20
ESADE	64	36
GSBA Zurich	80	20
Helsinki	60	40
Henley	84	16
Instituto de Empresa	60	40
IESE	78	22
IMD	78	22
Imperial College	72	28
INSEAD	80	20
ISA HEC	80	20
Judge Institute	70	30
London Business School	75	25
Manchester	74	26
Nijenrode	71	29
Rotterdam	78	22
Warwick	69	31

Note: Data are from 1997; consequently, they are subject to variations.

ORIGIN OF
STUDENT
BODY

TOP 20 SCHOOL	PERCENTAGE NATIONAL	PERCENTAGE INTERNATIONAL
Ashridge	50	50
SDA Bocconi	55	45
Cranfield	60	40
E. M. Lyon	55	45
ESADE	80	20
GSBA Zurich	35	65
Helsinki	62	38
Henley	50	50
Instituto de Empresa	34	66
IESE	56	44
IMD	5	95
Imperial College	32	68
INSEAD	20	80
ISA HEC	80	20
Judge Institute	20	80
London Business School	20	80
Manchester	30	70
Nijenrode	32	68
Rotterdam	15	85
Warwick	50	50

LENGTH OF PROGRAM

TOP 20 SCHOOL	MONTHS
Ashridge	10
SDA Bocconi	16
Cranfield	12
E. M. Lyon	12
ESADE	24
GSBA Zurich	24
Helsinki	12
Henley	12
Instituto de Empresa	15
IESE	21
IMD	11
Imperial College	12
INSEAD	12
ISA HEC	16
Judge Institute	12
London Business School	21
Manchester	18
Nijenrode	13
Rotterdam	18
Warwick	12

AGE OF STUDENT BODY

TOP 20 SCHOOL	AVERAGE AGE
Ashridge	34
SDA Bocconi	29
Cranfield	31
E. M. Lyon	30
ESADE	26
GSBA Zurich	28
Helsinki	29
Henley	33
Instituto de Empresa	27
IESE	27
IMD	31
Imperial College	29
INSEAD	30
ISA HEC	29
Judge Institute	29
London Business School	29
Manchester	28
Nijenrode	28
Rotterdam	28
Warwick	29

TOP 20 SCHOOL	AVERAGE YEARS' EXPERIENCE
Ashridge	12
SDA Bocconi	3
Cranfield	9
E. M. Lyon	7
ESADE	2
GSBA Zurich	6
Helsinki	3
Henley	6
Instituto de Empresa	3
IESE	3
IMD	7
Imperial College	3
INSEAD	5
ISA HEC	4
Judge Institute	5
London Business School	6
Manchester	5
Nijenrode	5
Rotterdam	2
Warwick	5

STUDENT
WORK
EXPERIENCE

SIZE OF CLASS

TOP 20 SCHOOL	STUDENTS PER YEAR
Ashridge	30
SDA Bocconi	130
Cranfield	50
E. M. Lyon	86
ESADE	125
GSBA Zurich	250
Helsinki	80
Henley	46
Instituto de Empresa	110
IESE	220
IMD	83
Imperial College	150
INSEAD	650
ISA HEC	250
Judge Institute	80
London Business School	70
Manchester	130
Nijenrode	60
Rotterdam	120
Warwick	60

ACCREDITA-TIONS

TOP 20 SCHOOL	AMBA	EQUIS	AASCB
Ashridge	Yes	Yes	No
SDA Bocconi	Yes	Yes	No
Cranfield	Yes	Yes	No
E. M. Lyon	Yes	Yes	No
ESADE	Yes	Yes	No
GSBA Zurich	No	No	Yes
Helsinki	Yes	Yes	No
Henley	Yes	No	No
Instituto de Empresa	Yes	Yes	No
IESE	Yes	Yes	No
IMD	Yes	Yes	No
Imperial College	Yes	No	No
INSEAD	Yes	Yes	No
ISA HEC	Yes	Yes	No
Judge Institute	Yes	No	No
London Business School	Yes	Yes	No
Manchester	Yes	No	No
Nijenrode	Yes	No	No
Rotterdam	Yes	Yes	Yes
Warwick	Yes	No	Yes

TUITION FEES

TOP 20 SCHOOL	U.S. DOLLARS
Ashridge	33,060
SDA Bocconi	20,000
Cranfield	29,834
E. M. Lyon	15,837
ESADE	27,650
GSBA Zurich	31,070
Helsinki	11,450
Henley	26,852
Instituto de Empresa	20,245
IESE	29,450
IMD	26,775
Imperial College	21,970
INSEAD	26,700
ISA HEC	20,950
Judge Institute	34,990
London Business School	50,797
Manchester	29,027
Nijenrode	19,512
Rotterdam	22,500
Warwick	27,415

A SAMPLE OF BUSINESS SCHOOOLS IN EASTERN EUROPE

COUNTRY	INSTITUTION	WEB SITE
Czech Republic	CMC Graduate School of Business	www.anet.cz/cmc/
Hungary	IMC Graduate School of Business	www.imc.hu
Poland	Leon Kozminski Academy of Entrepreneurship & Management	www.spiz.ed.pl
Romania	American Business School	www.asebuss.ae.ro
Russia	International Management School of St. Petersburg	www.wplus/pp/imisp/
Slovenia	University of Ljubljana Business School	www.ijs.si/slo/ljubljana

THE RANKING METHODOLOGY

OBJECTIVE AND FRAMEWORK OF THIS STUDY

This report aims to establish the most important differences in the appreciation that recruiters and both potential and current students have of European business schools. The report is centered on a group of the better-known and most prestigious business schools in Europe.

One of the fundamental problems with this type of study lies in the difficulty of finding individuals who have some knowledge, or even a vague idea, of all the schools in question. Generally speaking, one person can only provide information on a very small group of schools that he or she knows fairly well, but not all those that are included in the analysis. This means that the results of studies of this type may often be biased in one way or another.

METHODOLOGY

It was therefore essential that a special kind of methodology be used to overcome this type of problem. The result was a synthesis of methodologies which are described here in two sections: The first section deals with the content and processes involved in the survey, and the second section covers data analysis techniques.

THE SURVEY

The unusual methods employed in the course of this study began with the survey. The strategy consisted of carrying out separate surveys among the three main elements that make up this market: recruiters, potential students, and the business schools themselves.

Thus, it was possible to obtain a profile of what aspects or characteristics recruiters consider to be the most important, and what potential students are looking for. The business schools' contribution was based on the global content of the programs they offer, along with entry requirements and objective quality-related features.

The questionnaires aimed at recruiters and potential students provided evaluations of those characteristics or aspects that each of the two groups considered to be of interest. These evaluations were used to translate the characteristics of the different schools into a point-scoring system, and the score obtained by each one was the basis of the comparative analysis of the business schools included in the study.

The survey aimed at recruiters in organizations with a high demand for MBAs centered on aspects such as:

- Policies regarding the recruitment of MBA graduates
- Experiences with MBA graduates
- Qualities they look for in an MBA graduate
- Qualities they look for in a business school
- Future intentions with regard to the hiring of MBAs

Recruiters were also requested to indicate the stance of their clients with respect to the above points. The recruiter survey included the major European management consultancies and their clients in all industries. Thirty-one consultancies in all major European countries (EU and non-EU) completed the highly detailed questionnaire. The consultancies were mainly the European headquarters of the respective firms and responded for all of their offices. Given that consultancies are perhaps the largest recruiters of MBAs and they have intimate insight into their clients' recruiting patterns, the survey results reveal a lot about European recruitment of MBAs. The recruiter survey was jointly carried out with Management Consultant International.

The content of the survey aimed at candidates or potential students obviously had to be different. The main items were:

- The most appropriate country to carry out an MBA program
- Optimum structure and duration for an MBA program
- Evaluation of the teaching methods and learning processes (theory, practical work, case studies, electives, subjects, etc.)
- Exchange programs
- Qualification of the teaching faculty and research activities
- Language used in the classroom and other language skills
- How the school is run, national and international renown
- Funding a program

Over 200 students/potential applicants took part in the survey, of which 50 percent were from the field of economics and business

> The recruiter survey included 31 major European consultancies in all major European countries.

studies. The remaining 50 percent were studying or working in the field of civil engineering, math, chemistry, biology, medicine, design, etc. With regard to the age of the participants in this survey, the majority, some 90 percent, were aged between 21 and 27 years old, and 25 percent were women. The student/potential applicant survey was jointly carried out with *Audimax*, the monthly magazine with the largest circulation among university students (over 400,000).

The content of the surveys aimed at business schools covered three main areas:

- Questions related to the investment (time and expense) involved in undertaking a master's at the school, what financial aid was available, and what increase in income the participant could expect on completion of the program.
- Aspects related to the international character of the school, its program content, faculty, student body, etc.
- A series of items related to the excellence and quality of the program, entry requirements, links with the business community, etc.

ANALYSIS

The surveys directed at recruiters and potential students were used as a basis on which to estimate the importance, in their opinion, of a series of typical characteristics of a business school. These evaluations were used to translate the qualities and aspects of the different business schools into ratings.

The analysis is based exclusively on those features that were present in all the schools included in survey and which could therefore be evaluated based on the results of the survey questions aimed at recruiters and potential students. These limitations led to the inclusion of 15 variables:

1. Cost of enrollment
2. Duration of the program
3. Average salary on completion of the program
4. Financial aid and scholarships
5. Proportion of case studies related to global organizations
6. Number of nationalities in the student body
7. Use and acquisition of foreign languages
8. Different nationalities present among the teaching faculty

9. Projects offered in other countries
10. Number of international organizations that recruit MBAs from the program
11. Accreditations awarded to the program
12. Accreditations awarded to the school
13. Prestige among the national business community
14. Prestige among the international business community
15. Entry requirements (GMAT score, TOEFL score, years of experience, etc.)

The analysis of these scores was carried out with the intention of finding the combination of variables that made it possible to observe more easily the different scores that the business schools in the survey received for the variables listed above, that is, an axis that contained the maximum projected variant.

RESULTS OF ANALYSIS

The combination of variables that made it possible to achieve the desired objective via the method of analysis follows. The 15 variables have been placed in order of importance, according to their contribution to the definition of the most desirable combination.

- 10% Prestige among the national business community
- 10% Proportion of case studies related to global organization
- 9% Prestige among the international business community
- 9% Average salary on completion of the program
- 9% Different nationalities present among the teaching faculty
- 9% Entry requirements (GMAT score, TOEFL score, years of experience, etc.)
- 8% Number of nationalities in the student body.
- 8% Number of international organizations that recruit MBAs from the program
- 8% Projects offered in other countries
- 7% Financial aid and scholarships
- 6% Use of and learning process for foreign languages
- 3% Accreditations awarded to the program
- 3% Accreditations awarded to the school
- 1% Cost of enrollment
- 0% Duration of the program (contribution is less than 1%)

SCORES OBTAINED BY THE DIFFERENT BUSINESS SCHOOLS

SCORE	BUSINESS SCHOOL
965	INSEAD
961	London Business School
943	IMD
863	Rotterdam
854	Instituto de Empresa
848	Manchester
838	IESE
814	ISA HEC
806	Ashridge
763	SDA Bocconi
757	Cranfield
682	Nijenrode
669	GSBA Zurich
655	Warwick
616	E.M. Lyon
589	Henley
554	Judge Institute
528	ESADE
472	Imperial
470	Helsinki

THE MBA IN THE EUROPEAN CONSULTANCY BUSINESS

THE SURVEY METHOD

Together with the publication Management Consultant International, Cox Communications Consultants GmbH developed an extensive questionnaire consisting of two sections and covering 132 areas. The first section addressed the policies and attitudes of consulting firms toward MBAs and MBA schools. The second section covered the same points but from the viewpoint of the consultants' clients. The areas addressed included the following:

- Recruiting practices with regard to MBAs
- Experiences with MBAs
- Personal characteristics of MBAs
- Characteristics business schools should possess
- Plans with respect to MBAs

Cox Communications sent questionnaires to 250 consultancies in all the main European countries. Then Cox conducted three further follow-up mailings and two weeks of telephone follow-up work. Thirty-two major consultancies replied to the questionnaires.

The questionnaire consisted largely of closed questions in each area. Each question could be given 0, 1, 2, or 3 points, whereby 3 points was the highest number possible and indicated a strong agreement. The total number of points were added up for each area. The highest possible number of points for areas in the consultant section was 96. In the client section the highest was 53 points.

CONSULTANTS ARE THE LARGEST MBA RECRUITERS

Management consultancies are among the largest recruiters of persons with master of business administration (MBA) degrees, both in absolute terms and on a per capita employee basis. Perhaps the main reason is that business schools teach exactly what consultancies need: problem solving, strategy, creativity, internationalism, and project-oriented thinking. MBA graduates can be hired from business schools and directly employed in project teams at consultancies. In business school the students learn how to solve problems in hundreds of case studies in every business sector, which is what they are expected to do as consultants.

SURVEY PARTICIPANTS

Together with the specialized publication Management Consultant International of Lafferty Publications (London), we surveyed the large European consulting firms to determine recruiter attitudes. In a detailed questionnaire covering 132 areas, we asked the consultancies to tell us about their own policies and those of their clients toward MBAs and business schools.

SURVEY RESULTS

INCREASED RECRUITMENT OF MBAS IN EUROPE

Both consultancies and their clients plan to expand their recruitment of people with MBAs—in some cases quite strongly. Several consultancies reveal that they plan to hire over 100 MBAs next year. The 32 firms surveyed intend to recruit over 400 MBAs in total next year. Consultants' clients also plan to extend their recruitment of MBAs.

HIGH SATISFACTION WITH MBAS

Both consultancies and their clients think that MBAs are worth their money and generate profits for their companies. They need less training and, contrary to expectations, are not inclined to do much job hopping. However, the consensus is that they are more expensive than persons with other degrees.

MBAS ARE CREATIVE, SELF-CONFIDENT, AND ENTREPRENEURIAL

The highest scores in this survey are allocated to the strong "people skills" of MBAs. They are team players, self-confident, and creative, and they possess strong cross-cultural skills. They also are entrepreneurial and analytic. These skills are more important than a broad knowledge of business disciplines.

PREFERRED: ONE-YEAR FULL-TIME PROGRAMS TAUGHT IN ENGLISH AND A FOREIGN LANGUAGE

With respect to how an MBA program should be structured, both consultancies and clients strongly prefer one-year full-time programs, such as those of INSEAD, IMD, and Instituto de Empresa. A program should be bilingual and nationally and internationally reputed, and it should do well in rankings. Courses in entrepreneurship and mergers and acquisitions are important. The teaching approaches should be practical (hands on), and classes should be small. Much less important are courses on mid-sized firms. Although all agreed that one-year full-time programs were best, client firms preferred part-time programs over two-year full-time MBAs. Consultants gave two-year full-time programs second place. Top American schools were hardly mentioned. Harvard was not listed once. Stanford, Northwestern, and a few others received only one point. European firms seem to prefer European business schools. The reasons probably include that the U.S. programs are "too American" and too long (two years).

VIEWS OF MANAGEMENT CONSULT- ANCIES TOWARD MBAS

RECRUITING PRACTICES WITH REGARD TO MBAS

Most participants like to hire MBAs directly from business schools (61 points), of which the majority (52 points) hire from *specific* schools. The most popular schools include INSEAD, London Business School, and IMD—all schools which themselves claim that consultancies are either their largest or among their largest employers.

While the majority (51 points) prefer people entering the firm to have MBA degrees, nearly as many consultancies (47 points) are willing to pay for their employees to get an MBA. Those employees participating in part-time or executive MBA programs would still be working as consultants while going for their MBA degrees. Moreover, sponsored employees are likely to be people with specialized knowledge and/or extraordinary promise.

Nearly half of the respondents said that their recruitment of MBAs has increased over the past years (43 points).

Connections between consultancies and business schools are improving, with 26 out of 32 consultancies citing that they occasionally teach at business schools. However, these teaching engagements are relatively rare. The total number of points given to support of business schools amounted to only 47 out of 96 possible.

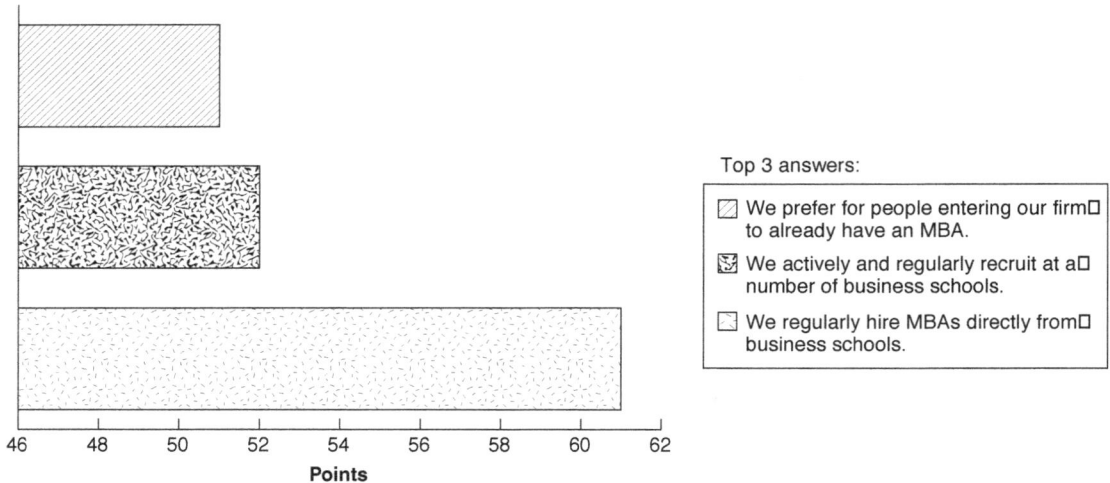

Top 3 answers:

- ▨ We prefer for people entering our firm to already have an MBA.
- ▧ We actively and regularly recruit at a number of business schools.
- ▢ We regularly hire MBAs directly from business schools.

EXPERIENCES WITH MBAs

The strongest consensus is that people with MBA degrees are more expensive than persons with other degrees (70 points). No firm disagrees with this statement while 16 firms strongly agreed. However, the higher costs seem to be justified. Most claim that MBAs are profitable for the consultancies (57 points) and that they need less on-the-job training than those lacking MBA degrees (55 points). In sum, consultancies feel that "MBAs are worth their salaries" (52 points) and that their "clients like MBAs" (51 points). Only one firm thought that clients did not like MBAs.

Surprisingly, the surveyed firms do not believe that MBAs need to work long hours. This area only receives 45 points. On the other hand, there is no strong support for the belief that MBAs do a lot of job hopping and do not remain with the firm for a long time. This aspect only gets 39 points.

PERSONAL CHARACTERISTICS OF MBAs

MBAs are expected to possess "soft" skills rather than knowledge. The surveyed consultancies agree strongly that MBA graduates should be self-confident, good at analysis and synthesis, and able to think conceptually. MBAs' team-working abilities (79 points out of 80 points maximum), creativity (77 points), and entrepreneurial skills (75 points) are considered most important, and cross-cultural skills are also considered highly important.

Consultancies think that people skills are more important than "practical knowledge of major management disciplines." This

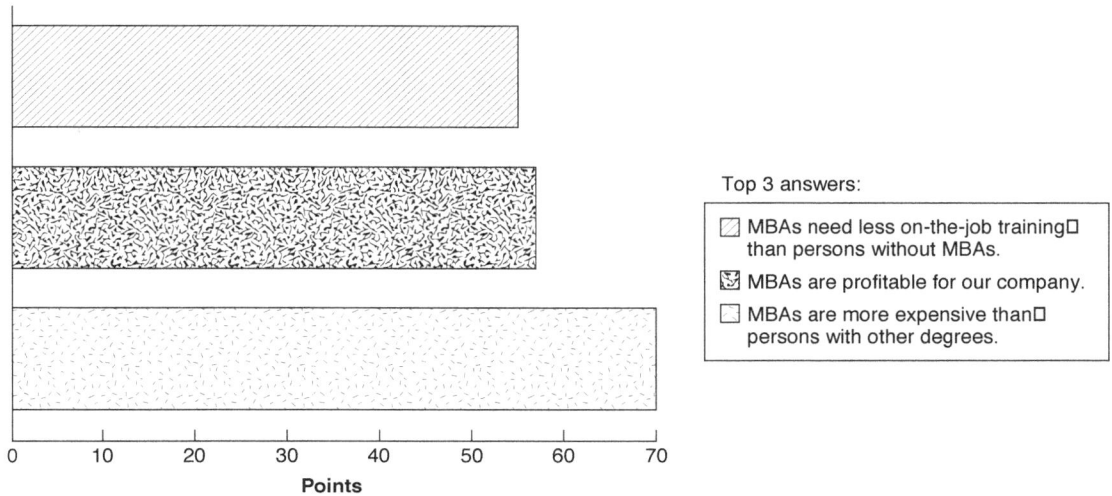

Top 3 answers:

☐ MBAs need less on-the-job training☐ than persons without MBAs.

☑ MBAs are profitable for our company.

☐ MBAs are more expensive than☐ persons with other degrees.

point scores lowest of all in this category (58 points). Surprising, the ability to use information technologies scores second lowest in this question (65 points).

Other characteristics ascribed to MBAs are:

- Cross-cultural skills (74 points)
- Decision-making and problem-solving skills (72 points)
- Knowing how to search for information (72 points)
- Integrity (69 points)
- Persuasive power (69 points)
- Identification with your company (68 points)
- People management (61 points)

CHARACTERISTICS BUSINESS SCHOOLS SHOULD POSSESS

This area addresses twenty business school characteristics, ranging from the MBA program structure (e.g., full-time one-year) to which specializations a program should offer (e.g., entrepreneurship).

MBA PROGRAM STRUCTURE AND LENGTH

Full-time MBA programs lasting roughly one year are the most popular MBA form (66 points). Europe has more or less pioneered this type of compact and intensive program, which contrasts with the traditional American two-year programs. Typical one-year programs include those of INSEAD, IMD, and Instituto de Empresa. These programs are short but intensive. Their philosophy is that an MBA should not interrupt one's career for too long because most applicants already have several years work experience and cannot afford to be away from the job world for a long time. This can mean a very scaled-down program, like INSEAD's, in which only core courses are covered in some depth. Or they can be programs which include extensive consulting projects (IMD) and entrepreneurial projects (Instituto de Empresa).

The second most popular (58 points) are two-year full-time MBAs such as those of London Business School, IESE, ISA-HEC, and Rotterdam. These programs involve exchange programs with other schools and allow students the time for more elective courses.

The final category are part-time programs (47 points). Part-time programs can be evening (London Business School), or weekend or modular (GSBA Zurich, WHU Koblenz). Their advantage is that students need not interrupt their careers and that in the case of modular programs, they need not necessarily live in the same city or country as the business school.

SCHOOL REPUTATION

A program must not just be good, it must be reputed. The consultancies gave the need for a strong international reputation 79 points. For more nationally oriented consulting firms, a school's national reputation is important (52 points). They also expressed strong preference for top European schools (65 points) over top American schools (53 points). All consultancies surveyed think schools should do well in rankings. Only four firms believe that rankings are less important. Schools with particularly strong international reputations include INSEAD, IMD, and London Business School. However, other schools with strong national reputations are gaining more global acclaim, e.g., Bocconi (Italy).

CURRICULUM

European consultancies still believe in the importance of language skills, given that most projects have national and interna-

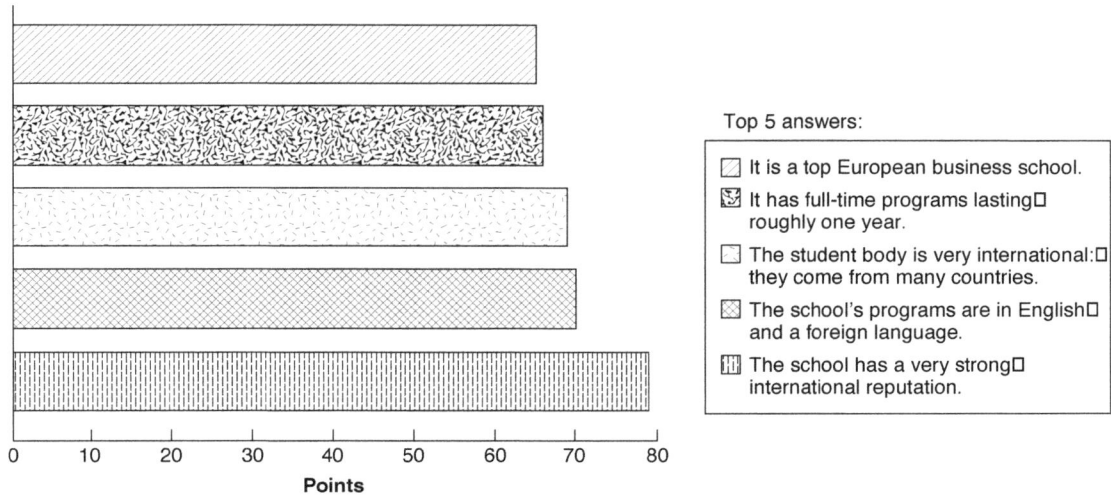

Top 5 answers:

- ☐ It is a top European business school.
- ☒ It has full-time programs lasting☐ roughly one year.
- ☐ The student body is very international:☐ they come from many countries.
- ☒ The school's programs are in English☐ and a foreign language.
- ☒ The school has a very strong☐ international reputation.

tional importance and client relations are often cultivated in the national language. Thus, MBA programs should be in English and a foreign language. Strongly bilingual programs can normally be found in countries with large domestic markets and clients such as Spain, France, and Germany. As such, strongly bilingual schools include Instituto de Empresa, IESE (both in Spain), ISA HEC (France), and GSBA Zurich/WHU Koblenz (Switzerland/ Germany).

Schools should offer courses in entrepreneurship (50 points) and mergers and acquisitions (47 points). The teaching approach should be "very practical" (62 points). "Very practical" normally means in-company projects or writing one's own business plan. In short, students should apply what they learn as they learn it. Classes should be small with up to 40 persons (64 points). Small classes improve the quality and intensity of the learning experience. Students get more chances to participate in class and are closer to the faculty. Perhaps to improve profit margins, many schools hold larger courses, while others stick to a 30 to 40 student maximum. Cambridge, for example, claims to have many small classes of around 10 students.

Courses on mid-sized companies (38) are less preferred by the blue-chip–oriented companies.

STUDENT BODY

An international student body is perhaps the most important aspect in acquiring a truly international business education, because MBA students participate frequently in class discussions and work in small project groups of roughly four people with other students. Resolving conflicts and generating a commonly acceptable result among students with different cultural, educational, and professional backgrounds is an important skill. Accordingly, an international student body receives 69 points.

SERVICES OFFERED BY BUSINESS SCHOOLS

Schools should have a large number of alumni (47). The big and famous schools, such as INSEAD and London, have nearly 20,000 alumni. These alumni can be found in companies around the world and in all industries. However, INSEAD, in particular, is known to graduate students mainly into the consulting business, while schools such as Instituto de Empresa, Manchester Business School, and Rotterdam supply various industries and service sectors with MBAs. Oddly, consultancies do not think that a professional alumni office, which normally makes the connection between MBA students and prospective employers, is very important (36 points). Interestingly, consultancies find it important (54 points) that schools offer executive development programs for more senior managers (short courses). These programs often serve to help the faculty keep in touch with business reality and further the schools' connections with the business world. Most top schools offer significant executive training. In particular INSEAD, IMD, London, Instituto de Empresa, IESE, and Ashridge are known to offer wide varieties of corporate training programs to blue-chip firms around Europe.

PLANS WITH RESPECT TO MBAS

Consultancies clearly plan to hire more MBAs in the future. Of the 32 consultancies that responded, 11 plan to strongly expand their hiring activities, 14 to increase their recruiting, and 3 firms want to only marginally raise recruiting efforts of MBAs. When asked how many MBAs they planned to hire annually in the future, one consultancy plans to hire 120, one 100, one 50, three 30, one 25, and two 15 MBAs. In total, the 32 companies surveyed intend to hire 415 MBAs next year.

When asked about which previous educational backgrounds

MBAs should have, the responses are as diverse as the number of educations available. However, many cite technical and scientific degrees such as engineering and information technology as ideal pre-MBA backgrounds.

VIEWS OF CONSULT-ANCIES' CLIENTS TOWARD MBAS

INDUSTRY SECTORS REPRESENTED

In this section, consultancies were invited to cite the likely attitudes of their clients toward MBAs. Although not all firms participating in the survey could fully respond, a wide range of industries in key European countries are represented, including:

- Small and mid-sized firms in Finland
- Services sectors in Switzerland
- Manufacturing in Germany
- Various industries in Scandinavia
- Banking in Switzerland
- Telecommunications in Europe
- Consumer and retail in the UK
- Finance in the UK and Europe
- Small and mid-sized firms in the Netherlands
- Telecommunications in France
- Mechanical engineering in Europe

RECRUITING POLICIES

Clients recruit both directly at business schools (40 points) and at particular business schools (39). Like the consultancies themselves, consultants' clients mostly recruit at INSEAD, London Business School, and IMD. Following this top group is an array of most of the best-known business schools in Europe.

Unlike the consultancies, clients prefer that people entering their firms already have MBA degrees (37 points). Only seven consultancies say that their clients would not pay for their people to go for MBAs. The total number of points for "clients paying for MBAs" is only 27—one of the lowest in this survey. However, clients have increased their recruitment of MBAs over the years (39 points). And some clients occasionally teach at business schools (32 points).

EXPERIENCES WITH MBAS

Clients think that MBAs are more expensive than persons with other degrees (53 points), can work long hours (45 points), and

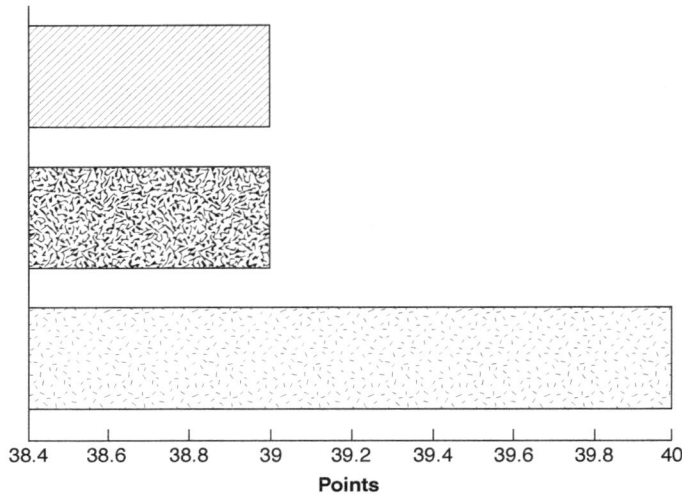

Top 3 answers:

- ▨ Clients' recruitment of MBAs has increased over the past years.
- ▨ Clients actively and regularly recruit at a number of business schools.
- ☐ Clients regularly hire MBAs directly from business schools.

are profitable for their companies (44 points). MBAs need less on-the-job training than those without MBAs (41 points), and consultancies are convinced that clients like MBAs (42 points).

PERSONAL
CHARACTERISTICS
OF MBAS

Analysis and synthesis skills (57 points), self-confidence (53 points), team ability (52 points), conceptual thinking (52 points), use of information technologies (51 points), knowing how to

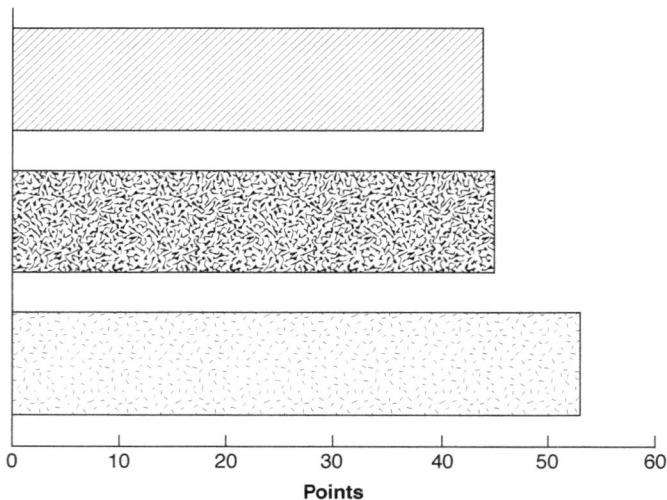

Top 3 answers:

- ▨ MBAs are profitable for the company.
- ▨ MBAs can work long hours.
- ☐ MBAs are more expensive than persons with other degrees.

search for information (51 points), cross-cultural skills (50), and decision-making and problem-solving skills (50 points) are characteristics which clients believe that MBAs possess. These results are practically identical to those of the consultancies own views of MBAs. Clients supposedly also think that MBAs have relatively little practical knowledge of major management disciplines.

Other important characteristics of MBAs are:

- Integrity (45 points)
- Creativity (45 points)
- Persuasive power (45 points)
- Identification with your company (44 points)
- Entrepreneurial skills (43 points)
- People management (42 points)
- Practical knowledge of major management disciplines (39 points)

CHARACTERISTICS BUSINESS SCHOOLS SHOULD POSSESS

MBA PROGRAM STRUCTURE AND LENGTH

Here too the one-year full-time MBA programs are most preferred (46 points). This time they are followed by part-time programs (37 points) and full-time two-year programs (25 points). Accordingly, clients are even more critical than consultancies toward

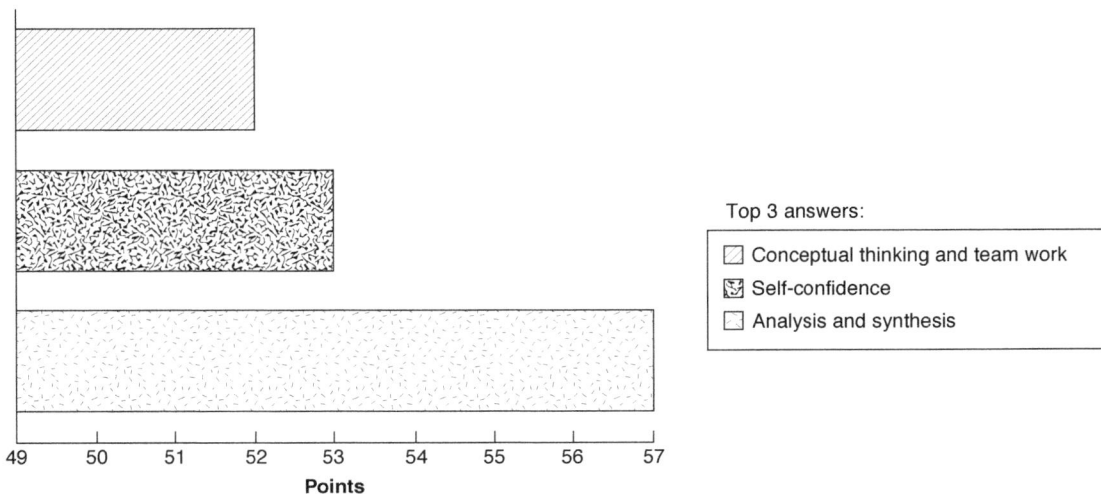

Top 3 answers:

☑ Conceptual thinking and team work
☒ Self-confidence
☐ Analysis and synthesis

Points

long, two-year MBA programs like those offered by London Business School, IESE, Rotterdam, and most American schools. Clients prefer short full-time or part-time MBA programs.

SCHOOL REPUTATION

Clients think that a school's national and international reputation are equally important (both 40 points). This suggests that clients are more nationally oriented than the consultancies. While consultants quickly move from one project to another, MBAs at client firms retain fixed (national) responsibilities longer. Top European schools are preferable (43 points) over their American counterparts (38 points).

CURRICULUM, STUDENT BODY, AND SERVICES OFFERED BY BUSINESS SCHOOLS

The preferences among clients in these areas are largely the same as those by the consultancies themselves: MBA programs should be in English and a foreign language (44 points); the teaching approach should be very practical (42 points); and courses in entrepreneurship should be required (36 points). Unlike consul-

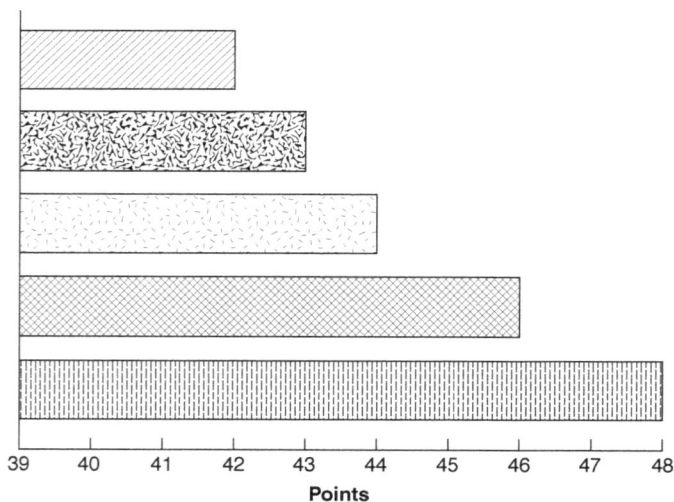

Top 5 answers:

- The school has a very practical teaching and learning approach.
- It is a top European business school.
- The school's programs are in English and a foreign language.
- It has full-time programs lasting one year or less.
- The school also offers many short courses for companies and executives.

Points

tants, clients do not think courses on mergers and acquisitions are that important (26 points). Clients are less likely to have much to do with mergers and acquisitions.

Clients moderately feel that the student body must be international and come from many countries (35 points). Equally, the number of alumni a school should have is not that important (32 points).

However, clients feel very strongly about the need that a school offer executive development courses (48 points), not just MBA programs. Placement offices are not seen as being very crucial (30 points).

PLANS WITH RESPECT TO MBAS

While clients also intend to hire more MBAs than before (40 points), they do not plan to change or expand the group of business schools from which they currently recruit MBAs (26 points).

These schools are also those preferred by consultants, such as INSEAD, IMD, and London Business School. However, clients give slightly higher scores to other, more national schools, such as Italy's Bocconi or Rotterdam, than do the consultants. Surprisingly, of the 22 top schools assessed by both consultants and their clients, the Manchester Business School, one of the UK's top schools, received the fewest points. Except for London Business School, the UK schools, including Ashridge, Cambridge (Judge), Cranfield, Henley, Oxford (Said), and Warwick received low scores, in several cases of only three points.

The top American schools do worst of all. Harvard is not mentioned once. Northwestern, California (Los Angeles), Wharton (Pennsylvania), Sloan (MIT), and Stanford all receive only one point. The overall orientation is clearly toward European business schools.

LISTING OF 50 LEADING EUROPEAN BUSINESS SCHOOLS

DENMARK	COPENHAGEN BUSINESS SCHOOL Solbjerg Plads 3 2000 Frederiksberg Tel: 45-38-153815 Fax: 45-38-152015 Web site: http://www.cbs.dk
ENGLAND/ **UNITED KINGDOM**	ANGLIA POLYTECHNIC UNIVERSITY ANGLIA BUSINESS SCHOOL Danbury Park Conference Centre Main Road, Danbury Chelmsford, Essex CM3 4AT Tel: 44-1480-323116 Fax: 44-1480-323011 Web site: http://www.anglianwater.co.uk/ ASTON UNIVERSITY ASTON BUSINESS SCHOOL Aston Triangle Birmingham B4 7ET Tel: 44-121-3593011 Fax: 44-121-3335774 Web site: http://www.aston.ac.uk/home.html THE BIRMINGHAM BUSINESS SCHOOL 46 Edgbaston Park Road Edgbaston Birmingham B15 3RT

Tel: 44-121-4146693
Fax: 44-121-4143553
Web site: http://www.bham.ac.uk/business

DE MONTFORT UNIVERSITY
SCHOOL OF BUSINESS AND LAW

The Gateway
Leicester LE1 9BH

Tel: 44-116-2577228
Fax: 44-116-2517548
Web site: http://www.dmu.ac.uk

DURHAM UNIVERSITY BUSINESS SCHOOL (DUBS)

Mill Hill Lane
Durham DH1 3LB

Tel: 44-191-3742211
Fax: 44-191-3743748
E-mail: mso.dubs@durham.ac.uk
Web site: http://www.dur.ac.uk/dubs/

KINGSTON UNIVERSITY
KINGSTON BUSINESS SCHOOL

Kingston Hill
Kingston-upon-Thames KT2 7LB

Tel: 44-208-5472000
Fax: 44-208-5477026
Web site: http://www.king.ac.uk

LANCASTER UNIVERSITY
THE MANAGEMENT SCHOOL

Lancaster
Lancashire LA1 4YX

Tel: 44-152-4593998
Fax: 44-152-43811454
Web site: http://www.lancs.ac.uk/users/manschool/

LEICESTER UNIVERSITY
MANAGEMENT CENTRE

The New Building
University of Leicester
University Road
Leicester LE1 7RH

Tel: 44-116-2525520
Fax: 44-116-2523949
Web site: http://www.leicester.ac.uk/lumc

LOUGHBOROUGH UNIVERSITY BUSINESS SCHOOL

Ashby Road
Loughborough, Leicestershire LE11 3TU

Tel: 44-150-9223147
Fax: 44-150-9223961
Web site: http://www.lboro.ac.uk/

MANCHESTER METROPOLITAN UNIVERSITY
FACULTY OF MANAGEMENT AND BUSINESS

Aytoun Building
Aytoun Street
Manchester M1 3GH

Tel: 44-161-2473701
Fax: 44-161-2476350
E-mail: m.b.faculty@mmu.ac.uk
Web site: http://www.man-bus.mmu.ac.uk

MIDDLESEX UNIVERSITY BUSINESS SCHOOL

The Burroughs
London NW4 4BT

Tel: 44-181-3625783
Fax: 44-181-3626011
Web site: http://www.mdx.ac.uk

OPEN UNIVERSITY BUSINESS SCHOOL
OPEN UNIVERSITY

Walton Hall
Milton Keynes MK7 6AA

Tel: 44-190-8655888
Fax: 44-190-8655898
Web site: http://www.oubs.open.ac.uk

THE ROBERT GORDON UNIVERSITY
ABERDEEN BUSINESS SCHOOL

Garthdee Road
Aberdeen AB10 7QE

Tel: 44-122-4263800
Fax: 44-122-4263838
Web site: http://www.abs.ac.uk

SHEFFIELD HALLAM UNIVERSITY
SHEFFIELD BUSINESS SCHOOL

Stoddard Building, City Campus
Sheffield S1 1WB

Tel: 44-114-2252820
Fax: 44-114-2255269
Web site: http://www.shu.ac.uk

UNIVERSITY OF BATH
THE SCHOOL OF MANAGEMENT

Bath BA2. 7AY

Tel: 44-122-5826742
Fax: 44-122-5826473
Web site: http://www.bath.ac.uk

UNIVERSITY OF BRADFORD MANAGEMENT CENTER

Emm Lane
Bradford, West Yorkshire BD9 4JL

Tel: 44-127-4234393
Fax: 44-127-4546866
Web site: http://www.brad.ac.uk

UNIVERSITY OF GREENWICH BUSINESS SCHOOL

Woolwich University Campus
Wellington Street
Woolwich, London SE18 6BU

Tel: 44-181-3319770
Fax: 44-181-3319616
Web site: http://www.greenwich.ac.uk/

UNIVERSITY OF LEEDS
LEEDS UNIVERSITY BUSINESS SCHOOL

Leeds, West Yorkshire LS2 9JT

Tel: 44-113-2334501
Fax: 44-113-2334355
E-mail: patmc@lubs.leeds.ac.uk
Web site: http://www.inst-mgt.org.uk

UNIVERSITY OF NEWCASTLE SCHOOL OF MANAGEMENT

Armstrong Building
University of Newcastle
Newcastle upon Tyne NE1 7RV

Tel: 44-191-2227440
Fax: 44-191-2228131
Web site: http://www.ncl.ac.uk/mgt

UNIVERSITY OF READING, THE MANAGEMENT UNIT

Building 22
London Road
Reading RG1 5AQ

Tel: 44-118-931-8180
Fax: 44-118-931-6539
Web site: http://www.rdg.ac.uk/mgt

UNIVERSITY OF SURREY
SURREY EUROPEAN MANAGEMENT SCHOOL (SEM)

Guildford
Surrey QUZ 5XH

Tel: 44-1483-259347
Fax: 44-1483-259511
E-mail: sems@surrey.ac.uk
Web site: http://www.sems.surrey.ac.uk

UNIVERSITY OF ULSTER MANAGEMENT INSTITUTE
FACULTY OF ULSTER BUSINESS SCHOOL

Shore Road
Newtownabbey
Co. Antrim BT37 0QB

Tel: 44-1232-368087
Fax: 44-1232-366843
Web site: http://www.ulst.ac.uk/

UNIVERSITY OF THE WEST OF ENGLAND
BRISTOL BUSINESS SCHOOL

Frenchay Campus
Coldharbour Lane
Bristol BS16 1QY

Tel: 44-117-9656261
Fax: 44-117-9763851
Web site: http://www.uwe.ac.uk/

UNIVERSITY OF WESTMINSTER
WESTMINSTER BUSINESS SCHOOL & HARROW BUSINESS
SCHOOL

35, Marylebone Road
London NW1 5LS

Tel: 44-171-9115000
Web site: http://www.wmin.ac.uk

FRANCE

CERAM SOPHIA ANTIPOLIS

B.P. 085
06902 Sophia Antipolis Cédex

Tel: 33-4-93954545
Fax: 33-3-20271294
E-mail: programme-esc@ceram.fr
Web site: http://www.ceram.fr/

ECOLE DE HAUTES ETUDES COMMERCIALES DU NORD
(EDHEC)

Rue du Port, 58
59046 Lille Cédex

Tel: 33-3-20154507
Fax: 33-3-20154508
E-mail: groupe@edu.edhec.asso.fr
Web site: http://www.edhec.asso.fr

ECOLE NATIONALE DES PONTS ET CHAUSSÉES (ENPC)

28, rue des Saints-Pères
75343 Paris, Cédex 07

Tel: 33-1-44582852
Fax: 33-1-40159347
E-mail: mib.admit@mail.enpc.fr
Web site: http://www.enpc.fr

ECOLE SUPÉRIEURE DE COMMERCE DE BORDEAUX (GROUPE)

Domaine de Raba
680 Cours de la Libération
33405 Talence Cédex

Tel: 33-5-56845555
Fax: 33-5-56845500
E-mail: Groupe.esc@esc-bordeaux.fr
Web site: http://www.esc-bordeaux.fr

ECOLE SUPÉRIEURE DE COMMERCE DE GRENOBLE (GROUPE)

Europole
12 rue Pierre Sémard—B.P. 127
38003 Grenoble Cédex 01

Tel: 33-4-76706060
Fax: 33-4-76706099
Web site: http://www.esc-grenoble.fr/esc.htm

ECOLE SUPÉRIEURE DE COMMERCE DE NANTES
ATLANTIQUE (GROUPE) (ESCNA)

Route de la Jonelière 8
B.P. 31222
44312 Nantes Cédex 3

Tel: 33-2-40373434
Fax: 33-2-40374530
Web site: http://www.escna.fr

ECOLE SUPÉRIEURE DE COMMERCE DE TOULOUSE
(GROUPE)

Boulevard Lascrosses, 20
31068 Toulouse Cédex 7

Tel: 33-5-61294949
Fax: 33-5-61294994
E-mail: info@esc-toulouse.fr
Web site: http://www.esc-toulouse.fr

INSTITUT D'ETUDES POLITIQUES DE PARIS (IEP)
MBA SCIENCES PO

27, rue Saint-Guillaume
75337 Paris Cédex 07

Tel: 33-1-45495050
Fax: 33-1-45496640
Web site: http://www.sciences-po.fr

THESEUS INSTITUTE

Rue Albert Einstein
BP 169
06903 Sophia Antipolis Cédex

Tel: 33-4-92945100
Fax: 33-4-67451356

E-mail: Info@theseus.fr
Web site: http://www.theseus.fr

IRELAND   UNIVERSITY OF DUBLIN
TRINITY COLLEGE MBA OF BUSINESS STUDIES

Trinity College
Dublin 2

Tel: 44-353-16081024
Fax: 44-3531-6799503
E-mail: append@tcd.ie
Web site: http://www.tcd.ie

THE NETHERLANDS   NIMBAS GRADUATE SCHOOL OF MANAGEMENT

P.O. Box 2040
3500 GA Utrecht

Tel: 31-30-2303050
Fax: 31-30-2367320
E-mail: nimbas@compuserve.com
Web site: http://www.nimbas.com

TSM BUSINESS SCHOOL CAMPUS UNIVERSITY OF
TWENTE

P.O. Box 217
7500 AE Enschede

Tel: 31-53-4898009
Fax: 31-53-4894848
Web site: http:/www.tsm.nl

NORWAY   HANDELSHOYSKOLEN BI
NORWEGIAN SCHOOL OF MANAGEMENT

P.O. Box 580
1301 Sandvika

Tel: 47-67-570500
Fax: 47-67-570570
E-mail: info@bi.no
Web site: http://www.bi.no

POLAND

LEON KOZMINSKI ACADEMY OF ENTREPRENEURSHIP
AND MANAGEMENT

59 Jagiellonska St.
P.O. Box 240
00-987 Warsaw

Tel: 48-22-5192112
Fax: 48-22-8113068

PORTUGAL

UNIVERSIDADE NOVA DE LISBOA
FACULDADE DE ECONOMIA

Travessa Estevao Pinto
1099-032 Lisboa

Tel: 351-1-3887480
Fax: 351-1-3871105
E-mail: jna@fe.unl.pt
Web site: http://www.fe.unl.pt

SCOTLAND

UNIVERSITY OF EDINBURG MANAGEMENT SCHOOL

7 Bristo Square
Edinburgh EH8 9AL

Tel: 44-131-6508077
Fax: 44-131-6506501
E-mail: management.school@ed.ac.uk
Web site: http://www.ems.ed.ac.uk

SLOVENIA

INTERNATIONAL EXECUTIVE DEVELOPMENT CENTER
BLED SCHOOL OF MANAGEMENT

Presernova cesta 33
4260 Bled, Slovenia

Tel: 386-64-792-500
Fax: 386-64-792-501
E-mail: center@iedc.si
Web site: http://www.iedc-brdo.si

SPAIN

ESCUELA DE ADMINISTRACIÓN DE EMPRESAS (EAE)

Avda. de la Catedral, 6-8
08002 Barcelona

Tel: + 34-93-3107184
Fax: + 34-93-3194436
E-mail: eae@eae.es
Web site: http://www.eae.es

ESCUELA DE ALTA DIRECCIÓN Y ADMINISTRACIÓN
(EADA)

Aragón, 204
08011 Barcelona

Tel: + 34-93-4520844
Fax: + 34-93-3237317
E-mail: info@eada.es
Web site: http://www.eada.es

ESCUELA DE ORGANIZACIÓN INDUSTRIAL (EOI)

Gregorio del Amo, 6
28040 Madrid

Tel: + 34-91-3495667
Fax: + 34-91-5542394
Web site: http://www.eoi.es

ESCUELA SUPERIOR DE GESTIÓN COMERCIAL Y
MARKETING (ESIC)

Avda. de Valdenigrales, s/n
28223 Pozuelo de Alarcón
Madrid

Tel: + 34-91-3527716
Fax: + 34-91-3527742
E-mail: ic.salprof.mad@esic.es
Web site: http://www.esic.es

UNIVERSIDAD PONTIFICIA COMILLAS DE MADRID
INSTITUTO DE POSTGRADO Y FORMACIÓN CONTINUA
ICAI-ICADE

Alberto Aguilera, 23
28015 Madrid

Tel: + 34-91-5422800
Fax: + 34-91-5596569
E-mail: mmerino@ip.upco.es
Web site: www.upco.es

SWEDEN

INSTITUTET FÖR FÖRETAGSLEDNING (IFL)
(SWEDISH INSTITUTE OF MANAGEMENT)

P.O. Box 45180
SE-104 30 Stockholm

Tel: 46-8-4571600
Fax: 46-8-314360
E-mail: ifl@ifl.se
Web site: http://www.ifl.se

THE STOCKHOLM SCHOOL OF ECONOMICS

Sveavägen 65
P.O. Box 6501
SE-113 83 Stockholm

Tel: 46-8-7369000
Fax: 46-8-318186
E-mail: info@hhs.se
Web site: http://www.hhs.se

UKRAINE   INTERNATIONAL MANAGEMENT INSTITUTE (IMI-KYIV)

19 Panasa Myrnoho Street
Kyiv, 01011

Tel: 380-44-2903352
     380-44-2904330
Fax: 380-44-2900495
E-mail: imi@mim.kiev.ua
Web site: http://www.imi.kiev.ua

THE TOP 20 EUROPEAN BUSINESS SCHOOLS—AT A GLANCE

SCHOOL	STARTING DATE
Ashridge	January
Cranfield	January and September
E. M. Lyon	September
ESADE	September
GSBA Zurich	Immediately after Admission
Helsinki	January
Henley	May
IESE	October
IMD	January
Imperial College	October
INSEAD	January and September
Instituto de Empresa	September
ISA HEC	January and September
Judge Institute	Late September
London Business School	September
Manchester	September
Nijenrode	August
Rotterdam	Mid-August
SDA Bocconi	September
Warwick	September

SCHOOL	APPLICATION DEADLINE
Ashridge	October
Cranfield	July
E. M. Lyon	June
ESADE	Rolling Basis
GSBA Zurich	Rolling Basis
Helsinki	Mid-September
Henley	Rolling Basis
IESE	Late April
IMD	Beginning September
Imperial College	End of July
INSEAD	April for the September Program and August for the January program
Instituto de Empresa	Late April
ISA HEC	Late May
Judge Institute	Rolling Basis
London Business School	Beginning April
Manchester	Late June
Nijenrode	Rolling Basis
Rotterdam	Mid-June
SDA Bocconi	Late April
Warwick	Late June

SCHOOL	NUMBER OF RECRUITING COMPANIES
Ashridge	Not available
Cranfield	80+
E. M. Lyon	100+
ESADE	150+
GSBA Zurich	Not available
Helsinki	130+
Henley	Not available
IESE	200+
IMD	50+
Imperial College	50+
INSEAD	250+
Instituto de Empresa	200+
ISA HEC	300+
Judge Institute	100+
London Business School	102+
Manchester	80+
Nijenrode	100+
Rotterdam	135+
SDA Bocconi	121+
Warwick	50+

SCHOOL	WEB SITE
Ashridge	http://www.ashridge.org.uk
Cranfield	http://www.cranfield.ac.uk/som
E. M. Lyon	http://www.em-lyon.com
ESADE	http://www.esade.es
GSBA Zurich	http://www.gsba.ch
Helsinki	http://hkkk.fi/mbafi
Henley	http://www.henleymc.ac.uk
IESE	http://www.iese.es
IMD	http://www.imd.ch
Imperial College	http://www.ms.ic.ac.uk
INSEAD	http://www.insead.fr
Instituto de Empresa	http://www.ie.edu
ISA HEC	http://www.hec.fr
Judge Institute	http://www.jims.cam.ac.uk/mba
London Business School	http://www.lbs.ac.uk
Manchester	http://www.mbs.ac.uk
Nijenrode	http://www.nijenrode.nl
Rotterdam	http://www.rsm.eur.nl/rsm
SDA Bocconi	http://www.sda.uni-bocconi.it
Warwick	http://www.wbs.warwick.ac.uk

INDEX